Summary of Forecast Methods and How and When to Use Them

Method	Classification	Forecast Time Frame	Patterns Treated	Resources Used/Cost 1 = lowest 4 = highest
Smoothing	Quantitative Time Series	short-term	cycle, trend	1
Seasonality	Quantitative Time Series	short-term	seasonal	1
Smoothing plus Seasonality	Quantitative Time Series	short-term	cycle, trend seasonal	1
Time Trends	Quantitative Time Series	short, med long-term	trend	1
Box-Jenkins	Quantitative Time Series	short, med term	cycle, trend seasonal	3
Indicators	Quantitative Time Series	short, med term	cycle	2
Simple Regression	Quantitative Causal	short, med long-term	cycle, trend	2
Multiple Regression	Quantitative Causal	short, med long-term	cycle, trend seasonal	3
Econometrics	Quantitative Causal	short, med long-term	cycle, trend seasonal	4
Growth Curves	Qualitative Technological	long-term	trend	3
Delphi Method	Qualitative Technological	long-term	trend	4
Jury of Executive Opinion	Qualitative Judgmental	short, med term	cycle, trend	3
Sales Force Composite Method	Qualitative Judgmental	short, med term	cycle, trend	3
Anticipatory Survey	Qualitative Judgmental	short, med term	cycle, trend	3
Subjective Assessment	Qualitative Judgmental	short, med term	cycle, trend	3

Chapter	Strength (S) and Weakness (W)
2	S – Easy to implement W – Does not identify factors influencing data patterns
3	S – Easy to implement W – Does not identify factors influencing data patterns
3	S – Easy to implement W – Does not identify factors influencing data patterns
4	S – Easy to implement W – Does not identify factors influencing data patterns
4	S – Can deal with intricate data patterns W – Does not identify factors influencing data patterns
4	S – Identifies cyclical turning points in a series W – Provides direction but not magnitude of series' path
5,6	S – Identifies factors influencing the forecasted series W – Requires more resources/time than most time series tools
5,7	S – Identifies factors influencing the forecasted series W – Requires more resources/time than most time series tools
8	S – Identifies factors influencing the forecasted series W – Requires considerable resources/time
10	S – Develops forecast with little or no historical data W – Difficult to determine shape and starting point of curve
10	S – Brings together expert opinions in a controlled setting W – Requires considerable resources/time
10	S – Can be developed quickly without rigorous analysis W – Judgmental biases can distort projections
10	S – Can be developed quickly without rigorous analysis W – Judgmental biases can distort projections
10	S – Directly surveys the customers who impact product sales W – Judgmental biases can distort projections
10	S – Attempts to explicitly examine possible outcomes W – Judgmental biases can distort projections

HANDBOOK OF
BUSINESS FORECASTING

Handbook of
Business Forecasting

Thomas W. Moore

1817

Harper & Row, Publishers, New York
BALLINGER DIVISION

Grand Rapids, Philadelphia, St. Louis, San Francisco
London, Singapore, Sydney, Tokyo, Toronto

International Standard Book Number: 0-88730-398-6

Library of Congress Catalog Card Number: 89-45771

Printed in the United States of America

Library of Congress Cataloging-in-Publication Data

Moore, Thomas W., 1945–
    Handbook of business forecasting / Thomas W. Moore.
      p. cm.
    Includes index.
    ISBN 0-88730-398-6
    1. Business forecasting.   I. Title.
  HS30.27.M66   1989
  658.4'0355–dc20   89-45771
                                 CIP

89 90 91 92 HC 9 8 7 6 5 4 3 2 1

To my parents
Thomas W. and Mollye G. Moore
and to
Heather and Courtney

Contents

3
SEASONALITY AND SMOOTHING 49

4
TIME-SERIES METHODS CONTINUED 75

5
REGRESSION ANALYSIS 109

6
CAUSAL MODEL BUILDING I 129

7
CAUSAL MODEL BUILDING II 153

8
FORECASTING FROM AN EQUATION AND ECONOMETRICS 207

9
TRACKING THE FORECAST/LOCATING DATA AND USING COMPUTERS 233

Preface

In today's business world, planning is a critical element of survival. As part of the company's daily operations, considerable resources are directed toward examining future paths that can improve the firm's long-term viability.

Within the planning function, forecasting is a key ingredient in arriving at an appropriate course of action. In addition, it is the starting point in the planning process. For example, the initial phase of introducing a new product requires an estimate of future demand and market penetration. Similarly, management's decision to purchase another firm will be based on a projection of that firm's growth potential.

Forecasting skills are also necessary in formulating labor and capital-spending policies. The commitment to add another work shift or to expand plant facilities will likely rest on a projection of industry business conditions.

Advertising campaigns, product promotions, investment decisions, research funding, production retooling, and other strategic considerations all begin with a forecast. In assessing any opportunity, the company will want to examine the future economic environment.

The purpose of this primer is to introduce the reader to the processes that underlie the more popular business forecasting methods. It approaches this task by going through all the steps, calculations, and decisions from the beginning to the end of a forecast. That is, it takes you from model inception to the final projection.

Real-life examples provide the vehicle for working through these methodologies. In fact, there are over twenty forecast situations described throughout the text. This should give the reader a flavor for the judgmental decisions and the mechanical procedures that constitute the art and science of forecasting. In addition, the methods are presented in enough detail so that they can be applied in a real-world situation.

The author is mindful that the individual's time is limited. Therefore, each discussion attempts to provide the necessary points as simply and succinctly as possible. To accomplish this, mechanics and practical application are stressed, while theorems and mathematical formulas are put aside. In addition, the concepts are discussed in clear, every-day language.

Texts will sometimes neglect to tie the various elements of forecasting together, making it difficult for the student to efficiently utilize the subject matter. In this primer, however, an attempt has been made to carefully connect the topics, with each chapter building on the previous ideas.

This book can be used as a reference guide when a question arises concerning a specific element of forecasting. On the other hand, it can also serve as a teaching tool since the steps and procedures can be applied to the manager's specific data series.

The methods presented in this text have been organized around the two major schools of forecasting—quantitative and qualitative. The quantitative category consists of time-series and causal techniques, while the qualitative group is made up of technological and judgmental methods. In Chapter One, we prepare for the journey by providing an overview of these two categories. In addition, we discuss the methods for measuring accuracy, which are the basis for evaluating forecast model performance.

Since the quantitative or mathematical procedures have generated the most research and interest, the majority of our text is devoted to their application. In Chapters Two through Four, the time-series techniques are presented. This discussion focuses on the use of these approaches to identify and treat the patterns in the data. Chapters Five through Eight address the causal methods of forecasting. This section starts with an explanation of regression analysis, the vehicle for building causal models. It proceeds through the modeling process, moving from simple structures to the more sophisticated methods. Chapter Eight develops projections from the equation models constructed in the previous pages.

Chapter Nine begins by tracking the forecast after its release to determine whether a revision is necessary. At this point, the steps involved in quantitative modeling have been covered, and the chapter concludes by discussing the supporting elements of locating data and using microcomputers. Chapter Ten is concerned with the qualitative methods, which are generally less rigorous than the quantitative techniques, but still have importance in the business world. Finally, Chapter Eleven draws the total body of knowledge together by examining the appropriate method to use in a given situation and explaining some important considerations in presenting a forecast.

Like other disciplines, forecasting has its own jargon and culture. Its importance, however, is in the supporting role it plays in the development of a company's business strategy. This book attempts to keep this vital consideration in mind. In the end, the businessperson or student will have obtained some basic forecasting skills to complement his or her management style.

Like most projects, this book has involved a greater degree of time and energy than I first imagined. Fortunately, I have had valuable assistance in bringing it to completion. Sally Moore Ng has provided me with editorial suggestions, and helpful ideas, as well as enthusiasm and support for the text. I am also grateful to John Glenn and Jonathan Shane, who played an important role in improving the structure and presentation of the material. I owe a great deal of thanks for the constructive criticism of John J. McAuley, R. H. Wrightson and Associates and Fordham University; John Broehl, Battelle Columbus Laboratories; Leon Hoke, University of Tampa; and Jack Gates, California State University; who unselfishly shared their forecasting insights. Finally, I want to thank Linda Kibbe Moore, who has provided a friendly forum for my economic "theories" over many years.

1

Introduction to Forecasting Methods and Measures

Your alarm rings at 6:15 A.M. You get up and get ready for work. All the time you keep looking at your watch, checking to see if you are on schedule. At 7:25, you get into your car and head for your job, arriving in the parking lot at 7:55. From the lot to your desk takes five minutes, bringing you into your office at 8:00. Nice going! You are right on target with your first forecast of the day.

That's right. You have been forecasting and didn't even realize it. We all make forecasts throughout the day; we estimate such things as how much research we need to finish a project at work or how long it will take to run an errand.

Let's go back to the beginning of the day. You decided to set your alarm for 6:15 because you knew you could get ready for work and be out of the house in one hour and ten minutes. You also expect the ride to work to take thirty minutes, plus five minutes from the parking lot to your desk. These are all estimates, or projections, on your part.

These forecasts are based on past observations or historical evidence. True, they are rough estimates because some days it might take longer to get dressed or to drive to work. Nevertheless, you are using both historical data and judgment in projecting the amount of time you need to get to work.

This type of forecasting goes under the heading of judgmental methods. But let's not worry about terms right now. The important thing to realize is that you

1

already have considerable experience in making projections.

Forecasting combines historical information with judgment, the objective with the subjective. A certain amount of common sense is always involved. In forecasting circles, the element of common sense is called reasonability. Therefore, the forecaster constantly questions whether or not the projection is reasonable, given past evidence, present considerations, and the future environment expected.

Reasonability is fine, but you want your projection to be based on more than that. After all, what people consider reasonable can cover a pretty wide area. Thus the critical ingredient in forecasting is a fair and unbiased analysis of past information to uncover significant patterns. For this reason the methods used in data analysis are the primary topic of this text.

The mathematical examination of past information is essential to forecasting. It can help us understand the past by revealing a series of patterns and relationships that we didn't realize existed. This understanding of recent history will, in turn, help us make an intelligent (or reasonable) future estimate.

The rigorous examination of past data has other benefits as well. First, a knowledge of the twists and turns in a data series helps the forecaster explain the future estimate to others. In addition, familiarity with the past boundaries of a series helps the forecaster determine whether a projection appears reasonable.

This book provides the beginning forecaster with some of the popular mathematical procedures used in identifying past patterns and making projections with them. It also touches on techniques that require more judgment and less statistical evaluation. The quantitative or mathematical methods, however, are by far the most popular procedures. Therefore, most of the text is dedicated to these approaches.

You have probably heard that forecasting is an art as well as a science. The *science* part entails the mathematical treatment of the data. This is usually the initial step in the forecasting process. The *art* is in the subjective decisions that the forecaster blends with the calculations to develop a projection. As you get a firmer grasp of statistical procedures and techniques, your ability to make subjective decisions will develop along with them.

Forecasting Methods

There are differing opinions about the best way to categorize and present forecasting methods. This primer divides the approaches into the two broad classes of *quantitative* and *qualitative*.

Quantitative

In the quantitative approach, forecasters use statistical methods of examining data to find underlying patterns and relationships. It is the most developed of the two groups and has benefited immensely from the widespread use of microcomputers.

The quantitative approach has two subcategories—the *time series* and *causal* methods. In most time series analysis, historical data of the series being projected is used for developing a forecast. For example, an investment researcher using a time series approach might try to forecast IBM sales for the coming year using only one data series—historic IBM sales.

The purpose of all time series methods is to examine historic data and isolate the trends or patterns in it. One reason that time series methods are so popular is that they are the least costly of the quantitative forecasting techniques. They are also simple and straightforward. However, they do not provide any rigorous explanation of the factors that influence the series being projected. That is, they do not deal with causality. We will more closely examine the advantages and disadvantages of time series approaches in a later chapter.

In the causal method the forecaster attempts to develop a mathematical relationship between the series being projected and the variables that have impact on it. The investment analyst in the previous example would seek to quantify the historical relationship between IBM sales and any factors that might explain its movements. These could include the national economy, the price of IBM computers relative to the competition, and IBM's advertising expenditures.

The causal approach has certain advantages over time series analysis. It provides (1) statistical proof that specific variables relate to the data series being forecasted and (2) a mathematical expression of that relationship. A drawback of the causal method is that its model development requires greater time, resources, and expenses than the simpler time series tools.

Qualitative

The qualitative category of forecasting techniques also has two subcategories—*technological* and *judgmental*. For the most part, historical data are either not available, not relevant, or not rigorously treated in qualitative forecasting. This is especially true of the technological methods, which forecasters use to project future products and innovations. In this area, past data are not useful because each new product or innovation is unique. As a result, expert opinion rather than statistical techniques provides the driving force behind a projection.

Judgmental methods also emphasize the intuition, experience, and expertise of individuals. They

Figure 1-1. Forecasting Methods.

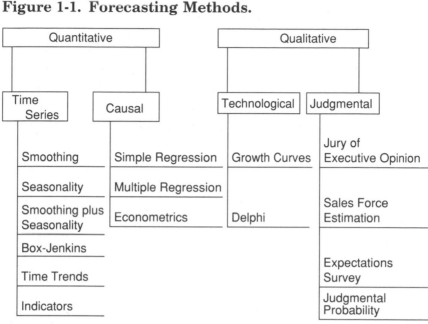

Quantitative			Qualitative	
Time Series	Causal		Technological	Judgmental
Smoothing	Simple Regression	Growth Curves		Jury of Executive Opinion
Seasonality	Multiple Regression			
Smoothing plus Seasonality	Econometrics	Delphi		Sales Force Estimation
Box-Jenkins				
Time Trends				Expectations Survey
Indicators				Judgmental Probability

are more applicable to everyday forecasting situations such as product sales than are technological methods. However, neither the judgmental tools nor the technological methods use rigorous statistical analysis.

Summary

At this point, let's stop and regroup. We have just viewed the "big picture" of forecasting. It consists of two schools: (1) quantitative and (2) qualitative. Just as their names imply, the quantitative uses mathematical and statistical techniques, and the qualitative relies on expert opinion. The quantitative school includes time series and causal methods, and the qualitative category includes technological and judgmental approaches. Figure 1-1 shows these groupings as well as the individual techniques that we will be studying.

Measuring Accuracy

No matter what method is used to generate a projection, the major barometer of success in forecasting is accuracy. This is most often management's bottom line for evaluation. Any comparison of individuals or firms that produce forecasts will likewise be based on accuracy. Whereas companies are graded on their profitability, forecasters are measured by their accuracy.

It should be noted, however, that accuracy measurements serve another purpose in the forecasting process: They play an important part in model building. This is especially true in the quantitative category in which the forecaster develops models from an examination of historical data. In fact, the forecaster usually chooses the model that best replicates past data. Accuracy measurements show which model has the smallest historical forecasting error. If a model does a good job of projecting the past, the assumption (and hope) is that it will also do well in the future.

Because past and future accuracy are so important, it is useful to know something about the most popular measurements of forecasting error. We will introduce you to four measurements of accuracy, including (1) average error, (2) mean absolute error or deviation (MAD), (3) mean squared error (MSE), and (4) mean absolute percentage error (MAPE).

Average Error

The example in Table 1-1 helps to illustrate the four measurements of error and their individual strengths and weaknesses. The *average error* is calculated from the differences between the actual data (column 2) and the corresponding forecasts (column 3). The individual forecast errors (column 4) are -1 in time period 1, 4 in time period 2, and -3 in time period 3. The table

Table 1-1.   Measuring Accuracy.

(1)	(2)	(3)	(4)	(5)	(6)	(7)
Time	Actual	Forecast	Error	Absolute Error	Squared Error	Absolute Percentage Error
1	10.0	11.0	−1.0	1.0	1.0	10.0%
2	20.0	16.0	4.0	4.0	16.0	20.0%
3	15.0	18.0	−3.0	3.0	9.0	20.0%
		Sum	0.0	8.0	26.0	50.0%
	Mean or Average		0.0	2.7	8.7	16.7%

shows that the average or mean of these three errors is 0 because the negative variations have offset the positive variation. Because of its offsetting effect, the average error is inappropriate for measuring the accuracy of a forecast. In this example, the average error measurement tells us that the forecasting error was 0 when in fact it was 1 or higher in each of the time periods.

Mean Absolute Deviation (MAD)

A better measurement of variance in forecasting is the *mean absolute deviation*, or MAD. The MAD takes the absolute value (without considering positives and negatives) of the errors calculated in column 4, thus removing the possibility of offsetting signs. This is illustrated in column 5, where the sign on the error term calculated in the previous column is removed. Now the errors do not wash each other out. As the table shows, the sum of the absolute errors is 8 and the average, or MAD, is 2.7. This, of course, provides a fairer evaluation of the forecast.

The average error (column 4), however, still has value even though it can't be used to measure forecasting accuracy. Economists like to examine the average error to see if the forecasting model is providing unbiased projections (projections that are equally likely to fall above or below the actual data points). Unbiased model results should fall both over and under the historical data. In the table, the forecast has fallen above the actual values twice and below them once, giving the forecaster some comfort as to its unbiased nature.

Mean Squared Error (MSE)

Like the MAD, the *mean squared error* (MSE) removes the sign on the error term in column 4. It does this by squaring the column 4 error to produce the value in column 6. Once again, the reason for removing the sign is to guard against offsetting errors. The MSE, however, has another effect. By squaring the errors, it penalizes large variations more than small variations.

This impact can be seen in Table 1-2. In this example, the MAD is exactly the same as in Table 1-1. In each case, the total absolute error is 8 and the MAD is 2.7. However, there are three small errors in Table 1-1 and one large error in Table 1-2. Despite the identical MADs, the MSE in Table 1-2 is 21.3, significantly higher than the 8.7 MSE value in Table 1-1. The MSE is higher in Table 1-2 because squaring the variance penalized the one large error more than the three smaller errors.

Because of this characteristic, the MSE is pre-

Table 1-2. MAD and MSE.

Time	Actual	Forecast	Absolute Error	Squared Error
1	10.0	10.0	0.0	0.0
2	20.0	20.0	0.0	0.0
3	15.0	23.0	8.0	64.0
			8.0	64.0
		Sum	8.0	64.0
		MAD	2.7	MSE 21.3

ferred where large errors are more costly than small errors. Most forecasters, however, will examine both the MAD and the MSE in measuring the accuracy of a forecast. Usually, the projection with the lowest MAD will also have the smallest MSE.

Mean Absolute Percentage Error (MAPE)

Another popular accuracy measure is the *mean absolute percentage error* or MAPE. Like the MAD and MSE, the MAPE uses the absolute value of the variation so that offsetting errors do not occur. However, it takes the process one step further by measuring the error as a percentage. The MAPE takes the absolute difference between each actual value and its corresponding forecast, divides this variation by the actual value, and multiplies by 100 to put the variation in percentage form.

In Table 1-1, the absolute value of column 2 less column 3 is divided by column 2, then multiplied by 100. For time period 1, the absolute error of 10 minus 11 is 1. Dividing 1 by 10 and multiplying by 100 yields a 10 percent error for that period (column 7). The average of the three periods, or the MAPE, is 16.7 percent.

The MAPE's advantage is its percentage format. This format provides a vehicle for comparing divergent series because percentages represent a common denominator. The MAPE, therefore, allows us to compare the IBM sales forecast with a sales projection for Chrysler Corporation or any other corporation.

Standard Deviation

A discussion of variation is hardly complete without mentioning the *standard deviation*. While the standard deviation can be used for examining forecast accuracy, it is not often employed in this manner.

Instead, it is utilized to focus on the characteristics of a data set as it measures the variation of the individual elements in a series from the central value or mean of the series. The formula for the standard deviation is

$$\sqrt{\frac{\sum (X - \overline{X})^2}{n - 1}}$$

where X represents the individual data points, $\overline{X}$ is the average or mean of the series, and n is the total number of observations in the series. We will come across the standard deviation again when we discuss regression analysis.

Degrees of Accuracy

Now that we have examined the measurement of accuracy, we must ask what level of accuracy we should strive for in forecasting a series. Although no specific answer exists, we know intuitively that a series whose past data patterns are volatile is more difficult to project than a series with a smooth, constant course.

As an example, multifamily housing starts have been plotted in Figure 1-2(A), while U.S. population has been plotted in Figure 1-2(B). Although the housing graph exhibits wide swings, the population data graph follows a steady upward course. Naturally, the latter series is easier to project, and a higher degree of forecasting accuracy can be expected.

The same conclusion can be drawn when an individual series shows both a volatile and a smooth pattern over time. Table 1-3 contains the inflation-adjusted gross national product (real GNP) forecast of the *Blue Chip Economic Indicators*, developed by averaging the projections of over 50 economists. During the turbulent years 1982 to 1984, the mean absolute deviation was 2.3 percent while the percentage

Figure 1-2. Comparison of Data Patterns. (A) Multifamily Housing Starts. (B) U.S. Population.

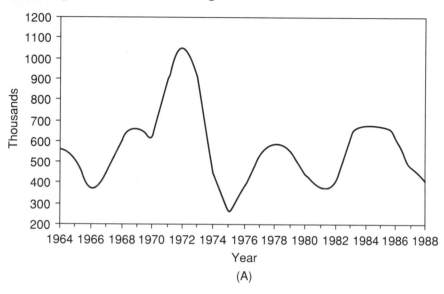

Year

(A)

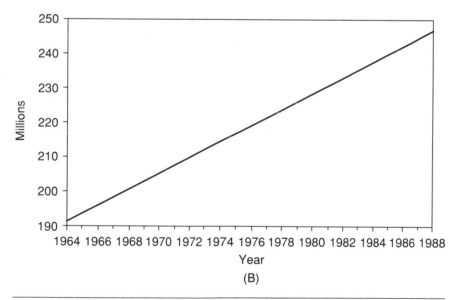

Year

(B)

Source: Bureau of the Census, Department of Commerce.

Table 1-3.   Forecasting Accuracy.

Forecast Year	Blue Chip Forecast Percentage Change	Real GNP Percentage Change	Absolute Deviation
1982	2.2%	−2.5%	4.7%
1983	3.2	3.6	0.4
1984	5.1	6.8	1.7
1985	3.5	3.0	0.5
1986	3.1	2.9	0.2
1987	2.7	2.9	0.2
		MAD 1982–1984	2.3
		MAD 1985–1987	0.3

Source: Bureau of Economic Analysis, Department of Commerce and *Blue Chip Economic Indicators.*

change in real GNP fluctuated between −2.5 percent and 6.8 percent. For 1985 to 1987 the average error was reduced to 0.3 percent while the economy maintained more stable growth.

As we see, the acceptable level of forecasting accuracy depends on the characteristics of the data set being projected. Most forecasters are constantly attempting to reduce variance in their forecasting through better procedures. Taking an optimistic view, an initially large error provides the forecaster with plenty of room to improve.

2

Time-Series Smoothing Approaches

> I know no way of judging the future but by the past.
>
> *—Patrick Henry*

We've seen that forecasters use time series methods to project a data set by examining its past movements. Statisticians often explain this process as the extrapolation of the data's underlying patterns into the future. However you say it, a substantial inventory of time series methods has been developed. Over the next three chapters, we will be discussing the most widely used of these, from the simple "naive" approach to the highly sophisticated Box-Jenkins method. It is always important to remember, however, that whatever their degree of rigor, all time series methods have the same general thrust—the examination of the patterns in the data series being projected.

Patterns in the Data

Let's explore the notion of patterns before going further. There can be as many as four patterns within any data series: (1) cyclical, (2) trend, (3) seasonal, and (4) irregular.

A *cyclical* pattern represents the ups and downs of business activity. This is the most difficult pattern to identify as well as the most difficult to anticipate. For example, the average national business cycle lasts about four years. However, a recent cycle, measured from recession to recession, lasted 20 months (November 1979 to July 1981), whereas the previous cycle covered six years.

The most familiar pattern is the *trend*. The trend represents the increasing, decreasing, or horizontal course of a data series over a period of time. This period usually encompasses at least one business cycle. Hence the cycle and trend patterns are interrelated: The general direction the cycle follows over a period of time is the trend. Many analysts, therefore, do not try to separate the cycle and trend patterns although decomposition time series analysis (Chapter Three) attempts to do this.

The third pattern in a data set is *seasonality*, the recurring movements within a year that are the result of social customs, holidays, and weather. Ice cream sales in New Jersey are always highest during the summer months, because of hot weather. This effect on sales as a result of the weather is the pattern of seasonality. Note, however, that seasonality offsets itself over a year. Therefore, annual data or data that are measured in increments of a year do not contain seasonal patterns.

An *irregular* pattern reflects unexplained variations in the data. These random movements may be the result of data collection errors or unexpected circumstances such as strikes or wars.

In summary, a data series can consist of *cyclical*, *trend*, *seasonal*, and *irregular* patterns. The purpose of time series methods is to remove the irregular and seasonal influences and project the series based on its cycle/trend pattern.

Overview of the Smoothing Approaches

Perhaps the most basic time series forecasting technique is the naive method. In its primary form, the naive approach uses the latest data point as the forecast for the next time period.

The naive approach can be appropriate if the series being projected is extremely stable or unchanging from observation to observation. Most series, however, do not display these characteristics. They tend to have irregular or random patterns and possibly seasonal influences. The naive process does not provide any adjustment for these factors.

Smoothing approaches, however, have the advantage of removing random variations from the data by averaging the observations in some fashion. These time series methods come in two general varieties: (1) simple, or first order, and (2) linear, or second order. Simple smoothing techniques, which will be discussed first, are best suited for data series that trend horizontally over time. Second-order smoothing is used for data that trends upward or downward.

Although smoothing removes random or irregular movements, it cannot adjust for seasonality. Therefore, any seasonal pattern in the data must be neutralized before smoothing can occur. We will learn about seasonal adjustment in Chapter Three. For now, we can get around this obstacle by examining annual data, which have no seasonality. That is, we will be analyzing annual data that have only cycle/trend and irregular patterns. The smoothing procedures will remove the irregular variations and forecast the series by identifying the underlying cycle/trend.

1. Simple Smoothing Techniques

Simple Moving Average (SMA)

The *simple moving average* method, or SMA, is a first-order, or simple, smoothing technique that averages a given number of observations and uses the result as the forecast for the next period.

In Table 2-1, a three-year SMA is being used where sales in years 1, 2, and 3 are 20, 60, and 40, respectively (column 2). The average of these three observations is 40 (column 3), which in this method becomes the forecast for the fourth period (column 4). As each new data point is obtained, we add it and drop the oldest observation. Therefore, an actual value of 50 in year 4 is added to the two previous values of 40 and 60 to arrive at an average of 50 [(60 + 40 + 50)/3 observations]. This new average becomes the forecast for the next period (year 5).

Now that you have the general idea of the SMA, let's confuse the issue just a little by providing a formula that embodies the calculations just completed.

$$F(t) = \frac{X(t - 1) + X(t - 2) + \cdots + X(t - n)}{n}$$

In this formula, $F(t)$ is the SMA forecast for the present period, where $X(t-1, t-2, \ldots, t-n)$ represents the actual values for past periods up to n. To apply this to our first calculation, just plug in the values of $40 + 60 + 20$ for $X(t-1) + X(t-2) + X(t-3)$, substitute 3 for n, and compute.

$$40 = (40 + 60 + 20)/3$$

Table 2-1.   Simple Moving Average.

(1)	(2)	(3)	(4)
	Actual	Three-Year	
Year	Sales	Moving Average	Forecast
1	20	—	—
2	60	—	—
3	40	40	—
4	50	50	40
5	—	—	50

There is yet another way to look at the SMA calculation. Here is the formula.

$$F(t + 1) = F(t) + \frac{X(t) - X(t - n)}{n}$$

This equation states that if we take the previous average, $F(t)$, and make an adjustment based on the difference between the most recent observation and the oldest (the one we are dropping), then we have the forecast for the coming period $F(t + 1)$. As the second calculation shows, the average of the first three periods (40) is adjusted by the difference between the most recent and the oldest data points divided by the number of periods [$(50 - 20)/3 = 10$] to arrive at a projection of 50.

$$50 = 40 + \frac{50 - 20}{3}$$

It is important to note that both formulas yield the same result. Therefore, either can be used in developing an SMA forecast.

SMA Characteristics. Let's now discuss the characteristics of the SMA method. First, moving averages (and all time series methods) are primarily suited for short-term forecasting. Another important characteristic is the equal weight given to each observation used in calculating the SMA forecast. In our example, the values of 20, 60, and 40 were averaged to arrive at a forecast of 40. Each of these three observations was given equal one-third representation in arriving at that forecast. Finally, when a new data value (50) was added, the oldest value (20) was dropped from the calculation. From this we see that observations outside of the moving average time frame have no weight at all.

Developing a Moving Average Model. Because the moving average method is largely mechanical, the forecaster follows a fairly standardized process in building a model. The only mechanism that can be altered is the number of observations being averaged. In our example, we arbitrarily chose a three-year period. In practice, the forecaster has complete control over whether the SMA model is based on three periods, four periods, or any other combination.

The SMA process, therefore, centers on determining the appropriate number of observations in the moving average. Forecasters generally choose the number that best recreates the historical series being projected. More specifically, the forecaster experiments with different combinations to see which provides the best historic accuracy (lowest MAD, MSE, or MAPE) and chooses it to project the data series.

A farm analyst at a Southern university provides a good example of this process. Like many of us, the analyst is perplexed and dismayed by the inaccuracy of weather forecasts. The analyst therefore decides to examine the weather for the past 14 years and generate an independent projection for the coldest daily temperature (24-hour average) to be experienced during the coming year. If accurate, the forecast will help farmers, electric utilities, and others cope with the weather.

Table 2-2 examines three- and five-year SMAs to see which best fits the actual past temperature data. The three-year SMA calculates an average of the first three observations (31, 44, 31). The resulting 35 becomes the forecast for period 4 (column 3). To calculate a new moving average for the period-5 forecast, the observation of 49 for period 4 is added, and the oldest observation (period 1) of 31 is dropped. This value of 41 becomes the projection for period 5. Moving down through the actual observations, the analyst calcu-

Table 2-2. Coldest Daily Temperature (Degrees Fahrenheit).

(1) Years	(2) Actual Temperature	Three-Year Moving Average			Five-Year Moving Average		
		(3) Forecast	(4) Absolute Error	(5) Squared Error	(6) Forecast	(7) Absolute Error	(8) Squared Error
1	31	—	—	—	—	—	—
2	44	—	—	—	—	—	—
3	31	—	—	—	—	—	—
4	49	35	14	196	—	—	—
5	28	41	13	169	—	—	—
6	25	36	11	121	37	12	144
7	21	34	13	169	35	14	196
8	35	25	10	100	31	4	16
9	44	27	17	289	32	12	144
10	37	33	4	16	31	6	36
11	28	39	11	121	32	4	16
12	32	36	4	16	33	1	1
13	22	32	10	100	35	13	169
14	41	27	14	196	33	8	64
15		32			32		
MAD			11			8	
MSE				136			87

lates forecasts for periods 4 through 14. (The forecast for period 15 represents the projection for the coming year.) This same procedure is used to calculate a five-year SMA. Again, the projections are contained in the forecast column (column 6).

At this point, the analyst measures the accuracy of the three- and five-year moving average projections, noting how well they replicate the historical data. To measure their accuracy, we employ the MAD and MSE measures with the lowest values representing the best fit. To calculate the MAD for the three-year SMA, we take the absolute value of the difference between each data point in column 2 and the corresponding projection in column 3. Summing these errors and computing their average, or mean, we get a MAD of 11. The MAD for the five-year SMA is 8, indicating a better reproduction of historical data. Examination of the MSE provides further support for the five-year method.

Because the five-year SMA assigns less weight to each observation than the three-year average (.20 versus .33), it has a greater smoothing effect on the data. Specifically, the five-year time frame reacts less to each data point. This points to a general rule: Where the data series exhibits wide variations around a stationary trend, a longer time period will always fit the data better. We will explore this idea further in the next discussion.

Although this example has supplied some insight into the SMA forecast process, real modeling situations involve additional procedures. One is the practice of plotting the data series before embarking on any calculations. A graphic view can provide the analyst with some early indication of the best-fitting combination.

For example, a plot of the 14 observed temperatures we have just examined (Figure 2-1) shows that

Figure 2-1. Coldest Daily Temperature.

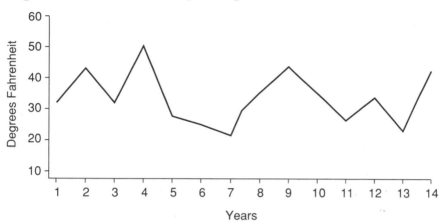

the series has sharp variations around a horizontal trend. Given this pattern, the analyst suspects, even before performing any calculations, that a longer-term moving average will probably provide a better fit.

It is also important that only two model combinations (three-year and five-year) were examined in our temperature exercise. In the real world, the analyst will try many combinations. By graphing the MAD of each combination, we can quickly identify the moving average with the smallest amount of historic error. In our temperature exercise, the seven-period SMA has the minimum MAD and thus best fits the actual data. Table 2-3 shows the moving average combinations and their MAD values, and Figure 2-2 plots these results.

Table 2-3. Accuracy Measurement (Degrees Fahrenheit).

SMA Period	MAD
3	11
5	8
7	6
9	7

Figure 2-2. MAD versus SMA.

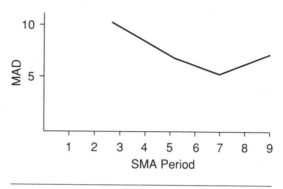

Interestingly, the moving average with the best historic fit (seven periods) has a MAD of 6. That is, the best historical replication still cannot come any closer than 6 degrees, on average, to the actual data. This experience should give the analyst a new appreciation for the difficulties of forecasting the weather.

Summary. Because we have covered a lot of ground, this is a good time to highlight the major points of the SMA.

1. The SMA method is used for short-term forecasting. The objective is to remove the random variations in the data and identify the underlying cycle or trend.

2. Each observation in the SMA carries equal weight. Thus a three-period moving average gives each value one-third weight.

3. Using a longer time frame for the SMA means giving each observation less weight. In our example, a five-period average provides only a one-fifth weight for each observation. Because the forecast is less affected by any individual data point, the longer term SMA is able to smooth the data.

4. Observations outside the SMA time frame have no weight in developing the forecast.

5. The forecaster controls the number of observations to be used in the moving average, choosing the combination that most accurately replicates the data series. The specification that comes closest to the actual data is the one with the lowest MAD, MSE, or MAPE.

Single Exponential Smoothing (SES)

The SMA has several limitations. Many people argue that the most recent observations of a data series should command more weight in the forecast than older values because they probably reflect the latest patterns in the data series. The moving average method, as we now know, gives equal weight to all observations.

Many analysts also believe that all values should have some weight in the forecast development. But the values outside the time frame of the average are removed from the calculation and have no impact on the forecast in the SMA.

To remedy these shortcomings, the *single exponential smoothing* (SES) method was developed. This approach is similar to the SMA since it also smooths the data by averaging them to remove random variations. However, SES also gives more recent data greater weight than their predecessors and allows all observations to influence the forecast.

Calculation. These enhancements have been accomplished through the ingeniously simple formula

$$F(t + 1) = \alpha \times X(t) + (1 - \alpha) \times F(t)$$

where the forecast for the coming period, $F(t + 1)$, is the product of alpha (α) multiplied by the last actual data value, $X(t)$, plus $1 -$ alpha $(1 - \alpha)$ multiplied by the last forecast, $F(t)$. Alpha, the key to SES, is a weighting factor between 0 and 1. Naturally, alpha plus $1 -$ alpha will equal 1. $F(t)$, or the latest forecast, represents a combination of all the previous values of the series. Thus all available data points are used in developing the forecast. This equation requires only three pieces of information: (1) the most recent actual value, (2) the most recent forecast, and (3) alpha.

Alpha. Alpha provides the forecaster with a valuable tool for assigning importance to recent data movements. Because alpha is multiplied by the latest data point in the SES equation, a higher alpha causes a greater weight to be assigned to the latest observation. If this new information seems to reflect a developing pattern, the analyst will give it a higher weight. If the point-to-point movements represent large random variations, alpha will be reduced.

The alpha mechanism has much the same effect as the number of observations chosen in the SMA method. As noted, *increasing* the alpha assigns greater weight to the most recent data point. In SMA, this same effect is accomplished by *reducing* the number of observations in the average. For example, decreasing the moving average from five to three periods increases the weight of each observation from .20 to .33. Therefore, alpha and the moving average period serve similar functions: Both provide the primary modeling mechanisms in their respective methods. In addition, they are inversely related because alpha $= 1/n$.

Comparison of SES and SMA. Before launching into a calculation of the SES, let's briefly review the advantages of this technique over the SMA. First, SES assigns current data greater weight and lets all values affect the forecast. Second, it requires only three pieces of information, substantially fewer than most SMA models. Third, the forecaster can fine-tune the weighting process, since alpha can range between 0 and 1. The moving average is less flexible, because the length of the period is limited to whole numbers. For example, a two-period average implies a weight of .50 for each data point, while each observation in a three-period average has a weight of .33. There is no mechanism, however, to employ values between .50 and .33 in the SMA methodology.

Developing an SES Model. As with the moving average approach, the forecaster constructs an exponential smoothing model by choosing the specification that best replicates the historical data. In the SMA methodology, this involves a trial-and-error process in which the analyst examines various combinations to arrive at a final model. The exponential method is exactly the same except the forecaster experiments with the alpha mechanism. The specific objective, once again, is to find the alpha that produces the best fit of the past data points, meaning the smallest MAD, MSE, or MAPE.

For the SES model, let's return to the farm analyst's search for the perfect temperature-forecasting technique. As you recall, the equation for calculating an SES forecast is $F(t + 1) = \alpha \times X(t) + (1 - \alpha) \times F(t)$, where $X(t)$ is the latest observation, $F(t)$ is the previous forecast, and α, or alpha, is the weighting mechanism. In Table 2-4, the analyst will compare the historical forecasting accuracy of two alphas, 0.1 and 0.9. An alpha of 0.1 gives only limited weight to the latest observation. An alpha of 0.9 attaches much more significance to the most recent observation.

In the initial forecast, a value for $F(t)$ is not available. Therefore, to get the process started, the

Table 2-4. Coldest Daily Temperature (Degrees Fahrenheit).

(1) Year	(2) Actual Temp	Alpha = 0.1			Alpha = 0.9		
		(3) Forecast	(4) Absolute Error	(5) Squared Error	(6) Forecast	(7) Absolute Error	(8) Squared Error
1	31	—	—	—	—	—	—
2	44	31	13	169	31	13	169
3	31	32	1	1	43	12	144
4	49	32	17	289	32	17	289
5	28	34	6	36	47	19	361
6	25	33	8	64	30	5	25
7	21	32	11	121	26	5	25
8	35	31	4	16	22	13	169
9	44	31	13	169	34	10	100
10	37	32	5	25	43	6	36
11	28	33	5	25	38	10	100
12	32	33	1	1	29	3	9
13	22	33	11	121	32	10	100
14	41	32	9	81	23	18	324
15	—	33	—	—	39	—	—
	MAD		8			11	
	MSE			86			142

analyst uses the first actual temperature of 31 (column 2) as the official forecast for the second period (column 3). This procedure is called initialization (the proof for which we will forgo here).*

Having initialized the forecast, the analyst is ready to project the points (using the SES formula) that will be compared with the historical data. In developing a forecast for period 3, the forecaster applies an alpha of 0.1 to the latest actual data point (period 2) of 44 to yield a value of 4.4. Then 1 − alpha, or 0.9, is multiplied by the latest forecast of 31 (period 2), which yields 27.9. Adding the values of 4.4 and 27.9, then rounding to a whole number, results in a projection for the third period of 32 (column 3). The same procedure is used to develop subsequent projections.

A close examination of the table indicates that the 0.1 alpha forecast remains fairly constant over time (column 3) with a narrow range of between 31 and 34. This smoothing influence of the low alpha results from the minimal impact given to the latest value. The effect is the same as including a large number of observations in the SMA, which also limits the influence of each (including the most recent) data point.

The 0.9 alpha projection has the opposite effect, since it reacts dramatically to the most recent data point by giving it considerable weight in the calculation.** This is similar to an SMA with a short averaging period.

---

* There are various approaches to initialization. In his book *Economic Forecasting for Business*, John J. McAuley averages the first two observations to initialize the model. A discussion of the elements behind the initialization process is contained in Wheelwright and Makridakis, 1985. *Forecasting Methods for Management, 4th ed.*, Wiley, New York.

** It is useful to note that if $\alpha = 1$, then the most recent data point becomes the next period's forecast. This, you might remember, is the naive method discussed earlier in this chapter.

Once the forecasts are completed, the forecaster measures the accuracy of the projected values compared with the actual values using the MAD and MSE. The results indicate that the historic forecast accuracy of the 0.1 alpha is superior to the 0.9 alpha because the former's MAD and MSE are smaller.

These findings are consistent with those of the SMA in our first look at forecasting the weather (Table 2-2). That is, the models that assigned lesser weight to the most recent observation (0.1 alpha and the five-year moving average) provide a better fit with the historical data.

In Figure 2-1, the analyst found that the data set displayed wide variations around a horizontal trend. A high weight given to the latest value produces a forecast that will always be out of sync with sharply fluctuating data because the movements in the projection will lag behind the observations by one time period. Therefore, a model that smooths the values (low alpha) will steer a course through the middle of the data set, minimizing the error and providing the better fit. The two graphs in Figure 2-3 illustrate this point by plotting the actual data with both the 0.1 and 0.9 alpha forecasts.

As in the SMA example, we have examined only two prospective models. In reality, the alphas between 0.1 and 0.9 would also be analyzed for accuracy. For this task, a microcomputer can save much time. The MAD or MSE corresponding to each alpha can then be reviewed, with the minimum error representing the best historical fit.

Summary

In this section we have presented the simple, or first-order, smoothing approaches, which remove the irregular patterns from the data to reveal the cycle/trend.

Figure 2-3. Actual Temperature versus SES Forecast.

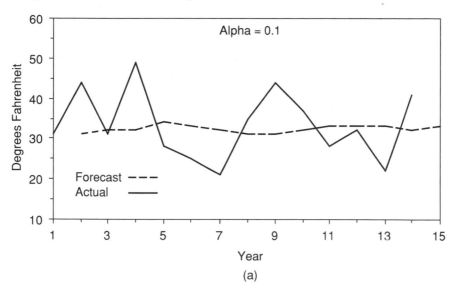

(a)

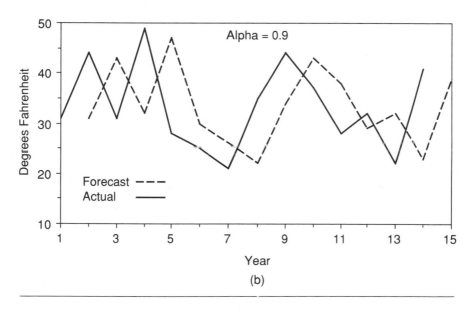

(b)

Once the cycle/trend patterns are identified, they form the basis for a one-period (short-term) projection.

Both the SMA and SES use the number of observations and alpha, respectively, as the primary mechanisms for model building. The forecaster arrives at the optimal model by determining which time period or alpha provides the best fit with the actual data. Most forecasters prefer SES to the SMA method because exponential smoothing (1) assigns the greatest weight to the most recent observation, (2) gives some influence to all data points, (3) requires minimal data, and (4) has more flexibility.

2. Higher-Order Smoothing

In the previous section, we presented the first-order smoothing approaches and determined that single exponential smoothing is preferable to the simple moving average. However, both these smoothing procedures work well only where the cycle/trend or underlying pattern is horizontal. If the data trend upward or downward, the performance of these methods falls off considerably.

Table 2-5 shows how this limitation occurs. In this table, the data series in column 2 has a steady upward trend. In the three-period SMA method, the forecast in column 3 falls below the actual data by a constant amount. (A plot of these values in Figure 2-4 illustrates this condition.) If the data trended downward, we would find the forecast line always above the actual data points. The problem is that first-order smoothing methods do not quickly adjust to upward or downward patterns.

Double Moving Average Method (DMA)

To remedy this difficulty, statisticians have developed the higher-order smoothing methods. One of these is

Table 2-5. Simple Moving Average versus Double Moving Average.

(1) Year	(2) Actual Demand	(3) Three-Period SMA Forecast	(4) Three-Period Double Moving Average Line	(5) Column 3 minus Column 4
1	5	—	—	—
2	10	—	—	—
3	15	—	—	—
4	20	10	—	—
5	25	15	—	—
6	30	20	—	—
7	35	25	15	10
8	40	30	20	10

the *double moving average* (DMA). This technique creates a second smoothed line, called the DMA line (column 4). In our example, it is a three-period moving average of the SMA line in column 3. Once it has been calculated, the difference between the SMA and DMA lines is added to the SMA line. The purpose of this adjustment is to close the gap between the actual values and the SMA forecast. But this adjustment also reflects the pattern or form of the original data. This

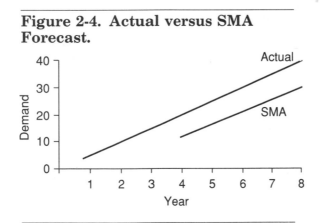

Figure 2-4. Actual versus SMA Forecast.

occurs because the DMA line is based on the SMA line, which in turn is based on the original data.

Table 2-5 illustrates how the DMA adjustment brings the forecast closer to the actual data line. In column 4, the DMA line is calculated by using the same three-period time frame as the SMA. However, the DMA, as we now know, is based on the single line.

The first double-line computation does not appear until period 7. Its value of 15 represents the average of the three SMA forecasts of 10, 15, and 20. The difference of 10 between the SMA and DMA lines (column 5) is added to the SMA forecast of 25 to arrive at a DMA projection of 35 for period 7. This projection matches the actual value of 35 for that period.

In actual use, the DMA method involves a step in addition to those outlined here. However, the purpose of this exercise is to explain the general structure and benefits of the higher-order smoothing procedures. The DMA provides an excellent vehicle for this task. As we will find out, however, there is an advanced exponential version that is a more efficient forecasting tool.

Summary

To review, the simple smoothing approaches will always lag behind the upward or downward trend in the original data. The DMA solution is to compute a double, or DMA, line from the simple line. By adding the difference between the simple and double lines to the simple line, the variance between the actual and the SMA forecast can be reduced. Once again, forecasters try to make this adjustment without destroying or altering the patterns embodied in the original data. This is accomplished by indirectly developing the new line from the actual observations.

Double Exponential Smoothing Method (DES)

The DMA process, however, has the same limitations as the SMA. That is, it lacks flexibility to increase the weighting of the latest observations, and the older data points have no influence on the forecast. Moreover, the DMA method needs twice as much data as the SMA. For these reasons, exponential smoothing is also the preferred technique at the higher order.

The DES method, also known as *Brown's linear exponential smoothing*, takes the same approach as DMA. First, a single exponentially smoothed line is developed. This line is adjusted by the difference between the single and double exponentially smoothed lines. Finally, a second adjustment adds a portion of the difference between the single and double lines. The purpose of these adjustments, like those of the DMA, is to close the gap between the forecast and actual data, while maintaining the form of the original data points.

Calculation Steps. With this background we can look at the steps for calculating the DES method. Although the discussion may be a bit plodding, it will prove rewarding because the DES is an all-purpose time series forecasting tool. The DES forecasting process can be broken into three steps.

1. Calculate the single exponentially smoothed line.
2. Develop the double line, calculate the difference between the single and double lines, and add this difference to the single line calculated in step one.
3. Add a portion of the difference between the single and double lines to the total from step two.

Now that the method has been outlined, we can examine the formulas contained in each of these steps.

1. As already discussed, the formula for the single exponential smoothed line is $F(t + 1) = \alpha \times X(t) + (1 - \alpha) \times F(t)$. $F(t + 1)$ represents the forecast for the coming period, α is alpha, $X(t)$ is the most recent data point, and $F(t)$ is the previous forecast.

2. Step 2 involves calculating the second smoothed line, called the double exponentially smoothed line. The formula is $F(t + 1) = \alpha \times F(t + 1) + (1 - \alpha) \times F(t)$ where $F(t + 1)$ represents the double exponential line forecast, $F(t + 1)$ is the single exponential line, and $F(t)$ is the previous double smoothed value. The differences between the single smoothed values calculated from the equation in step one and the double smoothed values derived from the equation in this step are next added to the single line.

3. The final adjustment of adding a portion of the difference calculated in step two can be shown mathematically as $[\alpha/(1 - \alpha)] \times [F(t + 1) - F(t + 1)]$.

At this point, the three steps of DES have been presented in a general format as well as in detailed formulas. Let's try an explanation somewhere between these two extremes. We will denote the single exponentially smoothed line as SES' and the double exponentially smoothed line as DES'. (The ' is to distinguish these acronyms from SES and DES, which represent the single and double exponential smoothing methods, respectively.)

1. Step 1 calculates SES'.
2. Step 2 calculates DES', then adds the differ-

ence between SES′ and DES′ to the original SES′. Mathematically, this is the same as SES′ + (SES′ − DES′).

3. Step 3 calculates the second adjustment or portion of the difference calculated in step 2. This can be shown as $[\alpha/(1 - \alpha)] \times$ (SES′ − DES′). As previously noted, this adjustment is added to the total from step 2.

By combining these steps, the analyst can present the DES calculation in simple mathematical fashion. The forecast for the coming period is

$$D(t + 1) = \text{SES′} + (\text{SES′} - \text{DES′})$$

$$+ \frac{\alpha}{1 - \alpha} \times (\text{SES′} - \text{DES′})$$

Again, two adjustments—SES′−DES′ and $[\alpha/(1-\alpha)]\times$ (SES′ − DES′)—have been made to the original SES line.

The Calculation. You are now prepared to develop a DES projection. Let's go ahead, then, and apply the steps already presented. In our example, the Associate Headmaster of Ivy Preparatory School wishes to project the number of students that will enroll during the coming year. This forecast, developed in Table 2-6, will serve as the basis for next year's revenue and expense budget.

Step 1 involves the calculation of SES′, or the single-smoothed line. As in the earlier smoothing example, the lack of a beginning forecast, $F(t)$ requires the use of the initialization process; that is, we take the first actual data point as our first SES′ value (column 3). Having used the first data point as the first SES′, we begin the calculation with period 2. Using the formula for step 1 and an alpha of 0.4, the SES′ value in line 2 is 0.4 × 498 (the latest actual value) plus

Table 2-6. Ivy Preparatory School—Double Exponential Smoothing (Alpha = 0.4).

(1) Year	(2) Actual Students	(3) (SES') Single Exponential Smoothing	(4) (DES') Double Exponential Smoothing	(5) (3) plus (3)−(4)	(6) Portion of (3)−(4)	(7) Forecast
1	450	450	450	—	—	—
2	498	469	458	480	7	—
3	530	493	472	514	14	487
4	480	488	478	498	7	528
5	455	475	477	473	−1	505
6	564	511	491	531	13	472
7	—	—	—	—	—	544

0.6 × 450 (the first SES' point), which equals 469 (column 3).*

The calculations of step 2 begin with the development of DES'. Again, we do not have an initial value for DES'. Therefore, the first actual observation also serves as the first DES' value. The calculation of the next DES' point in line 2 requires the alpha (0.4) that was used in the SES' computation. From the formula presented in step 2, DES' = 0.4 × 469 (the latest SES' value developed in step 1) plus 0.6 × 450 (the initial DES' point), which equals 458 (column 4). Having computed DES', we add the difference between SES' and DES' to the SES' value. This becomes 469 − 458, or 11, which we add to 469 to get 480 (column 5). An easier way to arrive at the same result is to use 2 SES' − DES'. Either way, the SES' − DES' adjustment to SES' is positive in this period (+11) since student enrollment has been trending upward. (When the observations trend downward, the SES' − DES' adjustment becomes negative. This downward trend occurs in period 5.)

Step 3 involves the final adjustment to the SES' line. This formula is $\alpha/(1 - \alpha)$—that is, 0.4/0.6 or 2/3—multiplied by SES' − DES' (11) for an adjustment of 7 (column 6). This result is added to the 480 derived in step 2 to arrive at a total DES forecast of 487. As in the single-smoothing methods, the projection covers the subsequent period, which is time period 3 (column 7).

An important feature of the DES method is that it lets the forecaster project more than one period with only one simple calculation. This can be accomplished

---

* For simplicity's sake, all values will be rounded to the nearest whole number in this and other examples. This is done at the expense of accuracy, however; our first forecast, without rounding, would be 488.4.

by using the step-3 adjustment. For a two-year forecast, the final adjustment (7) is multiplied by 2 and added to the 480 developed in column 5 to yield a projection of 494. If the forecast is for three periods forward, the adjustment factor (7) is multiplied by 3.

As with the first-order smoothing methods, the Associate Headmaster will experiment with various alpha combinations to arrive at a final DES forecast model. The minimum MAD, MSE, or MAPE will again be the determining factor. Assuming that the 0.4 alpha supplies the best fit with the historical data, the forecast for the coming year (period 7) is 544 students.

Although the DES method has been characterized as appropriate for data with increasing and decreasing trends, many forecasters also use it for horizontal patterns. Thus, DES can be used exclusively for all smoothing exercises. It should be noted, however, that there are other excellent higher-order smoothing approaches. These include the linear smoothing method developed by Holt and triple exponential smoothing. These methods are discussed in more advanced forecasting texts.* Still, the DES method is a proven and powerful tool.

Summary. We have discussed the concept of higher-order smoothing and have completed the rather detailed calculations behind the DES method. Here are the major points we have covered.

1. The single smoothing procedures studied in the previous chapter work only when the pattern of the data is horizontal or stationary. Once the data begin to trend upward or

---

* In *Forecasting—Methods and Applications* by Makridakis and Wheelwright, numerous higher-order smoothing methods are discussed.

downward, higher-order smoothing methods are required, because the simple techniques cannot quickly adjust to changing patterns.

2. Both the DMA and DES methods create a second smoothed line based on the simple smoothed line. The difference between the simple and the double smoothed line is then applied to the simple line to bridge the gap between the simple forecast and the actual data.

3. DES is preferable to its moving average counterpart for the same reasons that SES is the favored first-order technique. That is, the exponential method (1) allows the most recent actual value to have the greatest weight, (2) includes all data points in the forecast, (3) requires minimal data, and (4) is more flexible.

4. DES removes the irregular or random patterns (I) from the data and quickly adjusts to increasing or decreasing movements in the data series.

Exercise

In most instances, the forecaster will be working with data that have an upward or downward trend because horizontal data sets are unusual. Since the DES method is the preferred approach for projecting trended data, it's a technique the analyst will frequently use.

Because we extolled the virtues of the DES method, let's look at a concrete illustration of its advantages over the other smoothing techniques. We can do this by examining a trended data set and seeing how the DES approach better fits the series.

In this exercise, let's alter our emphasis slightly.

Up to now, we've concentrated mainly on the mechanisms for calculating the smoothing techniques. In fact, in previous examples we have given more importance to the calculations than to the forecast.

In real life, however, there are three important steps in model development and forecasting. The first, touched on in the previous section, is to plot and examine the historical data of the series being projected. The second step is to determine the model that best replicates the data. In most instances, this will be the method that provides the best historical fit (smallest amount of historical error). The final step involves examining the calculated forecast for reasonability. We do not want to blindly adopt a projection without analyzing it in light of past data trends and experience.

In this exercise, a demographic analyst just out of college is given the task of forecasting Florida's population for the coming year using a smoothing technique. The analyst will be examining the SMA,

Figure 2-5. Florida Population.

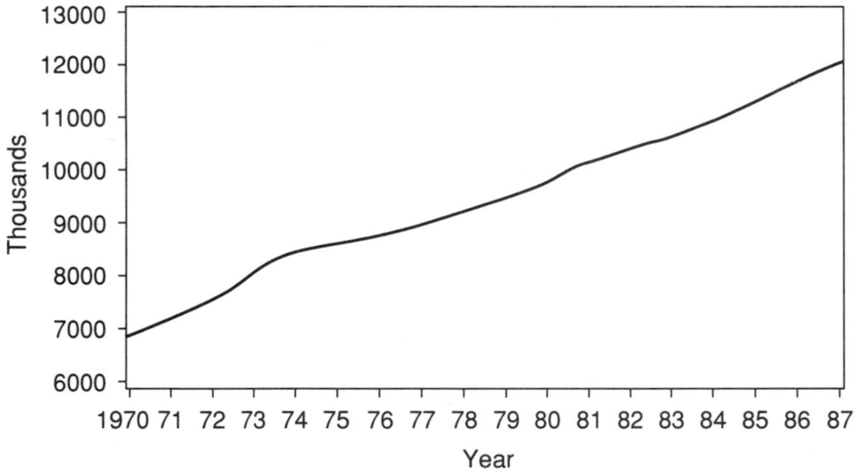

Source: Bureau of Economic and Business Research, University of Florida.

SES, and DES techniques to determine the approach that will best represent the data set.

In order to become familiar with the data set, the analyst plots the population series in Figure 2-5. The data exhibit a strong upward trend, indicating that a higher-order smoothing method will probably be most appropriate. However, the simpler smoothing techniques will also be tested since this is the analyst's first work assignment.

Looking first at the SMA technique, the analyst experiments with a five-year time frame. As before, MAD and MSE are the measurements of accuracy

Table 2-7. Florida Population Accuracy—Five-Year Moving Average.

Year	Population (Thousands)	Five-Year Moving Average Forecast	Absolute Error	Squared Error
1970	6,842	—	—	—
1971	7,194	—	—	—
1972	7,566	—	—	—
1973	8,042	—	—	—
1974	8,453	—	—	—
1975	8,619	7,619	1,000	1,000,000
1976	8,744	7,975	769	591,361
1977	8,920	8,285	635	403,225
1978	9,157	8,556	601	361,201
1979	9,449	8,779	670	448,900
1980	9,746	8,978	768	589,824
1981	10,106	9,203	903	815,409
1982	10,375	9,476	899	808,201
1983	10,592	9,767	825	680,625
1984	10,930	10,054	876	767,376
1985	11,279	10,350	929	863,041
1986	11,658	10,656	1,002	1,004,004
1987	12,044	10,967	1,077	1,159,929
1988	—	11,301	—	—
			MAD 843	MSE 730,238

used to evaluate the model's past performance. The results of the five-year SMA contained in Table 2-7 reveal some interesting developments. In this calculation, the population forecast for each year is considerably below its corresponding observation. This happens because the data set is rising rapidly and the five-year SMA procedure cannot sufficiently adjust to this phenomenon.

You might remember from our SMA discussion that a smaller number of observations in the calculation gives a greater weight to each observation. In the five-year SMA approach, each individual observation is assigned one-fifth, or 0.20, weighting. The analyst, therefore, believes that a three-year SMA, which would increase the weighting of the individual observations to 0.33, could possibly improve the historical fit. That is, raising the most recent observation's weight from 0.20 to 0.33 should produce a model that can better react to the data's rising trend.

The resulting fit of the three-year SMA in Table 2-8 indicates that the analyst has been partly successful. The greater weight implicit in the three-year moving average causes it to track the forward course of the population series more closely. This is reflected in the MAD and MSE of the three-year time frame, which are substantially lower than those of the five-year period.

Nevertheless, the forecasts for each individual year remain below the actual population values in the three-year SMA. In addition, the MAD and MSE continue to be high.

Because increasing the weight of the latest observation enhances the model's historical fit, the analyst proceeds to examine SES. The SES method, as we know, allows some flexibility in increasing the weight of the most recent data point. Therefore, the analyst tries the SES approach with an alpha of 0.60. This is

Table 2-8. Florida Population Accuracy—Three-Year Moving Average.

Year	Population (Thousands)	Three-Year Moving Average Forecast	Absolute Error	Squared Error
1970	6,842	—	—	—
1971	7,194	—	—	—
1972	7,566	—	—	—
1973	8,042	7,201	841	707,281
1974	8,453	7,601	852	725,904
1975	8,619	8,020	599	358,801
1976	8,744	8,371	373	139,129
1977	8,920	8,605	315	99,225
1978	9,157	8,761	396	156,816
1979	9,449	8,940	509	259,081
1980	9,746	9,175	571	326,041
1981	10,106	9,451	655	429,025
1982	10,375	9,767	608	369,664
1983	10,592	10,076	516	266,256
1984	10,930	10,358	572	327,184
1985	11,279	10,632	647	418,609
1986	11,658	10,934	724	524,176
1987	12,044	11,289	755	570,025
1988	—	11,660	—	—
			MAD 596	MSE 378,481

a greater weight than the 0.33 implied in the three-year SMA, and the analyst supposes that this should better track the data's upward movement.

The computation in Table 2-9 indicates that the SES method using an alpha of 0.60 fits the historical data set more effectively than either of the SMA configurations. The SES example has an MAD of 485 and an MSE of 249,345, considerably below the five-year and three-year errors. The reason, once again, is the greater weighting of the latest data point, which allows the method to track the series more closely.

Table 2-9. Florida Population Accuracy—Single Exponential Smoothing (Alpha = 0.6).

Year	Population (Thousands)	Single Exponential Smoothing Forecast	Absolute Error	Squared Error
1970	6,842	—	—	—
1971	7,194	6,842	352	123,904
1972	7,566	7,053	513	263,169
1973	8,042	7,361	681	463,761
1974	8,453	7,770	683	466,489
1975	8,619	8,180	439	192,721
1976	8,744	8,443	301	90,601
1977	8,920	8,624	296	87,616
1978	9,157	8,802	355	126,025
1979	9,449	9,015	434	188,356
1980	9,746	9,275	471	221,841
1981	10,106	9,558	548	300,304
1982	10,375	9,887	488	238,144
1983	10,592	10,180	412	169,744
1984	10,930	10,427	503	253,009
1985	11,279	10,729	550	302,500
1986	11,658	11,059	599	358,801
1987	12,044	11,418	626	391,876
1988	—	11,794	—	—
			MAD 485	MSE 249,345

The rapid upward movement of the series, however, continues to outpace the fitted forecast. In fact, this would be the case even with an alpha of 1.0. Assigning an alpha equal to 1.0 is the same as using the last observation for the forecast, which is the naive method. Yet it is interesting that even this maximum SES weighting arrangement will still lag behind an upward or downward trend.

The ultimate trend catcher, as previously noted, is the DES technique. The analyst again picks an alpha value of 0.6 as a starting point. The combination of DES and this high alpha leads to a dramatic improvement in the historical forecast (Table 2-10). The MAD and MSE fall to 130 and 26,817, respectively, a substantial reduction in the model's error. Moreover, the DES projection exceeds the actual population values in five instances (asterisked in Table 2-10). This does not occur with any of the simple smoothing methods. The complete calculation of the DES projection in Table 2-10 is provided at the end of this chapter.

Table 2-10.   Florida Population Accuracy—Double Exponential Smoothing (Alpha = 0.6).

Year	Population (Thousands)	Double Exponential Smoothing Forecast	Absolute Error	Squared Error
1970	6,842	—	—	—
1971	7,194	6,842	352	123,904
1972	7,566	7,263	303	91,809
1973	8,042	7,754	288	82,944
1974	8,453	8,335	118	13,924
1975	8,619	8,815*	196	38,416
1976	8,744	8,961*	217	47,089
1977	8,920	9,012*	92	8,464
1978	9,157	9,135	22	484
1979	9,449	9,360	89	7,921
1980	9,746	9,673	73	5,329
1981	10,106	10,001	105	11,025
1982	10,375	10,392*	17	289
1983	10,592	10,675*	83	6,889
1984	10,930	10,872	58	3,364
1985	11,279	11,209	70	4,900
1986	11,658	11,582	76	5,776
1987	12,044	11,986	58	3,364
1988	—	12,397	—	—
			MAD 130 MSE	26,817

Table 2-11. 1988 Florida Population Forecast Comparison (thousands).

Method	Observation Weight	1988 Forecast	1988 Actual	Variance
SMA	3 years	11,660	12,418	−758
SMA	5 years	11,301	12,418	−1,117
SES	0.6	11,794	12,418	−624
DES	0.6	12,397	12,418	−21

Fine-Tuning the Model

Table 2-11 compares the 1988 population projections from the four models with the actual population for that year. As expected, the DES method's forecast comes closest to the actual data. Therefore, the DES approach is not only the most accurate in replicating the historical observations but also in generating a future (1988) point. Moreover, the DES projection is the most reasonable because it is the only forecast higher than the actual 1987 population level. This is why most forecasters use the model that provides the best historical fit as the structure for projecting a series.

It should be noted that the best-fitting model does not always provide the best forecast. After all, there is always considerable uncertainty in forecasting. Still, it is reasonable to choose the forecasting structure that best tracks the past data.

The objective of this exercise has been to provide living proof that the advanced smoothing approaches are more effective than the simple methods in forecasting data series with increasing or decreasing trends. For our analyst, however, the model-building process is not complete. The alpha still needs to be fine-tuned to determine the most accurate replication of the historic series. Using a computer, our analyst

Figure 2-6. MAD versus Alpha.

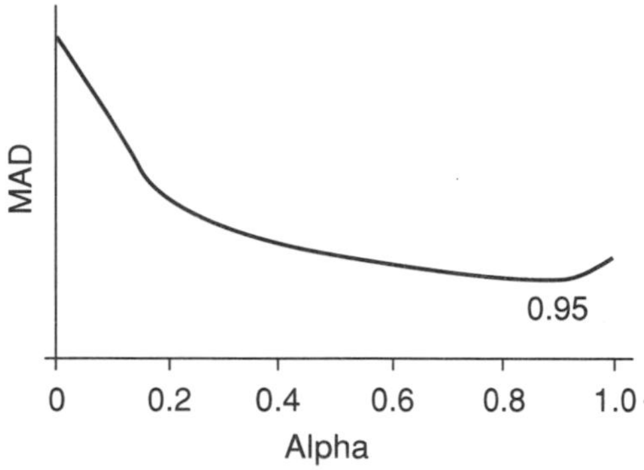

has programmed the DES calculations to generate a MAD and MSE for every alpha from 0.01 to 0.99.

Figure 2-6 contains a plot of the MAD values associated with the alphas examined. From this graph, the alpha with the smallest historic error is 0.95. The analyst, therefore, uses this specification for the DES forecasting model.

Having completed the higher-order smoothing methods, the reader now has a tool for examining and separating the cycle/trend from the irregular patterns. In the first section of Chapter Three, we will examine the final pattern of seasonality. We will then combine the seasonality and smoothing concepts in the second section to give the forecaster the ability to identify seasonality, remove the irregular pattern, and project the underlying trend of *any* data series.

Appendix to Chapter Two

Table 2A-1 provides the calculations behind the DES forecasts used in Table Ten. For a review of the steps, refer to the DES example on pages 35 to 38.

Table 2A-1. Florida Population Forecast—Double Exponential Smoothing (Alpha = 0.6).

(1) Year	(2) Population (Thousands)	(3) (SES') Single Exponential Smoothing	(4) (DES') Double Exponential Smoothing	(5) (3) plus (3)−(4)	(6) Portion of (3)−(4)	(7) Forecast
1970	6,842	6,842	6,842	—	—	—
1971	7,194	7,053	6,969	7,137	126	6,842
1972	7,566	7,361	7,204	7,518	236	7,263
1973	8,042	7,770	7,544	7,996	339	7,754
1974	8,453	8,180	7,926	8,434	381	8,335
1975	8,619	8,443	8,236	8,650	311	8,815
1976	8,744	8,624	8,469	8,779	233	8,961
1977	8,920	8,802	8,669	8,935	200	9,012
1978	9,157	9,015	8,877	9,153	207	9,135
1979	9,449	9,275	9,116	9,434	239	9,360
1980	9,746	9,558	9,381	9,735	266	9,673
1981	10,106	9,887	9,685	10,089	303	10,001
1982	10,375	10,180	9,982	10,378	297	10,392
1983	10,592	10,427	10,249	10,605	267	10,675
1984	10,930	10,729	10,537	10,921	288	10,872
1985	11,279	11,059	10,850	11,268	314	11,209
1986	11,658	11,418	11,191	11,645	341	11,582
1987	12,044	11,794	11,553	12,035	362	11,986
1988	—	—	—	—	—	12,397

3

Seasonality and Smoothing

In Chapter Two, we discussed the patterns that are likely to be found in a data series. As you remember, they encompass cycle (C), trend (T), seasonal (S), and irregular or random (I) movements. The smoothing approaches we discussed are able to remove the I pattern from the data and project the C/T. These methods, however, are not equipped to adjust for seasonality. To get around this obstacle, we used examples dealing only with annual data, which by definition do not contain seasonality.

In the real world, forecasters often work with weekly, monthly, and quarterly series. For these time periods, seasonal influence is a major consideration. In fact, forecasters must identify seasonality before determining the data's underlying trend. In the next section, we will present the concept of seasonality as well as the mechanics for quantifying this phenomenon. Following this, the chapter will conclude by combining the seasonal and smoothing techniques.

Seasonality

Seasonality represents movements in a series during a particular time of year (week, month, quarter) that recur year after year. Since seasonality consists of recurring patterns within a year, it is a consideration only where data is for a weekly, monthly, or quarterly period.

The removal of these patterns is called seasonally adjusting or deseasonalizing the data. When statisticians make this adjustment, they provide the notation *seasonally adjusted*, or *S.A.*, beneath the series name.

Seasonal patterns are the result of (1) climate/weather, (2) social customs/holidays, and (3) business policies. The impact of weather is often substantial and predictable. For example, convertible automobile sales are generally strongest in the spring, when the weather becomes milder. Weather also has a varying effect in different geographical locations. Housing starts in Maine during January are weak relative to other months of the year because of harsh winter weather. The impact of weather on January starts in Florida, however, is not nearly so dramatic because of its milder climate.

Social customs and holidays also have a major seasonal influence. Monthly retail spending is always greatest during December due to Christmas, Hanukkah, and the New Year. This end-of-the-year surge also explains why January sales are relatively weak. Specific products, of course, benefit from different holidays. Firecracker sales are strongest in June and early July as a result of Independence Day, and florists experience brisk activity around St. Valentine's Day.

Finally, business policy can also have an effect on the relationship among monthly sales. A good example is the domestic automobile industry, where the new models come out in the early fall, leading to consistently stronger sales during September/October than in July/August.

Where seasonality exists, it must be identified to separate it from the other data patterns. Once seasonality has been removed, different months and quarters within the year can be examined to determine the underlying trend. For example, a comparison between December and January retail sales is not particularly useful since December sales are always higher due to the seasonal impact just described. When the fore-caster adjusts for this seasonal difference, however, the remaining patterns in the series will include C/T and I. After smoothing to neutralize I, the forecaster can distinguish whether sales are trending upward or downward from December to January.

The mathematical expressions for seasonality are called seasonal factors. If you are analyzing quarterly data, there is a factor for each quarter, or a total of four. Similarly, there are 12 individual factors for monthly data and 52 for weekly data. Seasonal fac-tors are expressed as an index which varies around an average of 100 (in percentage terms) or 1.00 (in deci-mal terms). An index of 100 represents no seasonality. Over a year, the average of the weekly, monthly, or quarterly seasonal factors is 100, as there is no sea-sonality over a 12-month period.

The following example provides seasonal factors in decimal form for the four quarters of a year.

First	Second	Third	Fourth	Annual Average
.75	1.10	.95	1.20	1.00

The first-quarter value of 0.75 indicates that histori-cally this period has been 0.25 (or 25%) below the aver-age for the year due to a recurring seasonal pattern. The fourth-quarter factor of 1.20 quantifies this peri-od's historical pattern as being 0.20 (or 20%) above normal as a result of seasonal influences. Once again, the annual average (which is always 1.00) implies that although there are seasonal differences between the quarters, this process completes itself over a year.

In summary, seasonality takes account of the recurring patterns within a year. It is usually present in weekly, monthly, and quarterly series. However, annual data do not exhibit this pattern. Seasonality is the result of climate/weather, social customs/holidays, and business policy considerations. This impact is quantified through seasonal factors which vary around 100 or 1.00. Once data are seasonally adjusted, comparison of different months or quarters within a year can be made to identify the underlying trend (C/T).

Calculating Seasonal Factors

With this general description of seasonality, we can now measure its impact by calculating the seasonal factors related to a data series.

The basic technique for deriving seasonal factors is classical decomposition, also known as the ratio-to-moving average method. The objective of classical decomposition is to isolate the S (seasonal) pattern from the data. To accomplish this task, the process first removes the C/T pattern and then adjusts for the I variations. Usually three years of data are necessary for utilizing this approach.

In Table 3-1, Tampa International Airport passenger data are being examined. Since the series is quarterly, seasonality can be expected. The classical decomposition approach encompasses three major steps in analyzing this series.

Step One. The first step involves calculating the C/T pattern in the data. As review, the series in column 2 is composed of C/T, S, and I components. From this, the C/T can be identified by calculating a one-year moving average since, by definition, data of one year's duration have no seasonal pattern. (The moving average concept may be reviewed in Chapter Two.) For airport passengers, the initial moving average computation involves taking the mean of the first four observations (2.544, 2.051, 1.678, 1.956) in column 2. This average of 2.057 is then placed in column 3.

Table 3-1. Tampa International Airport Passengers (millions).

(1) Year	Qtr.	(2) Sales (C/T×S×I)	(3) One-Year Moving Average (C/T)	(4) Centered Moving Average	(5) Ratio-to-Moving Average (S×I)
1983	1	2.544		—	—
	2	2.051		—	—
			2.057		
	3	1.678		2.032	.826
			2.007		
	4	1.956		2.024	.966
			2.041		
1984	1	2.343		2.056	1.140
			2.070		
	2	2.187		2.078	1.052
			2.086		
	3	1.792		2.103	.852
			2.120		
	4	2.020		2.140	.944
			2.159		
1985	1	2.480		2.170	1.143
			2.181		
	2	2.345		2.200	1.066
			2.218		
	3	1.878		2.263	.830
			2.308		
	4	2.167		2.320	.934
			2.331		
1986	1	2.843		2.371	1.199
			2.411		
	2	2.436		2.428	1.003
			2.445		
	3	2.198		2.445	.899
			2.444		
	4	2.304		2.476	.931
			2.508		
1987	1	2.837		2.508	1.131
			2.508		
	2	2.691		2.505	1.074
			2.502		
	3	2.200		—	—
	4	2.280		—	—

Source: Hillsborough County Aviation Authority

The specific placement of this one-year moving average on the table is important. Because it represents the mean or average of the data points from the first to fourth quarter of 1983, it should be located in the middle of this period. In this instance, that would be between the second and third quarter (col. 3). From this starting point, the one-year or four-quarter moving average calculations will follow at one-period intervals. The objective of computing the C/T, however, is to compare it with the original series in column 2. This cannot yet be done since the values in columns 2 and 3 do not line up. However, a two-period moving average of column 3 centers this data set with the initial value in the third period of 1983. This new calculation, contained in column 4, is called the centered moving average. With this adjustment, the C/T can now be compared to the original values in column 2.

Step Two. As previously noted, the primary objective of classical decomposition is to separate the S pattern from the other elements in the data. In step one, we calculated the C/T. We can now begin to isolate seasonality from the passenger data by dividing the original series (C/T × S × I) in column 2 by the centered moving average (C/T) in column 4. Mathematically, dividing (C/T × S × I) by C/T results in cancelling the C/T patterns in both the numerator and denominator, leaving the S × I patterns from the original data. This division of the original passenger series by its centered moving average is called the ratio-to-moving average. The resulting S × I from this calculation is contained in column 5.

Reviewing the math:

$$\frac{\text{Sales}}{\text{Moving Average}} = \frac{\text{C/T} \times \text{S} \times \text{I}}{\text{C/T}} = \text{S} \times \text{I}$$

Once the ratio-to-moving average values for each

quarter are calculated, they need to be grouped together. This is done in Table 3-2.

Step Three. At this point, we have ratio-to-moving average values that reflect the S × I patterns. Since the goal is to completely isolate the S element, the I variations must be neutralized. We know from basic statistics that random or irregular variations fluctuate around zero and have a mean of zero. In other words, irregular movements offset each other over time. Therefore, the I pattern can be removed by taking the average of the ratio-to-moving averages for each quarter in Table 3-2.

There are two types of averages that can be utilized. The first is a simple average of the data which in Table 3-2 requires summing the four values for each quarter and then dividing by four. The second form is a medial average for which we drop the highest and lowest values for each quarter and take a simple average of the remaining observations. The purpose of a medial average is to remove values that may have been distorted by an unexpected event. For example, a strike could have dramatically reduced airline service during one of the quarters, which would lead to an

Table 3-2. Ratio-to-Moving Average Values.

Quarters	1	2	3	4	TOTAL
	1.140	1.052	0.826	0.966	
	1.143	1.066	0.852	0.944	
	1.199	1.003	0.830	0.934	
	1.131	1.074	0.899	0.931	
Simple Average	1.153	1.049	0.852	0.944	
Medial Average	1.142	1.059	0.841	0.939	
Convert to percentage form	115.3	104.9	85.2	94.4	399.8
Adjustment	115.4	105.0	85.2	94.4	400.0
(400.0/399.8 = 1.0005)					

aberration in that period's ratio-to-moving average. Dropping this extreme value keeps it from affecting the seasonal factor.

It is also important to have at least four ratio-to-moving average observations for each quarter before a medial average is utilized. The purpose of this requirement is to have at least two values available for averaging after removing the highest and lowest values.

The resulting values from the simple or medial average calculation are called seasonal factors and represent each quarter's seasonal influence based on the historical data. We must, however, make one further adjustment to these values in order to arrive at the final seasonal factors. We know that 100 implies no seasonality and that this represents the annual average of the four quarters or entire year. Since the annual average is 100, the total of this average over four quarters will be 400 (4 × 100). In our example, the factors developed from the simple average have been converted to percentage form in Table 3-2. The summation of these four preliminary quarterly values is 399.8. To adjust this total to 400, each quarterly value is multiplied by 400.0/399.8 (or 1.0005). Thus, each factor is increased by a similar amount (1.0005) to bring their average to 100 and their total to 400.*

The focus of our example has been on computing seasonal factors from quarterly data. This same three-step procedure can be applied in generating monthly or weekly seasonal factors. In fact, there are only minor differences between these three time frames.

---

* This same approach is used where the preliminary values exceed 400. For example, should the four quarterly values add to 401.0, each quarterly value is multiplied by 400.0/401.0 (or 0.9975). In this way, the preliminary factors are adjusted downward to bring their average to 100 and their total to 400.

First, X-11 has the ability to adjust for differences in the number of weekdays from month to month and also year to year. This correction, called a trading-day adjustment, can be important where sales of a product are strong on certain days. For example, a particular store may be open only from Monday through Friday. The X-11 program is able to adjust for the fact that the number of weekdays in February is different from the number in March. In addition, it also adjusts for the fact that the number of weekdays in February varies from one year to the next.

Interpretation and Utilization of Seasonal Factors

Seasonal factors provide valuable insight into the characteristics of the data. In the previous example, the highest value for any period is the first-quarter figure of 115.4. This value implies that passenger traffic in this quarter has historically been 15.4% above the average for the year due to seasonal influences. On the other hand, the lowest value for the four periods is the third quarter's seasonal factor (85.2), which indicates that passengers in this period have historically been 14.8% below the average due to seasonality.

The seasonal factors we have developed are consistent with the economics and geography of Tampa, Florida. During the winter months, northern tourists flock to this area because of its mild climate. This is reflected in the high seasonal factor during the first quarter. By the spring, the visitors begin to return home, as illustrated by a dip in the second-quarter seasonal factor. Summer is the lightest period for air traffic as the weather provides little incentive for visitors. Finally, fall's cooler temperatures bring a renewal in tourism.

Once seasonal impacts have been quantified, airport-traffic trends between the various quarters can be determined. Table 3-1 shows that the airport reported 2.280 million passengers during the fourth quarter of 1987, while the third-quarter level was 2.200. A cursory glance at these data might suggest that traffic trended upward during the final quarter. The historical data, however, show that this has always occurred, because of the start of the tourist season. To better understand how fourth-quarter airport activity fared in relation to the previous period, this seasonal influence must be removed—that is, the data need to be seasonally adjusted using the seasonal factors we have developed.

Seasonal adjustment is a straightforward procedure in which the unadjusted actual value is divided by the seasonal factor in its decimal form. In our example, the fourth-quarter 1987 passenger figure of 2.280 is divided by the fourth-quarter seasonal factor of 0.944 to arrive at a seasonally-adjusted value of 2.415. Note that dividing the seasonal factor into the actual number has adjusted its value upward. Specifically, the passenger figure has been raised by 5.9% (1.00/0.944) to adjust for the fact that fourth-quarter airport traffic has historically been below the average for the year (1.00).

The division of the third-quarter figure by its seasonal factor also yields a greater seasonally-adjusted value. In this calculation, the third-quarter actual activity has been upwardly adjusted by 17.4% to reflect this quarter's below-normal past activity.

Once the data have been seasonally adjusted, the fourth quarter can be compared to the third quarter. In Table 3-3, fourth-quarter passengers trend downward after seasonal adjustment, just the opposite of the actual data. This represents the fact that although actual fourth-quarter traffic was 3.6% above the prior

Table 3-3. Tampa International Airport Passengers (millions).

	Unadjusted / Seasonal Factor	=	Seasonally Adjusted
Quarter 4	2.280 / 0.944	=	2.415
Quarter 3	2.200 / 0.852	=	2.582
Quarter 2	2.691 / 1.050	=	2.563
Quarter 1	2.837 / 1.154	=	2.458

period $[(2.280 - 2.200)/ 2.200] \times 100$, it has histori-cally been 10.8% higher $[(0.944 - 0.852)/0.852] \times 100$ due to seasonality. After adjusting for this seasonal consideration, the fourth-quarter C/T points down.

It might be useful to determine how long activity has been on a declining course. This requires back-ing up to the first and second quarters of 1987 and calculating their seasonally-adjusted levels. While the third- and fourth-quarter passenger levels are adjusted upward by their seasonal factors, the effect is different for the first two periods. Dividing first-quarter passengers of 2.837 by its corresponding sea-sonal factor of 1.154 results in a seasonally adjusted figure of 2.458. That is, actual passengers are being "deflated" to remove the seasonal pattern where traffic has historically been 15.4% above normal. Since the second quarter's seasonal factor is also greater than 1.0, its seasonal adjustment has a similar downward impact on that quarter's original level.

The seasonally adjusted values in Table 3-3 indi-cate that the number of airport passengers rose steadily throughout 1987 until its fourth quarter decline. As we now know, the removal of the S pat-tern through seasonal adjustment has left the C/T and I elements. From this point, we can apply the smooth-ing procedures described in Chapter Two to remove I and identify the underlying trend in this series. This will be discussed later in this chapter.

Seasonal Factor Performance

The analyst usually wants to check the calculated seasonal factors for reasonability. This can be satisfactorily accomplished by comparing the seasonally adjusted series with the actual data. Since seasonality offsets itself over a year, summing the seasonally adjusted airline data for the four quarters of a given year should provide an annual value which closely corresponds to the actual annual data.

Going back to Table 3-3, the seasonally adjusted values for the four quarters of 1987 sum to 10.018 million passengers. The aggregation of the unadjusted traffic for this same period is 10.008 million. While this test is far from conclusive, it provides the forecaster a level of comfort that the seasonal factors, in totality, appear reasonable.

Deseasonalizing Difficult Series

In Table 3-2, the ordered ratios for each quarter have strikingly similar values. For instance, the first period ratio-to-moving averages of 1.140, 1.143, 1.199, and 1.131 are in close proximity. This implies that the data set has exhibited a stable seasonal pattern over time.

Certain series, however, do not respond to the classical decomposition approach because of extreme volatility or unusual patterns. In these situations, there are large variations between the individual elements within each ratio-to-moving average group. Where classical decomposition has been unsuccessful, there is a lack of uniformity or commonality within a period's factors, reflecting the method's inability to isolate the S pattern.

Multifamily housing permits for local areas is one example where the seasonal pattern is difficult to identify using decomposition. This is because the data often fluctuate greatly as large blocks of apartment or condominium permits may be reported in any month. Such sharp, random movements in the series can obscure the seasonal pattern.

Inflows and outflows from savings-and-loan associations are also difficult to treat for seasonality. In this case, the S pattern can change dramatically over time in response to new banking regulations and instruments which alter the consumer's savings patterns.

In these instances, an alternative method for removing the seasonal influence is to use a twelve-month moving average of the series. By definition, a 12-month average is free of seasonality. In addition, the longer time frame smooths the data, thus muting any irregularities. The drawback, however, is that this lengthy period responds slowly to upward or downward trends in the actual data since each new observation has only a one-twelfth impact.

The Census II Program

The classical decomposition method we have focused on is a simple and effective approach for seasonally adjusting data. However, more sophisticated procedures are also available.

One of these is the Census II method, developed by the Bureau of the Census during the 1950s. The latest version of Census II, called the X-11 program, is perhaps the most widely utilized method for calculating seasonality. It is used for adjusting most of the major U.S. economic series, including the Consumer and Producer Price Indices, as well as the National Income and Product Accounts (also known as the GNP accounts). This program, like the previous generation of Census II methods, is based on the classical decomposition framework. However, it employs a more rigorous examination of the data.

First, X-11 has the ability to adjust for differences in the number of weekdays from month to month and also year to year. This correction, called a trading-day adjustment, can be important where sales of a product are strong on certain days. For example, a particular store may be open only from Monday through Friday. The X-11 program is able to adjust for the fact that the number of weekdays in February is different from the number in March. In addition, it also adjusts for the fact that the number of weekdays in February varies from one year to the next.

Another important refinement in the X-11 method is that it eliminates extreme values, better known as outliers. The removal of these points is based on the supposition that they are likely the result of nonrecurring activities or data-collection errors. While the medial average presented in our example has a similar purpose, the X-11 approach is more rigorous.

Finally, the X-11 program attempts to identify and isolate the cyclical pattern in the data series. Care is necessary in interpreting these results, however, since the irregular nature of business cycles makes it difficult to monitor and project.

Combining Seasonality and Smoothing

Once again we return to our data series which has the patterns of C/T, S, and I. Smoothing methods to remove the I pattern were presented in Chapter Two. This was followed by a discussion of the mechanism for treating seasonality in the beginning of this chapter. We will now combine the procedures of seasonally adjusting and smoothing in order to identify the S component, eliminate the I variation, and project the underlying C/T.

Seasmooth—Dealing with Seasonality and Smoothing

There are several approaches for separating the S and I components from the data. The method presented here, named Seasmooth (from *sea*sonal and *smooth*ing), involves yet another three-step process which seasonally adjusts and smooths the series to arrive at a forecast. The first step removes the seasonal pattern. Step two smooths the data and provides a seasonally adjusted forecast. The final step then returns the seasonality to the projection. This process is a simple chore since we have already discussed the mechanics. Let's go through each step and see how we arrive at a projection.

Step One: Removing the Seasonality. The first step, which seasonally adjusts the original data, should be fresh in our minds from the previous discussion. In Table 3-4 we are again presenting the Tampa airport passenger data from the seasonal adjustment exercise. Column 1 contains passenger traffic in its original or unadjusted form. By dividing this column by the seasonal factors (col. 2) developed in the prior section, the seasonal impact is removed. That is, the series is seasonally adjusted (col. 3). Reviewing this calculation, first-quarter passengers of 2.837 divided by its seasonal factor of 1.154 yields a seasonally adjusted value of 2.458.

Step Two: Smoothing the Adjusted Data. The neutralization of seasonality leaves the C/T and I patterns. Next, a smoothing technique is utilized to remove the irregular or random pattern. In this example, a two-period SMA has been chosen for ease of explanation. The moving average is applied to the seasonally adjusted passenger data in column 3. From

Table 3-4. Tampa International Airport Passengers (millions).

Yr. Qtr.	(1) Passengers	(2) Seasonal Factor	(3) Passengers S.A.	(4) Two-Period Moving Average	(5) Forecast S.A.	(6) Seasonal Factor	(7) Forecast Unadjusted
1987							
1	2.837	1.154	2.458	—	—	—	—
2	2.691	1.050	2.563	2.511	—	—	—
3	2.200	0.852	2.582	2.573	2.511	0.852	2.139
4	2.280	0.944	2.415	2.499	2.573	0.944	2.429
1988							
1	—	—	—	—	2.499	1.154	2.884

64

the table, the first- and second-quarter seasonally adjusted values of 2.458 and 2.563 are averaged to yield 2.511 (col. 4). This value becomes the third-quarter forecast. Thus, step two has generated a seasonally adjusted SMA passenger projection (col. 5).

Step Three: Reinstating the Seasonal Effect. Companies usually want projections that include the seasonal influence. The reason is simply that forecasts which contain seasonality are directly comparable to the actual (unadjusted) data, which also possess the seasonal pattern. If this is the format management desires, then the seasonal element must be returned to the projections in column 5. To do this, the forecasts in column 5 are multiplied by the appropriate seasonal factors for the individual quarters (col. 6). This yields forecasts in column 7 that correspond directly to the actual passenger data. Returning to Table 3-4, the third-quarter seasonally adjusted forecast of 2.511 in column 5 is multiplied by the third-quarter seasonal factor of 0.852 to provide an unadjusted projection of 2.139.

Removing the seasonality from the original data only to return it to the smoothed forecast might appear to be a circular operation, but it is not. In fact, neglecting to seasonally adjust the original data can have a disastrous impact on forecast accuracy, as well as career advancement.

Vivid proof of the perils related to bypassing the seasonal adjustment process is provided in Table 3-5. In this table, a forecast is generated for the third and fourth quarters based on data that have not been seasonally corrected. This projection is then compared to the forecast developed in Table 3-4. As the MADs for these projections show, the variance resulting from the incorrect method (unadjusted for seasonality) is considerably higher than from Seasmooth (.365 vs. .105).

Table 3-5. Forecast Accuracy—Unadjusted versus S.A. (Seasmooth), (millions).

Year Quarter	Incorrect Forecast Based on Unadjusted Passengers			Correct Forecast Based on Seasonally Adjusted Passengers		
	Forecast	Actual	Absolute Variance	Forecast	Actual	Absolute Variance
1987						
3	2.764	2.200	.564	2.139	2.200	.061
4	2.446	2.280	.166	2.429	2.280	.149
1988						
1	2.240	—	—	2.884	—	—
Mean Absolute Deviation			.365			.105

Also noteworthy are the projections for the first quarter of 1988. Historically, first-quarter passenger traffic has been considerably higher than fourth-quarter traffic due to the winter tourist season in Tampa. Yet, the forecast developed from the unadjusted passenger data anticipates first-quarter traffic to be below the previous period (2.240 vs. 2.280). By comparison, the first-quarter 1988 Seasmooth forecast of 2.884 looks reasonable. The "unusual" unadjusted projection has been based on actual third- and fourth-quarter passenger figures which have not been altered to reflect their seasonally influenced lower level of activity. The process has incorrectly rolled this slower seasonal pattern into the first-period forecast.

Exercise

To put Seasmooth into practice, let's take as an example the Maze Department Store. As a member of Maze's planning department, our analyst is asked to examine recent sales history and project the store's revenues for the coming quarter. This revenue forecast will become the cornerstone for the company's short-term purchasing, inventory, and hiring policies.

In Table 3-6, the analyst has gathered four years

Table 3-6. Maze Department Store Sales (thousands of dollars).

Year	Quarter		Year	Quarter	
1984	4	371			
1985	1	218	1987	1	259
	2	272		2	349
	3	266		3	326
	4	410		4	496
1986	1	243	1988	1	282
	2	307		2	368
	3	282		3	352
	4	461			

Figure 3-1. Maze Department Store Sales.

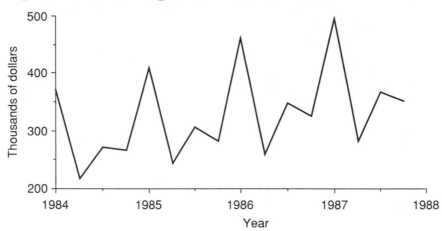

of quarterly information. The analyst starts by attempting to understand the patterns in the data. As we have seen, a good way to obtain initial familiarity with the series is to plot the values (Figure 3-1). From this picture, the analyst can identify a probable seasonal pattern as well as an upward trend.

Following these initial impressions, the analyst can proceed to the forecast stage using the three steps we've outlined.

Step One: Removing the Seasonality

Once again, the purpose of this step is to identify and remove the S pattern in the original data. As a starting point, the analyst calculates the seasonal factors, utilizing the classical decomposition approach. Table 3-7 contains the complete process. A simple rather than a medial average is used to compute the seasonal factors since there are only three ratio-to-moving average observations for each quarter. (Medial calculation requires at least four values since you need to have two or more observations to average after dropping the highest and lowest values.)

Table 3-7. Maze Department Store—Seasonal Factor Calculation (thousands of dollars).

Year	Quarter	Sales	One-Year Moving Average	Centered Moving Average	Ratio-to-Moving Average
1984	4	371		—	—
1985	1	218		—	—
			282		
	2	272		287	.948
			292		
	3	266		295	.902
			298		
	4	410		303	1.353
			307		
1986	1	243		309	.786
			311		
	2	307		317	.968
			323		
	3	282		325	.868
			327		
	4	461		333	1.384
			338		
1987	1	259		344	.753
			349		
	2	349		354	.986
			358		
	3	326		361	.903
			363		
	4	496		366	1.355
			368		
1988	1	282		372	.758
			375		
	2	368		—	—
	3	352		—	—

Quarters	1	2	3	4	Total
	0.786	0.948	0.902	1.353	
	0.753	0.968	0.868	1.384	
	0.758	0.986	0.903	1.355	
Simple Average	0.766	0.967	0.891	1.364	3.988
Adjustment	0.768	0.970	0.894	1.368	4.000
(4.000/3.988 = 1.0030)					

We have not included a step-by-step explanation of the seasonal calculations because the process was already covered in detail. However, it will be useful for the reader to go through the computations as a review. The calculated seasonal factors for this series (Table 3-7) exhibit the expected patterns of a retail establishment. Specifically, the fourth-quarter factor of 1.368 indicates that sales have historically been 37% above the average for the year due to the December holiday season. In addition, the first quarter has been the slowest period as sales activity has been 23% below normal.

After deriving the quarterly seasonal factors, the analyst adjusts the sales data to remove the seasonality. As before, this involves dividing the quarterly unadjusted sales figures by the appropriate seasonal factor. In Table 3-8, all fourth-quarter sales in column 1 are divided by 1.368. This seasonal adjustment deflates the actual data by recognizing that this quarter's activity has historically been well above normal. On the other hand, all first-quarter sales are increased to remove the seasonal effect of this quarter, which is always below the rest of the year.

Step Two: Smoothing the Adjusted Data

With seasonality removed, the remaining patterns in the sales series are C/T and I. At this point, we want to eliminate the I pattern and isolate the C/T. All smoothing techniques are capable of achieving this goal. However, the analyst feels that the DES method is most suitable for quickly capturing the upward trend of the data observed in Figure 3-1.

In the model-building process, analysts normally experiment with several alpha values to determine the one that most closely replicates the seasonally adjusted series (lowest MAD). Our example, however,

Table 3-8. Maze Department Store—Seasonal Adjustment of Sales (thousands of dollars).

Year	Quarter	(1) Unadjusted Sales	/	(2) Seasonal Factors	=	(3) Seasonally Adjusted Sales
1984	4	371		1.368		271
1985	1	218		0.768		284
	2	272		0.970		280
	3	266		0.894		298
	4	410		1.368		300
1986	1	243		0.768		316
	2	307		0.970		316
	3	282		0.894		315
	4	461		1.368		337
1987	1	259		0.768		337
	2	349		0.970		360
	3	326		0.894		365
	4	496		1.368		363
1988	1	282		0.768		367
	2	368		0.970		379
	3	352		0.894		394

only examines an alpha of 0.6. The DES historical fit and forecast for the fourth quarter of 1988 are provided in Table 3-9.

Step Three: Returning the Seasonality to the Forecast

The seasonally adjusted forecasts for the individual quarters are contained in column 7 of Table 3-9. Although the SES and DES calculations in columns 3 and 4 are shown to the nearest tenth, the forecast has been rounded to match the precision of the actual series.

As previously noted, companies usually want the seasonal pattern returned to the forecast so that it can be compared with the actual sales figures. In this exercise, the fourth-quarter 1988 sales projection of

Table 3-9. Maze Department Store—Double Exponential Smoothing (thousands of dollars) (Alpha = 0.6).

(1) Time Years		(2) Actual S.A. Sales	(3) Single Exponential Smoothing	(4) Double Exponential Smoothing	(5) (3) + (3) − (4)	(6) Portion of (3) − (4)	(7) Forecast S.A.
1984	4	271.0	271.0	271.0	—	—	—
1985	1	284.0	278.8	275.7	281.9	4.7	—
	2	280.0	279.5	278.0	281.0	2.3	287.0
	3	298.0	290.6	285.6	295.6	7.5	283.0
	4	300.0	296.2	292.0	300.4	6.3	303.0
1986	1	316.0	308.1	301.7	314.5	9.6	307.0
	2	316.0	312.8	308.4	317.2	6.6	324.0
	3	315.0	314.1	311.8	316.4	3.5	324.0
	4	337.0	327.8	321.4	334.2	9.6	320.0
1987	1	337.0	333.3	328.5	338.1	7.2	344.0
	2	360.0	349.3	341.0	357.6	12.5	345.0
	3	365.0	358.7	351.6	365.8	10.7	370.0
	4	363.0	361.3	357.4	365.2	5.9	376.0
1988	1	367.0	364.7	361.8	367.6	4.4	371.0
	2	379.0	373.3	368.7	377.9	6.9	372.0
	3	394.0	385.7	378.9	392.5	10.2	385.0
	4	—	—	—	—	—	403.0

$403 is multiplied by the corresponding seasonal factor (1.368) to generate an unadjusted forecast of $551. After examining for reasonability, the analyst would present this forecast to management.

Winters' Method

There is an alternative to Seasmooth for seasonally adjusting and removing the irregular pattern in the same process. This method, called Winters' Linear and Seasonal Exponential Smoothing, was developed by Peter Winters and described in his article in the April 1960 issue of *Management Science*. In addition, Wheelwright and Makridakis' book, *Forecasting Methods for Management*, has an excellent explanation of this procedure.

Winters' approach is based on three equations. One equation removes seasonality, and another identifies the trend. The third equation concentrates on smoothing the irregular, or random, element. This technique is quite similar to the DES Seasmooth procedure utilized in our forecasting example. As in Seasmooth, trial and error is necessary to determine the weighting factor that best recreates the historical series.

Summary

The completion of Chapter Three is a major milestone in your exploration of forecasting. You now have in your arsenal several time-series tools for making projections. The most powerful of these is Seasmooth, which has the versatility to deal with the numerous patterns encountered in forecast situations.

You are now ready to try your wings and generate a time-series projection. A suggested approach is to apply the steps from our examples to a specific data set of particular interest to you. As a reminder, utilize the DES method by itself where the data series is annual. For data of shorter duration (monthly and quarterly), Seasmooth with the DES procedure is the most appropriate technique.

In the next chapter, we will complete our examination of time-series methods by discussing indicators, time trends, and the Box-Jenkins approach. After that, we will move into causal modeling, which is the second group of quantitative forecasting techniques.

4

Time-Series Methods Continued

A trend is a trend is a trend, but the question is
where will it end?

—Leo's Lament

We spent the past chapter developing and combining
the concepts of seasonality and higher order exponential smoothing. We will now shift to other important
time-series approaches, including time trends, Box-
Jenkins, and economic indicators. While there are
numerous time-series methods, these are among the
more popular and widely used.

Time Trends

The time trend is usually one of the first methods
learned by the beginning forecaster. It involves fitting
a trend line to a data series which best reflects the
shape of the series. The line can be either linear or
curvilinear, depending on which form best represents
the data.

In years past, the common method for developing
a linear time trend was to draw a line through the
center of the plotted data using a ruler. The advent of
microcomputers, however, allows for a more accurate
fit.

The means for developing this line is a regression equation. Regression analysis will be presented
in detail in Chapters Five through Eight, but for now

we will discuss the fundamentals necessary to understand its application to time-trend development. As we will find in later chapters, regressions are the primary vehicle for generating causal models. Trending, however, is the only group of time-series methods developed using regressions.

Trends are also differentiated from other time-series approaches in their forecast-time horizon. As we have noted, the general class of time-series techniques is mainly used for short-term projections. The exception, however, is time trends, which can be employed for long- as well as short-term forecasts.

The objective of time trends, like the smoothing devices, is to remove the I pattern from a data series and reveal the C/T. Because trending (like smoothing) is not utilized for treating seasonality, data series with seasonal patterns must be adjusted before the underlying trend can be determined. Just as in Chapter Two, we'll avoid the obstacle of seasonality by using examples with annual data.

Three of the more popular time trends are linear, exponential, and polynomial functions. We will begin our discussion by explaining these three groups and showing how to apply them in developing a projection.

Linear Trend Line

The linear time trend assumes a constant, annual change in a series. The mathematical form of this line is $Y = a + bx$ where Y is the series to be projected, a is the y–intercept, x is time, and b signifies the constant annual increase or decrease. The b value is the most important element of the equation as it represents the yearly nominal change in the series that the equation is projecting. In addition, the equation line developed from the regression represents the best fit to the data series. The trend-fitting approach is similar to the smoothing methods in that the model chosen is the one that best recreates the past values of the series.

Figure 4-1(A) shows an increasing linear trend line. The straight fit reflects the fact that the series is being increased every year by a constant value (b).

Exponential Trend

In the linear trend, the b coefficient of the $Y = a + bx$ equation measures a constant change in a series based on its previous performance. Sometimes, however, a curvilinear line might best describe the trend. One of the more widely used is the exponential trend, which expresses the data/time relationship in terms of a constant-percent change.

The equation for an exponential trend is $\ln Y = a + bx$ where $\ln Y$ represents the natural logarithm of Y. This form is somewhat similar to the linear trend except that the Y is replaced by $\ln Y$. In addition, the b value represents a constant rate of percent change rather than the absolute change of the linear function.

Figure 4-1. Trend Lines.

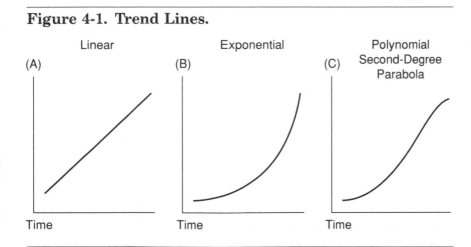

Linear	Exponential	Polynomial Second-Degree Parabola
(A)	(B)	(C)
Time	Time	Time

Figure 4-1(B) shows an increasing exponential trend. In this example, the series curves upward. This is because the constant growth rate applied to an expanding base results in increasing absolute additions over time. This concept is comparable to the effect of compound interest rates. For example, an 8% return on a $100 investment adds $8.00 to the base in the first year. In the next year, the 8% rate on the expanded base ($108) generates $8.64 of interest. By the tenth year, the annual contribution from the 8% is $16.00.

Polynomial Trend

Another curvilinear form is the fitted polynomial, whose standard equation is $Y = a + b_1x + b_2x^2 + \cdots b_nx^n$ where x, as always, is time. A common form is a second-degree polynomial or parabola which has the equation $Y = a + b_1x + b_2x^2$. This functional form allows for varying incremental changes to the series from one period to the next.

Figure 4-1(C) illustrates an increasing parabolic trend line. In this example, the curve advances rapidly in the early years, then moderates in later years as incremental additions slow. This variation from year to year is the result of having two variables (x_1 and x^2) to represent time. At some point, the parabola will reach a peak and begin to decline.

A third-degree polynomial, where Y is modelled against time, time squared, and time cubed, can also be utilized by the forecaster in developing a time trend. Still another approach is for the analyst to examine a logarithmic second-degree polynomial (parabola) by taking the ln Y and fitting it against time and time squared. In this case, the equation allows for varying rates of change in the series being projected.

Choosing the Appropriate Trending Form

Prior to the mid-1970s, forecasting texts provided formulas so that the forecaster could calculate the a and b values of the $Y = a + bx$ equations. The advent of high-powered calculators and microcomputers, however, has left this task to machines. Many calculators include an internal program for generating a regression line. In addition, many statistical software packages such as Lotus 1-2-3® have an option for implementing this calculation.

This has freed the forecaster to concentrate on the appropriate functional form to give the time trend; that is, whether it should be a linear, exponential, or polynomial function. As with the smoothing techniques, most analysts look for the form that provides the best replication of the historic time series. In the smoothing methods, the determining measures are the lowest MAD, MSE, or MAPE. In time trends, analysts utilize a test called R squared (or R^2), also known as the coefficient of determination. It represents the portion of the movement in the historic Y series that correlates with the x, or time, variable. The R^2 ranges between 0 and 1: the closer its value to 1, the better the time variable has tracked the Y series movements, and the better the equation fits the historical data.

Exercise One

Like the smoothing methods, the historical fit is just one consideration in building a trend model. More specifically, three important elements are (1) plotting and analyzing the data, (2) finding the model which best fits the data, and (3) testing the calculated forecast for reasonability.

With this background, let's try our first forecasting exercise. In it, a government demographer is developing a 1990 trend-line projection for U.S. population. The objective is to arrive at the form that best represents the series.

As noted above, the first step is to plot and examine the data set—in this case U.S. population from 1963 to 1987. Figure 4-2 is a graphic representation of the data series. From it, we notice that population has increased at a steady pace through time. In addition, the course of the data appears to follow a straight line.

An examination of the R^2 values from the time regressions in Table 4-1 indicates that all three forms fit the data extremely well. In all cases, the R^2 is over .999, which is quite close to a perfect fit of 1.000. Thus, each of the three forms does a good job of replicating the past data.

Let's look at the 1990 population projections from each of these three trends based on the equations from annual data covering 1963 to 1987. The equation for

Figure 4-2. U. S. Population.

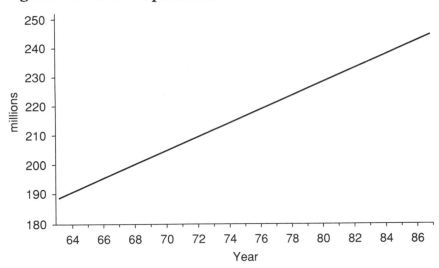

Source: Bureau of the Census, Department of Commerce.

Table 4-1.   U.S. Population Time-Trend Regressions.

	Type	R^2	1990 Forecast (millions)
1.	Linear	0.999	250.4
2.	Exponential	0.999	252.4
3.	Polynomial—Second-degree (Parabola)	0.999	251.1

the linear trend line is

$$\text{Population} = 189.4 + 2.26 \times \text{Time}$$

where time consists of years benchmarked from 0 (1963) to 24 (1987). The regression coefficient value of 2.26 represents an annual constant increase in population and is the slope of the line.

In order to project population, the demographer simply inserts the benchmarked year into the equation. Thus, a 1990 forecast (year 27) is derived from the equation

$$\text{Population} = 189.4 + 2.26 \times (27) = 250.4 \text{ million}$$

The exponential trend, as noted, represents a constant rate of change expressed in percent. In this form, the equation is presented as

$$\text{Natural log of Population} = 5.249 + 0.01045 \times \text{Time}$$

The rate of change implied by the equation can be calculated by taking the antilog of the equation's b value and subtracting 1. In this example, the antilog of the natural log 0.01045 is 1.01050. Subtracting 1 from this value and multiplying by 100 (to put in percentage form) yields a 1.050% constant growth rate projection for population based on the historic trend fit.

Using this equation to forecast 1990 population, the calculation is the natural log of Population

= 5.249 + .01045(27) = 5.531 or 252.4 million. This projection is a little higher than the 250.4 generated by the linear trend line.

The second-degree polynomial or parabolic line equation is expressed as

$$\text{Population} = 189.8 + 2.145 \times \text{Time}$$
$$+ .00465 \times \text{Time squared}$$

Plugging in values of 27 for Time and 729 for Time squared yields a population projection of 251.1 million for 1990, which falls between the linear and exponential forecasts.

In this exercise, the projection covers a relatively short time frame, and the results of the three trend lines all appear reasonable. Demographers, however, are also interested in long-term forecasts, and tend to be wary of exponential trend lines for longer time periods because the exponential form represents a constant percent change over time. For a population forecast, a constant rate of change applied (as in compound interest) to an increasing base results in accelerating population additions in future years. For a time period exceeding ten years this can produce an unrealistic projection.

In this case, the small annual rate of 1.050% does not appear to have much of a distorting influence. However, using an exponential trend for a rapidly growing state such as Florida or California could produce bizarre results over a long-term forecast.

At this point, our demographer has collected a considerable amount of information. First, a visual examination of the plotted data seems to indicate an upward linear function. Second, an exponential trend, though acceptable in the short term, is not appropriate since the demographer also plans to use this model for long-term projections. Third, all three forms appear to fit the historical data well, and produce short-term

(1990) forecasts that seem reasonable. In choosing a model, a useful rule of thumb is to utilize the simplest structure, which is the linear function, where the statistical evidence does not lean toward a clearly superior form. Accordingly, our demographer selects the linear trend model.

In our example, the demographer has examined only one time period (1963 to 1987). In the real world, several periods should be analyzed, as data can exhibit changing trends through time. Thus, the forecaster will want to test different time frames to be sure the model represents the most appropriate trend.

This is the first forecast example where we have seen judgment employed in the decision-making process. The use of judgment, however, is almost always necessary in forecasting. In fact, the forecaster is constantly making choices involving which time period to examine, decisions about whether the shape of the historical line might be changing, and about which forecast method is most appropriate. As in any other profession, judgment improves as the forecaster gains more experience.

Exercise Two

In this exercise, we extend the trending process to other functional forms as a trade association analyst wants to develop a 1997 trend projection for sales of microwave ovens. The data being examined cover 1970 to 1987, and the analyst is experimenting with a third-order polynomial as well as exponential polynomials.

Figure 4-3 provides a plot of the microwave series. The form is particularly interesting, as it starts out slowly, then accelerates. This shape corresponds to that of the upward-moving parabola in Figure 4-1(C).

The analyst has run time-trend regressions for

Figure 4-3. Microwave Oven Shipments.

Microwave Oven Shipments

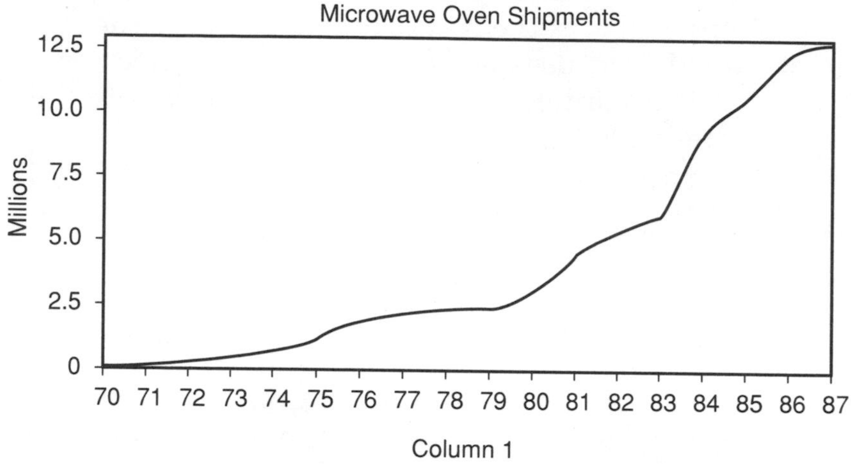

Source: Dealerscope Merchandising

the linear, exponential, and second-order polynomial (parabola) forms examined in exercise one. In addition, regressions were generated for a third-order polynomial plus a second- and third order exponential polynomial. We recall that the polynomial allows for varying absolute changes over time while an exponential polynomial provides for varying percent changes.

Table 4-2 contains the summary results, including the R squared and the 1997 forecast. The findings are consistent with the information obtained from the data plot. That is, the fitted polynomial trend lines have best replicated the historic microwave series.

An examination of the 1997 forecasts from the trending equations shows some unusual projections. The exponential function yields an unreasonably high forecast of 474.73 million. This projection is the result of the 43% average annual growth rate that the series has experienced. It is extremely doubtful that such rapid expansion could be expected in the future.

Table 4-2. Microwave Oven Trend Line Regressions.

	Type	R^2	Actual 1987 Level (Millions)	1997 Forecast (Millions)
1.	Linear	0.856	12.74	17.98
2.	Exponential	0.901	12.74	474.73
3.	Polynomial Second-Order	0.975	12.74	24.01
4.	Polynomial Third-Order	0.981	12.74	42.14
5.	Exp. Polynomial Second-Order	0.968	12.74	1.72
6.	Exp. Polynomial Third-Order	0.988	12.74	263448.91

However, the equation for the exponential forecast incorporates this past rapid growth.

The exponential polynomials have completely divergent projections. The second-order form generates a forecast which is exceptionally low, while the third-order projection is unrealistically high. This exercise highlights the potential difficulties with the curvilinear functions and the need to analyze projections for reasonability.

Also noteworthy in Table 4-2 is that the third-order polynomials have higher R^2 values than their second-order counterparts. This is always the case, as the fit must improve with each additional term or order. In fact, R^2 will reach 1.00 if a sufficiently high-order polynomial is utilized. The problem with increasing the order is that the equation begins to respond to the I pattern as well as the C/T. Once these random movements are ingrained in the model, forecast accuracy is endangered. Thus, the forecaster must make a judgment as to which polynomial degree to use. In most cases, the reasonability of the projection provides the needed guidance.

In our example the second- and third-order polynomials appear to be the most appropriate functions.
The analyst has chosen the second-order parabola
since its forecast of 24.01 for 1997 is closer to the modeler's expectations for sales.

Exercise Three

Trending equations are useful for data that have an
upward or downward C/T pattern. However, they cannot be applied to horizontally trended or stationary
series. In this exercise, a local business analyst wants
to derive a trend projection for manufacturing employment in the food-processing industry.

The data series, which covers 1970 to 1986, is
plotted in Figure 4-4, and indicates movement around
a stationary trend.

Regression analysis confirms this finding, as a

**Figure 4-4. Food Processing Employment, Hillsborough
County (FL).**

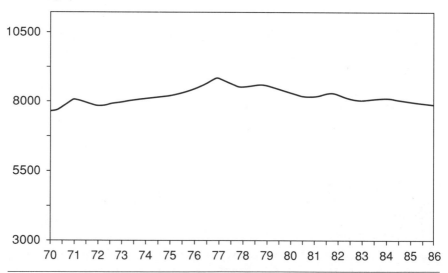

Source: Department of Labor and Employment Security, State of Florida

linear regression between the data and time produces an R^2 near 0. That is, there is no correlation between the stationary employment series and the increasing years which represent time.

Since there is no significant relationship, the trend approach cannot be utilized. Nevertheless, the analyst has other alternatives. A forecast can be developed by using the average (mean) of the data set or by applying the DES approach to smooth the series.

Summary

We see that the time-trend line has the same purpose as its smoothing brethren, which is to uncover the C/T pattern in the data. A visual examination of the basic series is the first step in finding the most appropriate time trend. In addition, different time periods as well as different forms (linear and curvilinear) should be analyzed.

The limitations of time-series analysis should also be kept in mind. That is, the trend line describes the path of the series being examined, not the causes or factors influencing that path. Because of this, extreme care should be taken in extrapolating trends into the future since some natural or economic phenomenon could change the historic trend in the coming years. As always, an examination of the forecast for reasonability is a necessary part of the process.

Table 4-3 reviews the various types of trends and their major characteristics.

Box-Jenkins Method

The Box-Jenkins (B-J) method, named after the two British statisticians who developed it, is one of the most sophisticated time-series techniques. The intricate nature of B-J has made it more popular in academic circles than in the business community. Still,

Table 4-3. Popular Trend Lines.

Type	Form	Characteristics
1. Linear	$Y = a + bx$	Constant change in the level or nominal value of the series
2. Exponential	$\ln Y = a + bx$	Constant percent change in the series
3. Polynomial	$Y = a + bx + bx^2 + \cdots$	Varying change in the level or nominal value of the series
4. Exponential polynomial	$\ln Y = a + bx + bx^2 + \cdots$	Varying percent change in the series

many companies have successfully utilized this technique for projecting data series.

Despite its rigorous theoretical framework, the objectives and general methodology of B-J are consistent with the other time-series approaches. First, B-J seeks to determine the underlying pattern of the data and to project these trends into the future. In addition, it is mostly utilized for short-term forecasting, and is especially appropriate for the 12- to 18-month time frame. Third, the primary goal of B-J is to develop a model which best recreates the historical series being analyzed. Finally, a wide range of coefficients are tested to determine the one that minimizes the historical error.

Special Characteristics

The development of a B-J model requires the initial step of creating subsidiary series from the original data set. These sub-series are developed by lagging the original observations. For a series with values 1, 2, 3, 4, and 5, a one-period lagged sub-series begins with the second observation in the original series. Therefore, the new series has the values 2, 3, 4, and 5. As we will see, the comparison of these sub-series serves as the basis for the derivation of B-J models.

The primary vehicle utilized for comparing these sub-series is autocorrelations, which measure the relationship between any two data sets from the same series. The measurement tool is called the autocorrelation coefficient (r), which ranges from -1 to $+1$. An r of $+1$ implies a strong direct relationship between the original and subsidiary series, whereas a -1 represents a strong inverse relationship. An autocorrelation value of 0 reflects complete independence between the original and subsidiary series.

The concept of subsidiary series helps us to understand the meaning of autocorrelation. Since *auto* means self, the term autocorrelation measures the relationship between various data sets of similar origin.

This is a good time to expand our discussion of time-series analysis. By far the dominant variety of time-series methods are those called univariate, which analyze only the series that is being projected. There are also multivariate methods which encompass other variables and are similar to the regression models we will study in the coming chapters. Multivariate time-series approaches, however, are rarely utilized in business because of their intricate nature.

Our discussion, therefore, will focus on the univariate B-J approach, which involves the examination of one basic data set. The sub-series (generated from the original data) and the autocorrelation vehicle provide the means to construct the optimal B-J model structure. Specifically, the analyst uses this information to identify one of three possible model types for explaining the original series.

1. The first possible structural form is called an AUTOREGRESSIVE (AR) model. In it the original series (Yt) is related to its past values $(Y_{t-1}, Y_{t-2}, \ldots, Y_{t-n})$.

2. The second type of model is where the original series (Y_t) is based on the previous error values or residuals $(e_t, e_{t-1}, e_{t-2}, \ldots, e_{t-n})$. This is called a MOVING AVERAGE (MA) model.

3. The third type is a combination of the first two, or an AUTOREGRESSIVE MOVING AVERAGE (ARMA) model. In this structure, projections are developed from past values as well as past errors.

In summary, the B-J model process begins with creating sub-series from the original data. The analyst examines this information, using autocorrelations to determine whether the most suitable model structure is an autoregressive (AR), a moving average (MA), or an autoregressive moving average (ARMA). With this background, we are ready to construct a model.

Identifying the Model

There are three steps in developing a B-J model. The first step is to identify a tentative model structure that the analyst believes best represents the patterns in the data. Following this identification, the analyst allows the computer to assign coefficients to the model terms which minimize the past forecast error. The third step is to examine the historic-model error to see if it is random. If it is not, the forecaster returns to step one and tests alternative structures.

The first step of identifying the model type is by far the most time-consuming and challenging. In it, the forecaster makes an initial determination as to whether the model is an AR, MA, or ARMA structure. To get to this point, however, all patterns (seasonal and cycle/trend) must be removed from the original data set. That is, the data set must be put in a constant, stationary, or horizontal form.

The removal of the patterns from the original series is achieved through a concept called differencing. It involves comparing the original data with a sub-series and the differencing, or subtraction, of their corresponding values to create a new stationary series. Using the previous original data set of $Y_t = 1, 2, 3, 4, 5$, the Y_{t-1} sub-series was 2, 3, 4, 5. Differencing of the Y_t and Y_{t-1} data sets creates a new stationary series 1, 1, 1, 1, (Table 4-4). This example is called the first difference. Most importantly, differencing has created a new stationary series devoid of pattern.

Two general types of differencing, called long and short, are used to remove patterns from the data. The purpose of long differencing is to remove the seasonal pattern. If the data are monthly, the analyst first determines whether the set has a seasonal pattern by examining the autocorrelations between the Y_t original series and the Y_{t-12}, Y_{t-24}, Y_{t-36} sub-series. If their autocorrelations are near $+1$, this indicates a seasonal pattern that must be removed. For quarterly data, a similar approach comparing Y_t to Y_{t-4}, Y_{t-8}, Y_{t-12} is used.

The objective of short differencing is to remove the cycle/trend patterns in the data. Similar to long differencing, it is first established whether a cycle/trend pattern exists. This is determined by analyzing the

Table 4-4. Differencing.

Original Y_t Series	Lagged Y_{t-1} Sub-series	New series
1	2	1
2	3	1
3	4	1
4	5	1
5		

autocorrelations between the Y_t original series and the Y_{t-1}, Y_{t-2} sub-series. If the autocorrelations are significant (near 1), a trend pattern exists. The computation in Table 4-4 provides an example of short differencing to remove the trend.

We now begin to see how sub-series, autocorrelations and differencing work together. Autocorrelations of the sub-series identify the seasonal and cycle/trend patterns in the original data set. From this point, differencing is employed to remove these patterns and establish a stationary or horizontal series.

This stationary data series is the raw material from which the analyst tentatively identifies the model type. The forecaster specifically examines the autocorrelations and the partial autocorrelations* of this new horizontal or differenced series. The model determination is based on the following guidelines.

1. If the autocorrelations of the differenced series drop off exponentially to zero, the model is AR.

2. If the partial autocorrelations of the differenced series drop off exponentially to zero, it is an MA model.

3. If both the auto and partial autocorrelations drop off exponentially to zero, the model is ARMA.

After making the initial identification, the ana-

---

* Partial autocorrelations are quite similar to autocorrelations. While the autocorrelation measures the relationship between two data sets from the same time series, the partial autocorrelation includes this effect as well as the impact of those series which fall between the two data sets. For example, an autocorrelation between Y_t and Y_{t-3} measures their statistical relationship. The partial autocorrelation for these two series also includes the influence of Y_{t-1} and Y_{t-2}.

lyst must also decide on the number of terms or the order of the model. A first-order AR model is based on the Y_{t-1} values while a second-order model is based on the Y_{t-1} and Y_{t-2} values. For an AR type, the order is decided by the number of significant partial autocorrelations. The MA order, on the other hand, is based on the significant autocorrelations.

Fortunately, B-J models are usually no greater than two terms. Moreover, the majority of models, whether AR, MA, or ARMA, are of the first-order variety. This simple fact has preserved the sanity of many forecasters.

At this point, the identification process has been completed. To summarize step one, autocorrelations of the sub-series identify the S and C/T patterns in the original data. After differencing to remove these elements, the analyst examines the autocorrelations and partial autocorrelations of the new stationary series. From this, the model's structure and order are tentatively identified.

Specifying and Checking the Model

Once the model is identified correctly, the most difficult part of building a B-J model has been completed. Step two involves the estimation of parameters. This is performed by the computer program, which through trial and error generates the coefficients that minimize the MSE between the fitted model values and the data series.

The third and final step is to analyze the historical error or residuals of the fitted model. This requires examining the autocorrelations of the residuals. If the residual autocorrelations are insignificant, then clearly the error terms are completely random and the model structure has accurately included all the patterns in the data series. If the errors are related, it is apparent that certain patterns have been omitted;

in this case the modeler must return to step one to identify a new structure.

Summary

The above discussion of the B-J methodology has outlined its general principles and mechanisms. Developing the actual model, however, would require considerably more detail and time than is available in this primer. There are excellent books on constructing a B-J model. These include *A Practical Guide to Box-Jenkins Forecasting*, by John C. Hoff, and *Forecasting with Univariate Box-Jenkins Models*, by Alan Pankratz. Both of these texts are presented in an understandable form with useful examples and practical pointers.

Other Advanced Time-Series Methods

There are other highly rigorous time-series methods that we have not discussed, including techniques with such exotic names as state space forecasting and spectral analysis. While such methods may have features differentiating them from the other advanced procedures, they all pursue the same time-series objectives. One of the more popular approaches is adaptive forecasting, which constantly respecifies the model coefficients as new data are recorded. This is the equivalent, in exponential smoothing, of computing a new alpha after each new observation is reported.

This feature of adaptive forecasting provides both advantages and disadvantages. First, the automatic adjustment process can save the forecaster considerable time where thousands of items are being projected. In addition, if the latest data point truly indicates a changing pattern, then the spontaneous respecification process will correctly adjust for this change. Should the most recent observation reflect random noise, however, the process can lead to a less optimal model. From this, we are again reminded that the forecaster's judgment and reasonability check are still an essential part of the process. Despite ever-improving techniques resulting from new technology, the analyst will always need to rely on the element of experience.

Indicators

> Business cycles are like snowflakes; no two are alike.
>
> *—Unknown*

Indicators are a time-series application that attempts to identify short-term cyclical turning points. An indicator can be based on one or several component series. Whichever the case, the goal is to generate a structure that correlates or moves in some fashion with the variable you are attempting to forecast.

Unlocking the Mysteries of the Business Cycle

The best-known indicators are those that anticipate movements in the national economy. The most popular is the Index of Leading Economic Indicators (ILEI). Comprised of 11 component series, the ILEI is released on a monthly basis and historically has moved in advance of national economic activity.

The leading indicators are closely monitored by the news media and the business world. This interest is fueled by the inability of forecasters to correctly anticipate cyclical turning points. As noted in Chapter Two, cyclical movements are the most difficult pattern to project because each business cycle is quite different in length and magnitude.

Another reason for the ILEI's popularity is the dramatic impact that economic fluctuations have on businesses and investors. Early warning of an impending recession gives businessmen a chance to reduce inventories, streamline expenses, and make plans for riding out the storm. Similarly, advance notification of an economic recovery allows companies to gear up production to meet increased demand. In each case, knowing in advance that an upturn or downturn is coming gives businessmen a competitive edge.

The ability to foresee the future course of business also has implications for investors. Stock and bond market movements are directly related to business profitability and the economic situation. Moreover, interest rates usually crest after the peak of the cycle and touch bottom after the recovery begins. Insight into the present cyclical phase of the economy, therefore, can help steer the investor in the right direction.

Because of this interest, *The Wall Street Journal (WSJ)*[*] and *Business Week* closely track those economic series which provide clues to the future course of the economy. The *WSJ*, in fact, contains numerous articles on the ILEI and its component series.

Other Applications

Indicators are not just limited to providing advance warning about the economy. Coincident indicators, for example, measure the present level of activity. They are particularly useful in monitoring regional economies since there are no timely yardsticks to quantify local business activity as the Gross National Product does at the national level.

Indicators also have other applications besides measuring national and regional activity. Many trade

---

[*] Every Monday *WSJ* discusses an economic topic of interest in a front page article entitled "The Outlook." In addition, page two of the same issue contains "Tracking the Economy," which previews the important economic series that are to be released that week.

associations develop indicators which follow important trends in their industry. In addition, individual firms can generate their own specific series. A popular approach is to measure the lead time between new orders and sales. From this, early trends in new orders provide the company with a leading indicator of future revenues.

Types of Indicator Structures

Two common types of indicators are diffusion and acceleration. In the diffusion structure, the number of component series that register an absolute increase from the previous time period are weighted against the number that fall. If the number of advancing series exceeds those retreating, the index is positive, which has favorable implications.

The acceleration index measures the percent of change in the components rather than the absolute change. That is, the index compares those series that are increasing at a faster rate against those that are growing more slowly. It is important to note that before the absolute value of a series reaches a peak and begins to decline, a slowdown will occur in its rate of growth. Therefore, movements in an acceleration index always lead a diffusion index, providing the user with an earlier warning system. Acceleration indices, however, usually contain more random fluctuations, as rates of change are generally more volatile than absolute movements. Given the strengths and weaknesses of these two approaches, many indicator methods attempt to blend both diffusion and acceleration characteristics.

Limitations of Indicators

While a good leading indicator can correctly anticipate cyclical turning points, there are limits to an indicator's usefulness. One important shortcoming is that indicators can tell us the direction of economic activity, but cannot quantify the magnitude of the movement. Thus, an increase in the ILEI during a recession implies that the economy will begin to improve. The index cannot, however, project the rate of growth that will occur.

Indicators can also suffer from changing relationships. For example, a component series which previously anticipated economic movements might no longer have that ability. This has occurred in retail sales, which was once an advance indicator of movements in national economic activity.

Another limitation is that certain indicators may give false signals. A frequently noted example is the stock market price series of the ILEI. Since World War II, the stock-price component has always turned down before an economic recession and turned up before an economic recovery. This indicator, however, has also risen and fallen at other times, causing one economist to note wryly that it has successfully predicted nine of the last five recessions.

A final problem that can develop in an indicator index is a change in the lead time between one of the components and the series to be projected. This has occurred in the money-supply series of the ILEI as its lead over economic activity has risen and fallen over the past several decades.

In summary, any indicator index should be reexamined periodically since the component series can (1) lose their close relationship, (2) give false signals, and (3) fall out of sync with the projected series. In all cases, the solution to these potential problems is to include a large number of series in your indicator index. By increasing the number of components, you reduce the reliance on any individual component and mute any distorting influence it might have on the index.

Exercise

The governing commission of Davis County is interested in producing an index that measures local economic activity. At this time, various series are reported which monitor area employment, building permits, and consumer purchases. Yet there is no single index or series that quantifies total economic activity in the county. The purpose of the indicator series is to provide such a measure for the county. This is expected to help guide the commission in making legislative decisions affecting the business community.

The local state university extension volunteers to construct the indicator index. The major steps of the construction process involve (1) determining the index type, (2) identifying the component series, (3) adjusting the data for seasonality and the impact of inflation, and (4) calculating and interpreting the index results. Since there is no standard method for deriving an index, we will work through the example and discuss several available alternatives.

Determining the Index Type

The university's economic group decides to produce a diffusion index, which is to be called the Davis Index of Business Indicators (DIBI). This index will calculate changes in the absolute level of various components and serve as a coincident measure of local activity. That is, its movement will represent the latest trends in the local economy.

Identifying the Major Components

The group has chosen five component series for the index: (1) housing permits, (2) retail sales, (3) manufacturing employment, (4) total electricity sales, and (5) total employment. The objective of the selection is to have a representative series from the construction (housing permits), service (retail sales), and manufacturing (manufacturing employment) sectors, plus two aggregate or overall economic measures (total electricity sales, total employment).

The series used in the index also have to be reported on a timely basis and be easily obtainable. These criteria have been met since all the series chosen are released with a lag of only one to two months, and are available from public sources with the exception of electricity sales. This component is easily obtained from the local utility.

Removing Seasonality and Inflation

Since the indicator index is attempting to measure the C/T pattern in the local economy, the S element must first be removed from the five component series. This is initially attempted through classical decomposition. However, the economic group experiences difficulty in adjusting residential permits. The residential series is composed of single family and multifamily permits. As mentioned in Chapter Three, local multifamily authorizations are often difficult to adjust using the standard decomposition approach. This is because of extreme volatility in the data as large blocks of permits representing an apartment or condominium complex can appear in any given month. This dramatic impact makes it difficult to identify the seasonal pattern in the series.

The group decides that a 12-month moving average of the multifamily data should provide a solution to the seasonality problem. A 12-month average is devoid of seasonality, and the length of the term also serves to mute irregularities in the series. In order to maintain consistency throughout the index, the remaining series are also adjusted with a 12-month moving average.

It is also important that only unit volume or "real" economic activity be measured. Accordingly, any inflationary effects should be removed from the data. In this case, four of the five component series measure volume. The fifth series, retail sales, is reported in dollars, which reflects both changes in the quantity of retail items sold (volume) and product price increases (inflation). To remove the inflation effect, the series is divided by the Consumer Price Index. This procedure is provided in Chapter Nine's discussion on data.

Calculating and Interpreting the Index Results

At this point, the economic group's data base consists of five component series which are seasonally adjusted and reported in volume terms. From here, there are several possible approaches for constructing the DIBI.

The first approach rebases the five components to a specific time period, in this case January 1988. Economic change is measured from this starting point. Rebasing, also known as indexing, is accomplished by dividing each individual series point by its January-1988 value. In Table 4-5, residential building permits for January are 350. To index January and subsequent months, the values are divided by 350 and multiplied by 100. For example, February's permit index of 95.7 is arrived at by dividing 335 by 350 and multiplying by 100. Indexing places all the series in a common form; that is, standardizes the components. Without this procedure, adding dollars to permits to employees to gigawatt hours would be a messy process.

Once the components are indexed, the DIBI-1 calculation can be completed. In Table 4-5, the economic group has decided to give equal weight to the five components since any other method requires a number of tricky judgments. The process of equal weighting is

Table 4-5. DIBI-1 Calculation.

		12-Month M.A.		Indexed to Jan. 1988 = 100	
		Jan. 1988	Feb. 1988	Jan. 1988	Feb. 1988
1.	Residential Building Permits (Units)	350.0	335.0	100.0	95.7
2.	Retail Sales (Thousands of 1982–84 $)	130.8	133.2	100.0	101.8
3.	Manufacturing Employment (Thousands)	46.2	46.2	100.0	100.0
4.	Total Electricity Sales (Gigawatt Hours)	470.3	474.6	100.0	100.9
5.	Total Employment (Thousands)	215.1	216.1	100.0	100.5
		DIBI-1		100.0	99.8

done by taking a simple average of the sum of the five components. The DIBI-1 value for January 1988 is, naturally, 100, while the February 1988 index is 99.8.

An examination of the results, however, reveals certain weaknesses in the index format. Despite the fact that three of the five components increased between January and February and only one declined, the DIBI-1 has fallen slightly. This is the result of a drop in building permits, which fluctuate more than the other series. The volatility of the permit component has the potential to cause dramatic movements in the index.

It can also be argued that residential construction is a relatively smaller portion of total business activity than either services or manufacturing. Yet, the present format gives them equal representation.

The group's solution to this problem is to judgmentally assign weights to the components based on the group's perception of each series' relative importance to local economic growth. The weights given to the five components are

1.	Residential Permits	0.12
2.	Retail Sales	0.22
3.	Manufacturing Employment	0.16
4.	Electricity Sales	0.25
5.	Total Employment	0.25
	TOTAL	1.00 or 100%

The aggregate economic measures (components 4 and 5) are given the most weight because they reflect overall activity. Looking at the major sectors, services (component 2) are believed to be the major contributor to the economy, followed by manufacturing. Although the group is now using a weighting approach they originally dismissed, the results are more reasonable. Multiplying the individual component weights by their respective February values and summing the five weighted contributions yields a February DIBI-2 of 100.24 (Table 4-6). This represents a 0.24% rise in county business activity, which corresponds more closely with the individual series movements.

The Index of Leading Economic Indicators (ILEI) adjusts for the problem of volatile series in another manner. Specifically, it examines the monthly change in each of the individual components against a measure of their average long-term dispersion. Thus, it compares the monthly movements of a series to its normal volatility. In addition, the ILEI also weights each individual series based on its past performance in leading the national economy.

Certain group members are uncomfortable with the somewhat arbitrary method of assigning weights

Table 4-6. DIBI-2 Calculation (January 1988 = 100).

	February 1988	× Weight	= Weight-Adjusted Contribution
1. Residential Building Permits	95.7	0.12	11.48
2. Retail Sales (1982–84 $)	101.8	0.22	22.40
3. Manufacturing Employment	100.0	0.16	16.00
4. Total Electricity Sales	100.9	0.25	25.23
5. Total Employment	100.5	0.25	25.13
		DIBI-2	100.24

in DIBI-2. Therefore, they devise another approach (DIBI-3.). In this approach, each component receives a +1 when its level increases during the month. On the other hand, a decline in the series is noted by a −1, while a 0 represents no change in the level. Once the individual calculations are completed, the values are added together.

The potential range of DIBI-3 is from −5 to +5. A value of −5 represents a decline in activity, while a +5 shows solid economic growth.

Table 4-7 contains the DIBI-3 computations. For February 1988, the DIBI-3 reported value is +2, indicating that the local-area economy is on a moderate, upward course.

Summary

For the series used in our example, the DIBI-2 and DIBI-3 methods appear to offer the best tools for quantifying local economic activity. It should be noted, however, that this exercise has only scratched the surface of available procedures for generating economic indicators. For example, the Conference Board, a New

Table 4-7. DIBI-3 Calculation.

		12-Month M.A.		Change from Preceding Period
		January 1988	February 1988	February 1988
1.	Residential Building Permits (Units)	350.0	335.0	− 1
2.	Retail Sales (Thousands of 1982–84 $)	130.8	133.2	+1
3.	Manufacturing Employment (Thousands)	46.2	46.2	0
4.	Total Electricity Sales (Gigawatt Hours)	470.3	474.6	+1
5.	Total Employment (Thousands)	215.1	216.1	+1
	DIBI-3			+2

York economic research firm, has built a mechanism into their indices which allows the most recent data points to have the greatest weight.

Perhaps the most extensive research on economic indicators is taking place in the Department of Commerce, which produces the leading (ILEI), coincident, and lagging national indicators. Its methodology for developing these series is contained in the *Handbook of Cyclical Indicators*. In addition, the Department produces the monthly *Business Conditions Digest*, which provides the latest information on the component-indicator series.

Considerable work in this area has also been done by Geoffrey Moore, one of the founding fathers of the ILEI. As head of the Center for International Business

Cycle Research in New York, Moore has expanded his studies into international economic indicators. In addition, he has developed a weekly set of U.S. leading economic indicators for *Business Week*.

Kondratieff—The Ultimate Time-Series Forecaster?

The past three chapters have presented the major elements of time-series analysis. Although many of these methods and concepts have only recently been developed, one of the greatest time-series analysts made important contributions long before the advent of calculators and computers. Nicholai Alexandrovich Kondratieff was a Russian economist who served as a professor at the Agricultural Academy and as the leader of the Business Research Institute in Moscow. Kondratieff's major research took place in the 1920s, right after the Russian Revolution.

Kondratieff was extremely interested in examining movements in economic data. In his work, he identified a long-run cyclical behavior in price and economic activity. This pattern, later called the Kondratieff Wave, was discovered by smoothing price and production data for coal, iron, and other products. All his data series came from the capitalist countries of the United States, England, France, and Germany.

The wave portrayed these countries as experiencing a series of expansions and contractions, with each cycle involving a rise and fall encompassing approximately 55 years. At the time of his work, he had identified two and a half of these long-wave cycles. His theory correctly anticipated the Great Depression of the 1930s, which represented the contractionary part of the third cycle.

Kondratieff found that while the capitalist countries were prone to fluctuating economic activity, their economies were inherently stable, as every downturn was followed by an expansion. His conclusions did not endear him to the Marxist philosophy prevailing in Russia. His Russian critics objected that his theory depicted the capitalistic economic system as self-correcting. This "heresy" led to Kondratieff's banishment and death in Siberia.

Despite Kondratieff's unfortunate end, his work lives on and has become quite popular in recent years. The reason for this new surge of interest is that during the 50-plus years since the Great Depression, the capitalist economies have experienced extraordinary prosperity, following the up-phase of Kondratieff's fourth wave. The Western world, however, is now passing into the contractionary phase of the cycle's timetable. The major debate is whether the fourth wave will complete itself.

Whether or not this occurs, Kondratieff is still remembered for his groundbreaking work in studying data patterns. With today's emphasis on information analysis and research, he would be in great demand as a consultant.

5

Regression Analysis

Congratulations! Completion of Chapters One through Four qualifies you as a time-series forecasting expert. An updated perspective on where we have come and where we are going will be useful at this point. As we've discussed, there are two major categories of forecasting techniques: quantitative and qualitative. Within the quantitative school there are two further subdivisions: time-series and causal. Through the first four chapters, we have studied a variety of popular time-series methods. These methods examine the patterns in the data and are used primarily for short-term projections. We have found them to be rather straightforward and simple to implement.

Now we will begin to examine the second category of quantitative tools—the causal methods. These techniques develop projections based on the mathematical relationship between the series being examined and variables which influence that series. The vehicle for measuring this relationship is called regression analysis. Causal techniques are extremely flexible and are used for making short, medium, and long-term projections.

In the following pages, we will introduce causal modeling, regression analysis and the major statistical tests for determining the optimal forecasting equation. This involves a substantial amount of information. However, it's not necessary to commit all the details to memory. The purpose of this chapter is to serve as a foundation and reference guide for the exercises which follow. For now, simply familiarize yourself with the main ideas. Chapters Six and Seven will apply these concepts to real-life examples.

The development of causal models involves three major steps.

1. The forecaster attempts to hypothesize the structure of the model. Thus, a theoretical framework is developed which includes those series which may explain the variable being projected. For example, if an analyst is charged with forecasting company sales, the first step is to make a list of those factors that are believed to influence sales.

2. The forecaster develops a data set and utilizes regression analysis to quantify the relationships between the hypothesized variables and sales. This includes statistical testing to determine which variables can be empirically related to sales.

3. The forecaster uses the resulting mathematical equation from regression analysis to derive a forecast.

Of these three steps, the first is most critical. A sound understanding of those factors that influence sales is the key to a successful forecast model. Fortunately, this is an area in which you, as an informed student or employee, already have some knowledge. Steps two and three, covering regression analysis and the forecast calculation, primarily involve mechanical procedures. These latter steps can be picked up quickly, but the understanding of an industry's dynamics necessary for hypothesis development can only be gained by years of experience.

Regression Analysis

Regression analysis is the procedure for estimating the mathematical relationship between a series, such as sales, and the variables that are thought to impact on it. Regressions utilize a functional form to present these relationships. This form is $Y = f(X)$ where Y is the dependent variable to be forecasted and X represents the independent variable(s) influencing Y. In our example, sales are the dependent variable, and those factors hypothesized to influence sales are the independent variables.

It is important to note that while a regression quantifies the relationship between variables, it cannot prove causality. That is, the regression cannot confirm that the independent variables influence the dependent variable. The equation results can only determine whether a significant quantitative relationship exists between the series being examined.

Regression equations can take two forms. The first is the simple regression, which has one dependent and one independent variable. The second is the multiple regression, which has more than one independent variable. The simple regression is expressed as $Y = f(X)$. For the multiple regression, the form is $Y = f(X_1, X_2, \ldots, X_n)$, where X_n represents any number of independent variables. You may have noticed that the difference between simple and multiple regressions is only in the number of independent variables. All regressions have only one dependent variable.

There are also two data formats in regression analysis. The first, called time-series regression, develops an equation using historical data from a given period of time. For example, we might examine the relationship between a company's sales and the variables thought to influence it based on data from 1970 to 1988. In this way, we can identify the prominent factors and their impact over a specific time frame.

The second type is cross-sectional regression. Here, the data period is fixed at one point in time. An example would be an analysis of the sales of multiple companies selling a similar product at a certain time, perhaps the year 1988. In this study, the sales of each company for that year are regressed against variables such as the product price and advertising expenditures. In such a case, cross-sectional analysis allows us to determine the factors that differentiate the companies, and compare the firms' relative strengths.

The time-series format is by far the most common of the two categories in business forecasting, and the focus of our discussion in the following chapters will be on this type of regression. However, a cross-sectional exercise is included in Chapter Seven to show the objectives and uses of this approach.

Regression analysis, therefore, takes the historical data such as sales (dependent variable) and the series you believe are an influence on sales (independent or explanatory variables) and delineates a mathematical relationship between them. This relationship is embodied in a linear equation $Y = a + bX$ where Y represents the series to be projected and X is the explanatory variable. The a value, called the constant or intercept term, is the point where the equation line intersects the vertical Y-axis. When X is set at zero, the Y value is equal to the constant.

The b value is the slope of the regression line and the most crucial element of the equation. Called the regression coefficient, it represents the change in the Y (or dependent) variable that results from a one-unit change in X, the independent/explanatory variable. In a multiple regression with more than one independent variable, the format is $Y = a + b_1 X_1 + b_2 X_2 + \cdots + b_n X_n$. Thus, each independent variable has its own coefficient.

With these highlights of the $Y = a + bX$ regression equation, we need to understand how the parameters, or values, of a and b are determined. This is accomplished by fitting the equation line through the historical data points using a procedure called ordinary least squares.

The objective of least squares is to develop an equation line that best represents the historical relationship between the data being regressed. To achieve this, an equation is derived that minimizes the squared distance between the actual data and the corresponding points on the regression-equation line.

Figure 5-1 will help illustrate this procedure. In the figure, the equation line $Y = a + bX$ is directed through the historic data points which represent corresponding values for Y and X. Each of the points Y_i is an actual value of Y corresponding to an actual X_i. Y_{if} is the calculated value of Y obtained by substituting the actual X_i into the fitted equation line. The e_i term is the error or difference between the actual Y_i and the calculated Y_{if}.

The equation has been fit through the actual data points so that it minimizes the squared e_i variations. In mathematical terms, the objective is to minimize Σ

Figure 5-1. Least Squares Fit.

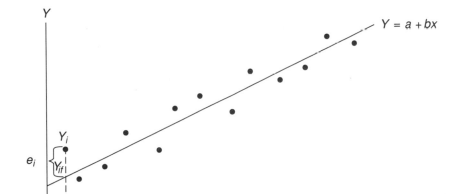

$e_i^2 = \Sigma(Y_i - Y_{if})^2$. That is, we need to minimize the total squared errors between all the calculated and actual Y values in order to produce the line with the smallest or "least squared" error.

As part of the minimization process, the actual data points are evenly dispersed above and below the fitted equation. In mathematical terms, this appears as $\Sigma \, e_i = 0$ where the total of all variances above the line offset those below the line.

Measuring Model Equation Significance

In step one of causal modeling, the forecaster contemplates those factors believed to explain movements in the series being projected. Step two begins with gathering the pertinent data series, then proceeds to the development of regression equations which mathematically express the hypothesized relationships. At this point, the analyst examines the equations to determine if they can be used for forecasting. This testing process is referred to as evaluating the statistical significance of the equations.

As one would expect, there are numerous approaches to evaluating an equations's significance. Here are eight major tests for determining a model's validity.

1. Coefficient of determination (R^2)
2. t-ratio
3. Standard error of the estimate
4. F-statistic
5. Multicollinearity test
6. Serial correlation test
7. Heteroskedasticity test
8. Stability test

In building time-series models, our main criterion was to find the specification that most accurately recreated the past series. The best-fitting model was the one that produced the smallest historic variance.

The same approach is utilized in developing causal models. Here, the primary objective is to construct a regression equation which best replicates the past movements in the dependent variable (Y). As before, the measuring stick is the minimization of past forecast variance.

Tests One through Four in the list above are specifically aimed at examining an equation's past track record. Called "goodness of fit" measures, they analyze how well the equation's independent variables have explained the past data for the dependent (Y) variable.

Coefficient of Determination (R^2).

Any discussion of the coefficient of determination (R^2) should be preceded by consideration of its close statistical cousin, the coefficient of correlation (r). In our Box-Jenkins analysis, autocorrelations were used to examine the relationship between series created from the same original data set. The r value, or coefficient of correlation, utilized in regression analysis is quite similar in concept. The difference is that in causal modeling more than one series is being examined.

The purpose of r is to measure the relationship between any two series. An r can be computed between a dependent and independent variable, as well as any two independent variables.

The coefficient of correlation has a range between -1 and 1. A value of 1 indicates a strong direct relationship between the two variables. For example, the correlation between the Gross National Product and the money supply is likely to be close to 1. That is, both of these variables move together. At the opposite end of the spectrum, an r value of -1 represents a strong inverse relationship. The correlation between mortgage rates and housing starts fits this situation, as starts usually accelerate when borrowing costs decrease, and decelerate when borrowing costs increase. In the middle, an r value of 0 implies that the two variables are unrelated. Therefore, the best situation is where r is either close to 1 or -1. The R^2, often referred to as the premier "goodness of fit" measure, is simply the square of the coefficient of correlation (r). Looking back to Figure 5-1, R^2 equals $\Sigma (Y_{if} - \bar{Y})^2 / \Sigma (Y_i - \bar{Y})^2$ where $\bar{Y}$ is the mean or average of the dependent variable Y. The $Y_{if} - \bar{Y}$ term represents the dependent variable's movement from its mean (explained by the equation), while $Y_i - \bar{Y}$ is its total actual variation. R^2, then, stands for the explained variation/total variation, or the percent of the past movement in the dependent variable which is explained by the movement in the independent variable(s) of the equation.

R^2 has a range between 0 and 1. Therefore, an R^2 value of .80 means that 80% of the historical movement in the dependent variable Y has been accounted for by the regression equation and the independent variables within that equation. The closer the R^2 is to 1, the better the equation replicates the historical dependent variable. If the R^2 is near zero, the explanatory power of the equation is poor.

An illustration will tie together the relationship between R^2, the actual data points and the equation line. In Figure 5-2(A), the data points are interspersed around the equation line. You remember from Figure 5-1 that the distance between the actual data points (Y_i) and the equation line (Y_{if}) for a given X is called the unexplained variation (e_i). That, in essence, is the portion of the historical Y values that the equation cannot explain. The closer the actual data points are to the regression equation line, the smaller the unexplained, and the greater the explained, variation in

Figure 5-2. Relationship of R^2, Data Points, and Equation Lines.

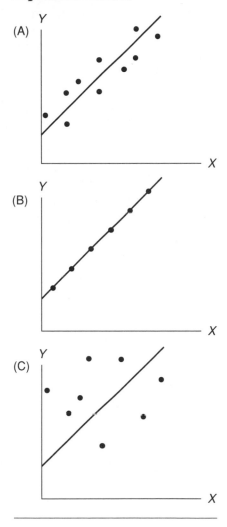

the equation. This greater explained variation represents a higher R^2 value (explained variation/total
variation). If the actual data points coincide exactly
with the equation line (an unusual occurrence), the R^2
has a value of 1 because all of the variation has been

explained—see Figure 5-2(B). Finally, the R^2 declines as the data points are further from the regression line—as in Figure 5-2(C).

Most analysts use a variation of the R^2, called the adjusted R squared or $\bar{R}^2$, to measure the fit of the equation. The $\bar{R}^2$ is almost identical to the R^2, except that the adjusted version allows for a fairer comparison of regression equations that have a differing number of independent variables. This is because the $\bar{R}^2$ considers (and adjusts for) the constraints on the data sample that result from having extra (independent) variables in the equation. Because of this feature, the $\bar{R}^2$ is particularly important when examining multiple regressions. Due to the preferred status of the $\bar{R}^2$, we will use it as the coefficient-of-determination measure in the exercises over the next two chapters.

t-Ratio. While the R^2 measures the fit of the regression equation, the *t*-ratio, or *t*-statistic, examines the significance of each independent variable. The *t*-ratio performs this task by determining whether the regression coefficient (the *b* value in the equation) of each independent variable is more significant than zero. If the coefficient is not significantly different from zero, the variable should be dropped from the equation.

The first step in this process is to compute the standard error or typical variation in the coefficient. Next, the coefficient value is divided by the standard error. This calculation, called the *t*-ratio, represents the distance, in number of standard errors, of the coefficient from zero. The greater this distance (the more standard errors), the greater the likelihood that the coefficient is significantly different from zero.

The final step is to compute a minimum acceptable *t*-ratio that serves as the standard for comparing the *t*-ratio of each independent variable. When we build equation models in the next chapter, a specific minimum t-ratio will be developed. For now, a common rule of thumb is that the t-ratio for an independent variable should have an absolute value greater than 2. That is, if the variable's coefficient is significant, it should be at least two standard errors from zero.

The absolute value is used because the t-ratio for a given coefficient can be positive or negative. In fact, the t-ratio for an independent variable always has the same sign as its regression coefficient. In an earlier example, we noted that housing starts and interest rates tend to have a strong inverse relationship. That is, their coefficient of correlation (r) should be negative. Therefore, an equation delineating housing starts (dependent variable) as a function of interest rates (independent variable) should be defined as housing starts $= a - b \times$ interest rates. From this we see that the coefficient sign on the interest-rate variable is negative. Moreover, the standard error is always measured as a positive value. Since the t-ratio represents the coefficient divided by the standard error, the t-ratio for the interest-rate coefficient is negative.

The preceding discussion brings to light another important point in checking the significance of the individual independent variables. Not only should the t-ratio of the independent variables be significant (absolute value greater than 2), but the sign on the independent variable coefficient should conform to economic theory and the forecaster's expectations. In the above example, you would not use the equation with a positive interest-rate coefficient, even if the coefficient were significant.

Standard Error of the Estimate (SEE). The standard error of the estimate (SEE) is similar to the R^2 (and $\overline{R}^2$) in that it measures the ability of the model to replicate the historical dependent variable. The SEE does this by examining the unexplained variations (e_i in Figure 5-1) or differences between Y_i, the actual Y values, and Y_{if}, the calculated Y values from the fitted-equation line. An equation with a good fit to the historical data will have a relatively small unexplained variation and SEE.

Since the SEE and R^2 both measure the equation's fit, they are likewise statistically related. Specifically, the SEE calculates the historical forecast error, identified above as the unexplained variation in the dependent variable. The R^2 value, as noted, measures the explained variation as a percent of the total variation. We see that the two measures are presented in different formats: the R^2 is calculated as a ratio, while the SEE is not. Still, as the explained variation or R^2 improves, the unexplained variation of SEE should decline. Thus, we expect the R^2 and the SEE to be inversely related. And this is true where the number of observations in the equation does not change.

Some forecasters key on the R^2 in developing their regression models, while others target the SEE. The former desire a high R^2, while the latter look for a low SEE. These two variables are closely related, however, and the use of either test should bring the forecaster to the same decision when choosing the best equation.

The SEE also is used in model development to provide a means for placing a band or range around the equation model forecast. In statistics, a normally-distributed data series has 67% of its values within one standard deviation of the mean, and 95% of its values within two standard deviations of the mean. It also can be shown that the SEE represents the standard deviation of the regression data. Therefore, to place a range around the forecast which approximates

95% of the probable future values, the forecaster has only to add + and − 2 SEE to the projection. This will be examined further in Exercise One of Chapter Six and in step three of model building (Chapter Eight).

F-Statistic. As we have seen, the R^2 and the SEE values both quantify the success of the equation in reproducing the historical values of the dependent variable Y. The F-statistic provides yet another measure for evaluating an equation's fit. In its simplest form, the F-statistic examines the equation's explained variance as a ratio of its unexplained variance. Since the R^2 measures the ratio of explained to total variation and the SEE calculates the unexplained variation, all three tests are closely intertwined.

The relationship between these three tests is easily illustrated. If an equation's explanatory power or fit improves, the effect is to increase the numerator and decrease the denominator of the F-statistic, causing a rise in its total value. Since the R^2 value also increases in this situation, the F-statistic and the R^2 tests are directly related. They both increase when the equation fit improves, and both decrease when the equation fit deteriorates. The SEE, on the other hand, always moves in the opposite direction of the F-statistic and the R^2.

While the R^2, SEE, and F-statistic all measure an equation's fitness, the R^2 and SEE cannot easily provide a minimum standard for determining whether the equation is acceptable for forecasting. For the t-ratio test, a rule-of-thumb value of greater than 2 serves as a minimum. Any t-statistic below this point implies that the independent variable is not statistically significant. No such benchmark exists for the R^2 and SEE tests, making it difficult to decide if a specific equation is appropriate for forecasting.

The *F*-statistic, however, provides such a test. Moreover, it uses the same general methodology as the *t*-ratio by comparing the equation's significance to zero. The common rule of thumb is that an *F*-statistic above 5 indicates that the regression equation is more significant than zero and can be utilized for forecasting. The specific determination of the minimum *F*-statistic will be saved until our model-building exercises in the next chapter.

A final note is needed on the relationship between the *t*-statistic and the *F*-statistic. The *t*-test is utilized for determining the significance of each independent variable in a regression equation. The *F*-value, on the other hand, measures the significance of the total equation. There is plenty of common ground, however, in that the addition of a significant (high *t*-statistic) explanatory variable enhances the fit of an equation, thus improving the *F*-statistic as well as the R^2 value. Clearly, there are close ties between the four tests utilized for examining the equation's historical fit.

Multicollinearity. Having completed the major "goodness of fit" measures, we can move on to four other criteria needed to ensure an equation's forecasting validity. The first of these is the test for multicollinearity. Although this term sounds more like an intestinal disorder than a statistical condition, it is an important consideration in any equation with more than one independent variable. In other words, multicollinearity is a potential concern in a multiple regression, but not in a simple regression.

Multicollinearity occurs where two or more independent variables of the regression equation are closely correlated. Where this occurs, the regression procedure is unable to separate the impact of these variables on the dependent variable, which can result in incorrectly assigned coefficients to the independent variables.

In order to understand the importance of a correct coefficient, recall the section on regression analysis. In that discussion, the coefficient was defined as representing the change in the dependent variable Y that results from one unit of change in the independent variable. Thus, the projection for the Y variable is determined by future estimates of the independent variables multiplied by their assigned coefficients. An inappropriate coefficient on an independent variable, therefore, can have a disastrous effect on the Y variable forecast.

There is no universally accepted test for multicollinearity. A common rule of thumb, however, is that multicollinearity can be a potential problem when the coefficient of correlation (r) between any two independent variables is greater than .7. It is important to emphasize that multicollinearity applies only to independent variables. A high r value between the dependent and any independent variable is desired in regression analysis.

The greatest sources of multicollinearity are data series which trend upward. In the event that any two independent series have an r of .7 or above, the analyst can drop either the independent variable that is less closely related to the dependent variable, or the independent variable that is most difficult to forecast. If the analyst believes that both variables are important to the equation, the form of a series can be changed rather than removed. In this regard, a common solution is to model the variable's change from period to period rather than its level. All of these approaches will be further examined in our model-building exercises.

Serial Correlation. It has been noted that one of the primary objectives in forecast-model development is to generate an equation with a small historic error. In addition, an equation with this characteristic should also have a high R^2, a strong F-statistic and a low SEE.

While minimal historical variance is desirable, the pattern of the error term over time should also be considered. For an equation to be statistically valid, the error (residual, or unexplained variance) should be randomly distributed from observation to observation. That is, the error term in one period should not be related to the error term in the previous time period. If the errors are related, then a pattern exists and the residuals are said to be serially correlated or autocorrelated.[*] This problem, if severe enough, can invalidate the R^2, as well as the coefficient values.

Earlier in the chapter, the two data formats of time-series and cross-sectional regression were presented. Since cross-sectional analysis deals with a fixed point in time, autocorrelation is not a consideration. Time-series regressions, however, can be vulnerable to this problem since they use data over a specific time period. Therefore, cross-sectional regressions *do not* have to be examined for serial correlation, whereas time-series regressions *should be* tested.

There are several ways to check for serial correlation. One approach is to plot the residual, or unexplained, variations. If the terms cluster in groups of positive and negative variations, there is a pattern in the error terms. The most common test, however, is the Durbin-Watson (D-W) statistic. This measure, whose value ranges between 0 and 4, examines the error terms to see if there is a close correlation

---

[*]   We are talking here about first-order serial correlation, where the error term is related to the previous period's error. This is the most common type of autocorrelation. In our exercises, we will be attempting to identify and adjust for this variety.

between them. When the D-W is 2.0, the error terms are completely independent, meaning there is no problem of serial correlation. A D-W of 2.0, however, is as rare as an R^2 of 1. Thus, a rule of thumb has been developed to guide the forecaster for values on either side of 2.0. A D-W value in the 1.5 to 2.5 range implies that we can be reasonably sure no serial correlation exists in the residuals. A D-W value that falls between 1.0 to 1.5 or 2.5 to 3.0 implies a gray area where one cannot be sure whether the error terms do, or do not, have a pattern. Finally, a D-W value below 1.0 or above 3.0 indicates reasonable probability that serial correlation exists in the residuals.

If the residual terms are determined to be closely related, there are several solutions available. In many instances, a pattern indicates that another independent variable is needed in the equation. The correlated error terms reflect the missing independent series, and the inclusion of another variable in the model usually resolves the situation.

Another solution is to alter the form of the series by modeling its difference from one time period to another, rather than its level. This is the same approach that was presented for dealing with multicollinearity. The problem with this solution is that while the D-W statistic improves, the R^2 value usually suffers. We will examine this further in our model-building exercises.

Heteroskedasticity. As explained above, the D-W statistic checks to see whether the error terms are interrelated. It is also important that the error or residual is not increasing or decreasing over the data set. That is, the error terms should have a constant variance from observation to observation. Should the error indicate a rising or falling pattern over the set of observations, the problem of heteroskedasticity exists.

Like serial correlation, severe heteroskedasticity can produce incorrect goodness-of-fit results and a mis-specification of the equation.

Heteroskedasticity is also similar to autocorrelation in that this nonconstant pattern in the residuals can represent an explanatory variable that has been omitted from the equation. The solution, therefore, is to identify the missing series.

Cross-sectional regressions often relate data series which encompass a wide range of values. Consequently, heteroskedasticity is a potential danger in this type of regression and the equation should be tested to determine if this problem exists. In time-series regressions, nonconstant variations in the error terms are generally not a problem. Therefore, most forecasters do not examine a time-series regression for heteroskedasticity.

There are several possible methods of testing for heteroskedasticity. One popular approach is the Park Test. In this technique, the residuals of the regression equation are correlated to an explanatory series in the regression. Since the explanatory variable has a wide range of values, a strong correlation between the two series indicates that the residuals have a similar increasing or decreasing pattern and thus are heteroskedastic. Exercise 5 in Chapter Seven, which constructs a cross-sectional model, covers the steps involved in testing for heteroskedasticity.

Stability. Before discussing stability, we need to explain an important principle. We know from basic statistics that a correctly drawn sample provides an understanding of the total population's characteristics. Further, a larger sample better reflects the actual characteristics of this population. A regression equation is similarly drawn from a sample that seeks to represent real-world characteristics and relationships. As in a survey, a sufficient number of observations is necessary for the equation to accurately estimate the actual relationship. If too few data points are used, the equation coefficients will not reflect the real world.

The importance of an equation's coefficients to a successful regression model has been emphasized on several occasions. It is the forecaster's obligation to make sure that the coefficients accurately represent the true relationships being modeled. As stated above, a sufficient number of observations enhances the probability of realizing this objective.

From the above discussion, it has been noted that the coefficients are critical to the equation, and that a sufficiently large data base is necessary for the coefficients to be accurately specified. The objective of the stability test is to determine whether the regression "sample," or number of observations, is sufficient to ensure the coefficients' accuracy.

Instead of discussing the number of observations, however, statisticians use the term degrees of freedom. Degrees of freedom represents the number of observations in the data set adjusted for the number of regression variables. For example, if there are 50 observations in the data base and there are four variables (one dependent and three independent) in the regression equation, then there are 46 degrees of freedom $(50 - 4)$. Analysts believe that this better measures the size of the regression "sample" because the specification of the equation's coefficients and intercept places a constraint on the data set. In fact, this adjustment for the number of variables is what differentiates the $\bar{R}^2$ from R^2. From this, the benchmark for measuring stability becomes a sufficient number of degrees of freedom.

Although an appropriate number of observations or degrees of freedom is necesary for equation stability, there is no specific rule enumerating the exact requirement. Some forecasters desire at least 15 degrees of freedom, and others may require 30. Certainly the forecaster should check the model for stability if the degrees of freedom are at the lower end of this range. But as the degrees of freedom increase, stability should be less of a concern.

If the degrees of freedom are inadequate, the equation coefficients may fluctuate dramatically as observations are added to the data set. In other words the model coefficients are unstable. The method of testing for this possible flaw is straightforward. Simply remove the latest observation from the data base and rerun the regression. Should the coefficients undergo a marked change, the regression is unstable.

The solution for instability is also simple. Additional data points usually lend more stability and accuracy to the equation's specification, but only to a point. If data points that embody obsolete trends (such as pre-OPEC relationships) are added, the latest developments can become blurred in the equation specification.

Summary

We now have a foundation on which to move forward into Chapters Six and Seven. In the upcoming model-building discussions, many of the points just presented will be reviewed and reinforced. Moreover, further important aspects of regression analysis will be uncovered as we go about the task of developing forecasting equations. In presenting this part of your causal model training, Chapter Six will examine the simple regression, while Chapter Seven will cover the more intricate multiple regression. By the end of Chapter 7, you will have the tools to develop your own quantitative techniques.

6

Causal Model Building I

Having examined the major statistical tests for analyzing regression equations, we are ready to apply this information to the model-building process. The next two chapters will explore the use of these tests in a real-world setting. This will involve specific exercises which proceed through the development of forecasting equations. By the time this discussion is completed, you will have a firmer grasp of the role these criteria play in constructing forecasting tools.

As explained, the three major steps of model building include (1) hypothesizing a structure by listing potential explanatory variables, (2) utilizing regression analysis to quantify the historical relationships in the hypothesis, plus measuring the resulting equations for statistical validity, and (3) developing a forecast from the best equation. Chapters Six and Seven will deal primarily with step two, or the examination of the regression equations for statistical validity. However, step one is also encompassed in the exercises since it is a necessary precursor to the equation analysis.

Exercise One

An analyst for a municipality is attempting to develop a technique for projecting local manufacturing employment. From past experience, the analyst is aware that manufactured products are almost always sold in markets which extend outside the local area. Therefore, the analyst has hypothesized that national economic activity might explain movements in local manufacturing. A popular measure of national economic activity is real (inflation adjusted) Gross National Product.

The analyst also believes that manufacturing might be influenced by local demand. A surrogate for local area business activity is population, since people purchase goods. Therefore, a regression is run with local manufacturing employment (MANEMP) as the dependent variable, and real Gross National Product (GNP82)[*] and local population (POP) as the explanatory variables.

Most forecasters develop regression models using a computer. There are numerous statistical packages for running regressions on computers, each with its own format. Table 6-1 presents the major tests using a hybrid approach which has chosen the best features from several packages. With this table, we will review each of the test results in evaluating the equation's statistical validity.

$\overline{R}^2$

In the previous chapter it was explained that the adjusted R squared or $\overline{R}^2$ is the most appropriate measure of the coefficient of determination. By way of review, the $\overline{R}^2$ represents the percent of the historical movement in the dependent variable (MANEMP) that is explained by the independent variables (GNP82, POP). In this equation, the .92 seems impressive since we know that the maximum value is 1.0. Still, this does not provide a formal test of whether the equation has significantly explained the dependent series. For this, we will look at the F-statistic.

---

[*] Real or inflation-adjusted Gross National Product represents volume movements in economic activity as prices are held constant at a base year level, which presently is 1982.

Table 6-1. Regression Results: MANEMP = f(GNP82, POP).

Sample:	1966–1987
Equation:	MANEMP = $a + b_1 \times$ GNP82
	$+ b_2 \times$ POP
	MANEMP = 5.67 + .0116 $\times$ GNP82
	$(t = 3.8)$
	$- .015 \times$ POP
	$(t = -1.1)$
$\bar{R}^2$:	.92
F-statistic:	119.20
D-W:	1.30

Correlation Matrix:

	MANEMP	GNP82	POP
MANEMP	1.00	0.96	0.93
GNP82	0.96	1.00	0.98
POP	0.93	0.98	1.00

Number of Observations:	22
Degrees of Freedom:	19

t-statistic

Before examining the *F*-statistic, however, let's evaluate the significance of the individual explanatory variables. As previously discussed, the *t*-statistic measures the significance of each independent variable by examining the importance of its coefficients. Although an absolute value above 2 represents a general standard of comparison, the minimum acceptable *t*-value for this specific equation will be calculated using Table 6-2.

To understand the table, it should be noted that statisticians test whether each coefficient is *not* significant rather than if it *is* significant. This phenomenon, known as the null hypothesis, seeks to prove the variable's importance by *refuting* the

Table 6-2. Critical Values of the *t*-distribution.

Degrees of Freedom	Probabilities					
	.40	.20	.10	.05	.02	.01
1	1.376	3.078	6.314	12.706	31.821	63.657
2	1.061	1.886	2.920	4.303	6.965	9.925
3	0.978	1.638	2.353	3.182	4.541	5.841
4	0.941	1.533	2.132	2.776	3.747	4.604
5	0.920	1.476	2.015	2.571	3.365	4.032
6	0.906	1.440	1.943	2.447	3.143	3.707
7	0.896	1.415	1.895	2.365	2.998	3.499
8	0.889	1.397	1.860	2.306	2.896	3.355
9	0.883	1.383	1.833	2.262	2.821	3.250
10	0.879	1.372	1.812	2.228	2.764	3.169
11	0.876	1.363	1.796	2.201	2.718	3.106
12	0.873	1.356	1.782	2.179	2.681	3.055
13	0.870	1.350	1.771	2.160	2.650	3.012
14	0.868	1.345	1.761	2.145	2.624	2.977
15	0.866	1.341	1.753	2.131	2.602	2.947
16	0.865	1.337	1.746	2.120	2.583	2.921
17	0.863	1.333	1.740	2.110	2.567	2.898
18	0.862	1.330	1.734	2.101	2.552	2.878
19	0.861	1.328	1.729	2.093	2.539	2.861
20	0.860	1.325	1.725	2.086	2.528	2.845
21	0.859	1.323	1.721	2.080	2.518	2.831
22	0.858	1.321	1.717	2.074	2.508	2.819
23	0.858	1.319	1.714	2.069	2.500	2.807
24	0.857	1.318	1.711	2.064	2.492	2.797
25	0.856	1.316	1.708	2.060	2.485	2.787
26	0.856	1.315	1.706	2.056	2.479	2.779
27	0.855	1.314	1.703	2.052	2.473	2.771
28	0.855	1.313	1.701	2.048	2.467	2.763
29	0.854	1.311	1.699	2.045	2.462	2.756
30	0.854	1.310	1.697	2.042	2.457	2.750
40	0.851	1.303	1.684	2.021	2.423	2.704
60	0.848	1.296	1.671	2.000	2.390	2.660
120	0.845	1.289	1.658	1.980	2.358	2.617
∞	0.842	1.282	1.645	1.960	2.326	2.576

This table is used for two-tailed tests, or the testing of a coefficient's significance where the coefficient has either a negative or a positive value.

Source: M. Merrington, "Table of Percentage Points of the *t*-Distribution," *Biometrika,* Vol. 32, 1941–42, p. 300. Reprinted with permission of the Biometrika Trustees.

premise that the coefficient is *not* significant. The figures across the top of Table 6-2 represent the probability that the coefficient's *t*-statistic exceeds the minimum values underneath each column if the variable is *not* significant.

Since this can be confusing, let's convert the probabilities at the top of the table into a level of confidence by subtracting these values from 1. For example, the probability of .05, or 5%, in column 6 changes to a confidence level of 95%. Now it can be said that if a variable's *t*-statistic exceeds the values in this column, we are 95% confident that the coefficient (and variable) is significant.

We still need to identify a specific minimum value from the 95% column by examining the degrees of freedom (observations less total variables) on the left hand side of Table 6-2. Using the 19 degrees of freedom in the equation and the confidence level of 95%, we see that the acceptable minimum *t*-value for this equation is 2.093. That is, if an independent-variable coefficient has a *t*-statistic whose absolute value is greater than 2.093, we can be 95% confident that the variable is significant in explaining movements in the dependent series.

From the equation, GNP82 has a *t*-statistic of 3.8. Since this exceeds the lower limit of 2.093, this variable is significant. POP, however, is below the acceptable 95% limit since the absolute value of its *t*-statistic is 1.1. Looking across the 19-degrees-of-freedom line, you see that the POP *t*-statistic falls within the 60 to 80% confidence range. That is, one can be 60 to 80% confident that the POP series is significant. Some forecasters might consider this acceptable and use it in their equation. Most, however, use the 95% confidence level criterion.

In the previous chapter, we noted that the absolute value of the *t*-ratio is used in measuring significance. While the *t*-test ignores the coefficient's sign, this latter element is nevertheless important in equation analysis. In fact, the coefficient assigned to the independent variable should have a sign that conforms to economic theory and the forecaster's expectations.

In this equation, the GNP82 coefficient has a positive sign. That is, an increase in GNP82 has a positive impact on MANEMP as calculated by the equation. This is intuitively logical since expanding economic activity should result in increased purchases and production of manufactured products, leading to more manufacturing employment.

Using similar reasoning, population growth should also translate into employment gains. This is not, however, reflected in the model equation. The sign on the POP variable is negative, implying an inverse relationship with employment. This negative sign does not conform to economic logic and appears to be incorrect.

Multicollinearity

A check for multicollinearity provides an explanation for this inconsistency. Multicollinearity, we recall, is a close relationship between two or more independent variables. That is, certain of the independent variables are highly correlated. Identifying multicollinearity involves examining the coefficient of correlation (r) between the independent series. This has been done in the correlation matrix in Table 6-1. The matrix includes the r or correlation between all the variables in the equation with a possible range of values from -1 to $+1$. However, only the independent variables are involved in the question of multicollinearity.

Looking at this matrix, the r between GNP82 and POP is .98. This is greater than the .7 rule of thumb mentioned in the prior chapter, and indicates an extremely close relationship between these two independent series. Because these variables are highly correlated, the regression program has had difficulty in assigning individual coefficients to GNP82 and POP. The result is that the POP variable has been incorrectly specified, including an erroneous sign on its coefficient.

When multicollinearity exists between two independent variables, a possible solution is to remove one of them from the equation. The forecaster usually drops the variable that has the weakest relationship with the dependent series (MANEMP). From the correlation matrix, GNP82 is more closely correlated with the dependent variable. Specifically, the r between GNP82 and MANEMP is .96, while the r between POP and MANEMP is .93. Under this criterion, POP would be removed from the equation.

Another approach is to keep the independent variable that is less difficult to project. This is important since a forecast of the independent variable is required to calculate a future value for MANEMP (the dependent variable). Since it is easier to locate projections for GNP82 than for local population (POP), the former series should be maintained.

Sometimes the modeler wants to retain both independent variables when they are theoretically appropriate in explaining the dependent variable. In this case, the form of one of the explanatory variables can be changed to reduce the close relationship between them. In this example, the population series can be adjusted to measure the year-to-year change rather than the level. Our analyst, however, makes the judgment that national demand, represented by GNP82, is the primary driver in determining local manufacturing activity and employment. After all, any local demand for industrial goods will likely be reflected in the GNP82 data. Therefore, the analyst is quite satisfied to leave the local surrogate (POP) out of the specification.

In summary, multicollinearity has been discovered among the two independent variables. In addition, it has been determined that GNP82 should be retained and POP removed from the equation because of (1) GNP82's closer relationship to MANEMP, and (2) the ready availability of GNP82 forecasts in newspapers, economic letters, and other sources. The equation is rerun as a simple regression with MANEMP as the dependent variable and GNP82 the independent variable.

Table 6-3 contains the major statistical tests for the resulting equation.

$\overline{R}^2$

The $\overline{R}^2$ remains at .92 in this equation. To determine if the equation is significant in explaining the dependent variable's historical movements, it is necessary to examine the F-statistic and the t-statistic.

F-statistic

We now know the rule of thumb that an F-value

Table 6-3. Regression Results: MANEMP = f(GNP82).

Sample:	1966–1987
Equation:	MANEMP = $a + b_1 \times$ GNP82
	MANEMP = 5.84 + .0085 × GNP82
	(t = 15.4)
$\overline{R}^2$:	.92
F-statistic:	235.92
SEE:	1.21
D-W:	1.26
Number of Observations:	22
Degrees of Freedom:	20

greater than 5 indicates that the regression is more significant than zero in explaining MANEMP. Nevertheless, let's calculate the minimum acceptable F-statistic based on the equation characteristics.

Table 6-4 contains the pertinent information for establishing the boundary for the F-test at the 95% confidence level. The left-hand column denotes the equation's degrees of freedom, while the row across the top represents the number of explanatory variables. In the latest regression there are 20 degrees of freedom and one explanatory variable (GNP82). Therefore, the equation is statistically significant if the F-test is greater than 4.35. The equation's F-test of 235.92 easily exceeds this critical or minimum value.

t-statistic

An acceptable F-test in a simple regression (one explanatory variable) also reflects a strong t-statistic for the explanatory series. The GNP82 t-test of 15.4 illustrates this point.

Multicollinearity

Multicollinearity is not a consideration where there is only one independent variable. This is the reason for omitting the correlation matrix from Table 6-3.

Serial or Autocorrelation

As discussed in the previous chapter, the unexplained variation in the regression equation must be random. That is, the error or residual terms, which are the difference between the actual and calculated MANEMP values from the regression equation, must be unrelated. The Durbin-Watson (D-W) statistic is used to determine whether the residuals are independent.

Table 6-4. Critical values of the F-Statistic—5% Level of Significance.

Degrees of Freedom for Numerator

	1	2	3	4	5	6	7	8	9	10	12	15	20	24	30	40	60	120	∞
1	161	200	216	225	230	234	237	239	241	242	244	246	248	249	250	251	252	253	254
2	18.5	19.0	19.2	19.2	19.3	19.3	19.4	19.4	19.4	19.4	19.4	19.4	19.5	19.5	19.5	19.5	19.5	19.5	19.5
3	10.1	9.55	9.28	9.12	9.01	8.94	8.89	8.85	8.81	8.79	8.74	8.70	8.66	8.64	8.62	8.59	8.57	8.55	8.53
4	7.71	6.94	6.59	6.39	6.26	6.16	6.09	6.04	6.00	5.96	5.91	5.86	5.80	5.77	5.75	5.72	5.69	5.66	5.63
5	6.61	5.79	5.41	5.19	5.05	4.95	4.88	4.82	4.77	4.74	4.68	4.62	4.56	4.53	4.50	4.46	4.43	4.40	4.37
6	5.99	5.14	4.76	4.53	4.39	4.28	4.21	4.15	4.10	4.06	4.00	3.94	3.87	3.84	3.81	3.77	3.74	3.70	3.67
7	5.59	4.74	4.35	4.12	3.97	3.87	3.79	3.73	3.68	3.64	3.57	3.51	3.44	3.41	3.38	3.34	3.30	3.27	3.23
8	5.32	4.46	4.07	3.84	3.69	3.58	3.50	3.44	3.39	3.35	3.28	3.22	3.15	3.12	3.08	3.04	3.01	2.97	2.93
9	5.12	4.26	3.86	3.63	3.48	3.37	3.29	3.23	3.18	3.14	3.07	3.01	2.94	2.90	2.86	2.83	2.79	2.75	2.71
10	4.96	4.10	3.71	3.48	3.33	3.22	3.14	3.07	3.02	2.98	2.91	2.85	2.77	2.74	2.70	2.66	2.62	2.58	2.54
11	4.84	3.98	3.59	3.36	3.20	3.09	3.01	2.95	2.90	2.85	2.79	2.72	2.65	2.61	2.57	2.53	2.49	2.45	2.40
12	4.75	3.89	3.49	3.26	3.11	3.00	2.91	2.85	2.80	2.75	2.69	2.62	2.54	2.51	2.47	2.43	2.38	2.34	2.30
13	4.67	3.81	3.41	3.18	3.03	2.92	2.83	2.77	2.71	2.67	2.60	2.53	2.46	2.42	2.38	2.34	2.30	2.25	2.21
14	4.60	3.74	3.34	3.11	2.96	2.85	2.76	2.70	2.65	2.60	2.53	2.46	2.39	2.35	2.31	2.27	2.22	2.18	2.13
15	4.54	3.68	3.29	3.06	2.90	2.79	2.71	2.64	2.59	2.54	2.48	2.40	2.33	2.29	2.25	2.20	2.16	2.11	2.07

Degrees of Freedom for Denominator

Degrees of Freedom for Denominator

16	4.49	3.63	3.24	3.01	2.85	2.74	2.66	2.59	2.54	2.49	2.42	2.35	2.28	2.24	2.19	2.15	2.11	2.06	2.01
17	4.45	3.59	3.20	2.96	2.81	2.70	2.61	2.55	2.48	2.45	2.38	2.31	2.23	2.19	2.15	2.10	2.06	2.01	1.96
18	4.41	3.55	3.16	2.93	2.77	2.66	2.58	2.51	2.46	2.41	2.34	2.27	2.19	2.15	2.11	2.06	2.02	1.97	1.92
19	4.38	3.52	3.13	2.90	2.74	2.63	2.54	2.48	2.42	2.39	2.31	2.23	2.16	2.11	2.07	2.03	1.98	1.93	1.88
20	4.35	3.49	3.10	2.87	2.71	2.60	2.51	2.45	2.39	2.35	2.28	2.20	2.12	2.08	2.04	1.99	1.95	1.90	1.84
21	4.32	3.47	3.07	2.84	2.68	2.57	2.49	2.42	2.37	2.32	2.25	2.18	2.10	2.05	2.01	1.96	1.92	1.87	1.81
22	4.30	3.44	3.05	2.82	2.66	2.55	2.46	2.40	2.34	2.30	2.23	2.15	2.07	2.03	1.98	1.94	1.89	1.84	1.78
23	4.28	3.42	3.03	2.80	2.64	2.53	2.44	2.37	2.32	2.27	2.20	2.13	2.05	2.01	1.96	1.91	1.86	1.81	1.76
24	4.26	3.40	3.01	2.78	2.62	2.51	2.42	2.36	2.30	2.25	2.18	2.11	2.03	1.98	1.94	1.89	1.84	1.79	1.73
25	4.24	3.39	2.99	2.76	2.60	2.49	2.40	2.34	2.28	2.24	2.16	2.09	2.01	1.96	1.92	1.87	1.82	1.77	1.71
30	4.17	3.32	2.92	2.69	2.53	2.42	2.33	2.27	2.21	2.16	2.09	2.01	1.93	1.89	1.84	1.79	1.74	1.68	1.62
40	4.08	3.23	2.84	2.61	2.45	2.34	2.25	2.18	2.12	2.08	2.00	1.92	1.84	1.79	1.74	1.69	1.64	1.58	1.51
60	4.00	3.15	2.76	2.53	2.37	2.25	2.17	2.10	2.04	1.99	1.92	1.84	1.75	1.70	1.65	1.59	1.53	1.47	1.39
120	3.92	3.07	2.68	2.45	2.29	2.18	2.09	2.02	1.96	1.91	1.83	1.75	1.66	1.61	1.55	1.50	1.43	1.35	1.25
∞	3.84	3.00	2.60	2.37	2.21	2.10	2.01	1.94	1.88	1.83	1.75	1.67	1.57	1.52	1.46	1.39	1.32	1.22	1.00

Degrees of freedom for numerator = Number of independent (explanatory) variables

Degrees of freedom for denominator = Degrees of freedom in the regression equation

Source: M. Merrington and C. M. Thompson, "Tables of Percentage Points of the Inverted Beta (F) Distribution," *Biometrika*, Vol. 33, 1943, pp. 73–83. Reprinted with permission of the Biometrika Trustees.

To review, the rule of thumb is that a D-W of 1.5 to 2.5 implies that the error terms are independent. If the D-W ranges between 1.0 to 1.5 and 2.5 to 3.0, the status of the residual terms is uncertain. Finally, a D-W below 1.0 and above 3.0 indicates a pattern or interdependence in the error terms.

Despite this general rule, calculating the specific D-W limits of the equation is still a useful exercise. Table 6-5 provides the raw material to compute the acceptable D-W at the 95% confidence level. The far-left column represents the number of observations, while the heading across the page ($k = 1$ to $k = 5$) represents the number of explanatory variables. In the latest equation, there are 22 observations and one explanatory variable ($k = 1$). The intersection of these two points yields a d_l value of 1.24 and a d_u value of 1.43.

The interpretation of d_l and d_u is somewhat complex. If the D-W statistic is below d_l (1.24), one can be 95% confident that positive autocorrelation exists. That is, the residuals have a pattern. If the D-W statistic is above 1.43, then there is 95% confidence that no positive serial correlation exists. That is, the residuals are independent. A D-W between d_l and d_u (1.24 to 1.43) is inconclusive or in the gray area. Should the D-W statistic exceed $4.0 - d_l$ ($4.0 - 1.24 = 2.76$), then the equation has negative autocorrelation. A D-W value of less than $4.0 - d_u$ ($4.0 - 1.43 = 2.57$) indicates no pattern in the residuals. Finally, values between $4.0 - d_u$ (2.57) and $4.0 - d_l$ (2.76) are inconclusive. To summarize these statements

No pattern (good): 1.43 to 2.57

Inconclusive: 1.24 to 1.43 and 2.57 to 2.76

Autocorrelation (bad): Less than 1.24 and greater than 2.76

Table 6-5. Critical Values of the Durbin-Watson Test Statistics of d_l and d_u: 5% Level of Significance.

	$k=1$		$k=2$		$k=3$		$k=4$		$k=5$	
n	d_l	d_u	d_l	d_u	d_l	d_u	d_l	d_u	d_l	d_u
15	1.08	1.36	0.95	1.54	0.82	1.75	0.69	1.97	0.56	2.21
16	1.10	1.37	0.98	1.54	0.86	1.73	0.74	1.93	0.62	2.15
17	1.13	1.38	1.02	1.54	0.90	1.71	0.78	1.90	0.67	2.10
18	1.16	1.39	1.05	1.53	0.93	1.69	0.82	1.87	0.71	2.06
19	1.18	1.40	1.08	1.53	0.97	1.68	0.86	1.85	0.75	2.02
20	1.20	1.41	1.10	1.54	1.00	1.68	0.90	1.83	0.79	1.99
21	1.22	1.42	1.13	1.54	1.03	1.67	0.93	1.81	0.83	1.96
22	1.24	1.43	1.15	1.54	1.05	1.66	0.96	1.80	0.86	1.94
23	1.26	1.44	1.17	1.54	1.08	1.66	0.99	1.79	0.90	1.92
24	1.27	1.45	1.19	1.55	1.10	1.66	1.01	1.78	0.93	1.90
25	1.29	1.45	1.21	1.55	1.12	1.66	1.04	1.77	0.95	1.89
26	1.30	1.46	1.22	1.55	1.14	1.65	1.06	1.76	0.98	1.88
27	1.32	1.47	1.24	1.56	1.16	1.65	1.08	1.76	1.01	1.86
28	1.33	1.48	1.26	1.56	1.18	1.65	1.10	1.75	1.03	1.85
29	1.34	1.48	1.27	1.56	1.20	1.65	1.12	1.74	1.05	1.84
30	1.35	1.49	1.28	1.57	1.21	1.65	1.14	1.74	1.07	1.83
31	1.36	1.50	1.30	1.57	1.23	1.65	1.16	1.74	1.09	1.83
32	1.37	1.50	1.31	1.57	1.24	1.65	1.18	1.73	1.11	1.82
33	1.38	1.51	1.32	1.58	1.26	1.65	1.19	1.73	1.13	1.81
34	1.39	1.51	1.33	1.58	1.27	1.65	1.21	1.73	1.15	1.81
35	1.40	1.52	1.34	1.53	1.28	1.65	1.22	1.73	1.16	1.80
36	1.41	1.52	1.35	1.59	1.29	1.65	1.24	1.73	1.18	1.80
37	1.42	1.53	1.36	1.59	1.31	1.66	1.25	1.72	1.19	1.80
38	1.43	1.54	1.37	1.59	1.32	1.66	1.26	1.72	1.21	1.79
39	1.43	1.54	1.38	1.60	1.33	1.66	1.27	1.72	1.22	1.79
40	1.44	1.54	1.39	1.60	1.34	1.66	1.29	1.72	1.23	1.79
45	1.48	1.57	1.43	1.62	1.38	1.67	1.34	1.72	1.29	1.78
50	1.50	1.59	1.46	1.63	1.42	1.67	1.38	1.72	1.34	1.77
55	1.53	1.60	1.49	1.64	1.45	1.68	1.41	1.72	1.38	1.77
60	1.55	1.62	1.51	1.65	1.48	1.69	1.44	1.73	1.41	1.77
65	1.57	1.63	1.54	1.66	1.50	1.70	1.47	1.73	1.44	1.77
70	1.58	1.64	1.55	1.67	1.52	1.70	1.49	1.74	1.46	1.77
75	1.60	1.65	1.57	1.68	1.54	1.71	1.51	1.74	1.49	1.77
80	1.61	1.66	1.59	1.69	1.56	1.72	1.53	1.74	1.51	1.77
85	1.62	1.67	1.60	1.70	1.57	1.72	1.55	1.75	1.52	1.77
90	1.63	1.68	1.61	1.70	1.59	1.73	1.57	1.75	1.54	1.78
95	1.64	1.69	1.62	1.71	1.60	1.73	1.58	1.75	1.56	1.78
100	1.65	1.69	1.63	1.72	1.61	1.74	1.59	1.76	1.57	1.78

k = Number of explanatory variables

n = Number of observations in the regression equation

Source: J. Durbin and G. S. Watson, "Testing for Serial Correlation in Least Squares Regression. II," *Biometrika*, Vol. 38, 1951, pp. 159–178. Reprinted with permission of the Biometrika Trustees.

If there is an autocorrelation problem, it is usually in the positive region (below 1.24). In the latest equation, the D-W statistic of 1.26 is right on the lower edge of the inconclusive, or gray, area. Some forecasters accept any D-W value above the lower limit of the gray area (1.24), while others do not accept anything below 1.43. In this example, those that tolerate a D-W in the gray zone accept this equation. Those that hold the higher standard require alterations to the model.

Assuming that this D-W is not acceptable to the forecaster, there are various alternatives for improving the equation. Since the residual term may include an explanatory variable that has not yet been identified, the first approach should be to provide additional variables on the right side of the equation. From our previous experience, the addition of POP yields a small improvement in the D-W, but is not acceptable since it results in multicollinearity. However, other variables can be tested. For example, the original hypothesis, which confined itself to national influences on local manufacturing, can be expanded to include series which measure foreign demand for U.S. industrial products. In Exercise 3, we will examine the process of adding variables to reduce the pattern in the error and enhance the D-W statistic.

Should this search prove unsuccessful, another approach is to alter the form of the variables. This can entail modeling the change in the series rather than their levels, or the use of a nonlinear function. The first concept will be described in detail during the next exercise, while the nonlinear approach will be pursued in Exercise 7.

A final alternative for eliminating the pattern is to use the Cochrane-Orcutt procedure. In this technique, the pattern in the error, called rho, is identified.

The equation is then reestimated to remove this serial correlation.[*]

To summarize, we are now able to calculate a specific D-W criterion based on the number of explanatory variables and degrees of freedom. Once an autocorrelation problem has been identified, the first approach is to determine if other explanatory variables can be located. If the problem cannot be resolved in this manner, the analyst can experiment with other forms for the variables. As a final resort, the Cochrane-Orcutt procedure offers yet another solution. In Chapter Eight's discussion of forecasting, however, a simpler alternative to Cochrane-Orcutt will be presented. This process, called addfactors, adjusts for autocorrelation and provides for a smoothed transition from the last actual data point to the forecast line.

Stability

Forecasters require that regression coefficients exhibit stability over time. Should an equation's parameters fluctuate dramatically when new data points are added, there are probably insufficient observations or degrees of freedom. The solution is to provide additional data points to the regression.

In the latest regression, there are 22 observations and 20 degrees of freedom. This is a fairly sizable sample, but the equation should still be tested for stability. The test involves the removal of the most recent data point and the respecification of the equation. If the parameters change considerably, the model is unstable and needs more observations. If

---

[*]   Other procedures with a similar objective include Hildreth-Lu and Theil-Nager.

the respecified equation is similar to its previous form, then the model is stable.

For the latest equation, the 1987 data points for MANEMP and GNP82 are removed and the regression is rerun. The equation, which now encompasses data from 1966 to 1986, has a new specification with MANEMP = 4.91 + 0.0088 × GNP82. A comparison with the previous equation where MANEMP = 5.84 + 0.0085 × GNP82 indicates no major variations in the model parameters. Therefore, the equation appears to have stability.

Standard Error of the Estimate (SEE)

The SEE, one of the four "goodness of fit" measures presented in Chapter Five, has been left to the end of this discussion because the $\bar{R}^2$ and the F-statistic are the primary means of examining the equation's ability to recreate the historical dependent series.

While other tests can be utilized for evaluating the equation fit, the SEE plays a unique role in providing bands around the forecast. There are times when management might want a range of possible values for the dependent or forecasted variable rather than a point projection. In these instances, the SEE is one tool for developing alternative outcomes.

The statistical basis for using the SEE was touched on in the previous chapter. We noted that a normally distributed data series has 67% of its values within one standard deviation of the series mean. In addition, 95% of the observations fall within two standard deviations of the mean.

Since the SEE is representative of the standard deviation, an approximate 95% confidence band can be developed by adjusting the point forecast in both directions by two SEE. This provides a boundary within which the manager can be 95% certain that the forecast will fall.

It should be stressed that the 95% confidence interval developed from the SEE is an approximate measure. A more statistically-rigorous approach to banding the forecast employs a variation of the SEE called the standard error of the forecast (SEF). The SEF is derived from the SEE, but also considers the number of observations in the regression and the distance between the independent variable (X) being used in the forecast calculation and its mean ($\overline{X}$). If the sample size of the regression is sufficiently large (over 30) and the X value used in calculating the forecast is near its mean, the SEF is equivalent to the SEE.

Let's develop a 95% confidence band around a forecast using the SEE approach. Going back to Table 6-3, the SEE for the regression is 1.21. Substituting the 1987 GNP82 value of $3816.9 into the equation, the projected MANEMP level is 38.3. Adding plus and minus two SEE (2.4) to this level results in a range of 35.9 to 40.7. Therefore, we are 95% confident that MANEMP will fall within this boundary should GNP82 be $3816.9. This is supported by the actual 1987 MANEMP level of 36.6, which falls within this range.

This example is useful because the number of observations in the MANEMP equation (22) are below the 30 considered to be substantially sufficient, and the GNP82 value of $3816.9 is well above its mean of $2897.7. Where the data sample is small and the X value is considerably different than its mean, the SEF and the actual confidence bands will be wider than the value obtained by our rule of thumb using 2 SEE. Still, the SEF-based confidence band (which requires considerable calculation) in the MANEMP example is ± 2.76, quite close to the ± 2.42 obtained from the

SEE method. Therefore, the SEE approach to developing confidence bands provides a simpler as well as an accurate alternative to the lengthier calculation.

Another method of producing multiple forecasts is to develop alternative scenarios for the explanatory variable. This will be discussed further in Chapter Eight, which presents methods for deriving a projection from the model equation.

Summary

From this exercise, you have become aware that model building is both an art and a science, which is the reason why a forecaster can pursue various paths in developing a regression equation. All involve both a general understanding of the technical aspects, as well as judgmental decisions on variables and time frames. While this example has followed only one of many possible courses of action, you have gained some experience in the dynamics of the process. Let's move on to another example.

Exercise Two

An economics professor is attempting to provide statistical support to the macroeconomic concept that consumption is related to disposable income. A forecast for consumer purchases is to be developed from the resulting equation.

The hypothesis step has evolved from economic theory, which states that consumption is a function of disposable income: $C = f(Y_d)$. This relationship will be statistically pursued by running a regression with real personal-consumption expenditures (PCE82) as the dependent variable and real disposable personal income (DPI82) as the independent, or explanatory, variable.

First, however, it is important to reemphasize the point made in Chapter Five that a regression cannot prove causality. That is, it cannot confirm that income determines consumption. This is because any close statistical relationship between these variables could either be the result of income influencing consumption or vice versa. Still, a regression can provide evidence that a significant quantitative relationship exists between these series.

Table 6-6 contains the pertinent statistical information from the regression. Since the major tests have been previously examined both in concept (Chapter Five) and in application (Exercise 1), we can be less formal in their presentation this time around.

The $\overline{R}^2$ value implies that 99.6% of the historic movement in PCE82 has been explained by the equation, which in this case is the independent variable DPI82. The F-statistic of 4950.54 confirms this excellent fit.

When a simple regression equation has a high $\overline{R}^2$ and F-statistic, the t-statistic on the independent variable should also be favorable. The t-ratio of 70.4 is so substantial that it isn't necessary to check its significance against a minimum value derived from Table 6-2.

The one problem posed by the equation is its D-W statistic. From Table 6-5, 22 observations with one explanatory variable yields a d_l of 1.24. Reviewing our previous discussion, any D-W value less than 1.24 implies 95% certainty that a positive autocorrelation problem exists. The D-W value of 0.84 in Table 6-6 is well below this limit.

As previously noted, the addition of another independent variable is the initial approach to resolving serial correlation. In this instance, however, this is not a viable option since the professor is interested only in specifying the relationship between PCE82 and

Table 6-6.   Regression Results: PCE82 = f(DPI82).

Sample:	1965–1986
Equation:	PCE82 = $a + b_1 \times$ DPI82
	PCE82 = $-69.1 + .939 \times$ DPI82
	($t = 70.4$)
$\bar{R}^2$:	.996
F-statistic:	4950.54
SEE:	22.37
D-W:	0.84
Number of Observations:	22
Degrees of Freedom:	20

DPI82. The Cochrane-Orcutt adjustment is a remedy, but only after all other avenues have been exhausted.

The next best solution is to model the changes in PCE82 and DPI82 from period to period rather than their levels. The change can be measured as either (1) the change in value (called the first difference) or (2) the percent change. For example, the values of PCE82 for 1985 and 1986 are $2324.5 billion and $2418.6 billion, respectively. To calculate the first difference, $2324.5 is subtracted from $2418.6. The result of $94.1 billion represents the difference for 1986. In computing the

Table 6-7.   Regression Results: CHPCE82 = f(CHDPI82).

Sample:	1966–1986
Equation:	CHPCE82 = $a + b_1 \times$ CHDPI82
	CHPCE82 = $13.3 + 0.7286 \times$ CHDPI82
	($t = 6.0$)
$\bar{R}^2$:	.63
F-statistic:	35.79
SEE:	19.49
D-W:	1.85

1986 percent change, the formula is [(1986 − 1985)/ 1985] × 100. Putting in the yearly values, the calculation becomes [($2418.6 − $2324.5) / $2324.5] × 100, which yields 4.05%. Therefore, the change in 1986 can be enumerated as $94.1 billion (first difference) or 4.05% (percent).

Table 6-7 contains the equation results where the first difference of PCE82 is regressed against the first difference of DPI82. The modeling of the differences has removed the problem of autocorrelation as the new specification's D-W of 1.85 is considerably above the 1.43 d_u value for 22 observations and one explanatory variable.

The adjusted R squared value, however, has fallen from .996 to .63. While this appears to be a loss of explanatory power, it should be noted that the change in a series is interpreted differently from its level. Specifically, assume that the equation relating the PCE82 and DPI82 levels estimates a PCE82 value of 103 for year t from 100 in year $t − 1$. If the actual level is 105, the model has roughly accounted for 98% (103/105) of the t-year value. Utilizing the first difference model of CHPCE82 versus CHDPI82, the expected increase in year t is 3 (103 − 100), with an actual change of 5 (105 − 100). This yields a rough explanatory ratio of 60% ($3/5$) . While the measurements in this example do not strictly adhere to the calculation of an $\overline{R}^2$, the point is clear. That is, a lower R^2 can be accepted in a difference model without compromising accuracy.

This can be further illustrated by comparing the historical performance of the PCE82-DPI82 and CHPCE82-CHDPI82 models. From previous discussions, we are aware that the SEE can be used to examine past performance because it measures the residual, or distance, between Y_i, the actual Y values, and Y_{if}, the equation's fitted values.[*] The PCE82-DPI82 equation, with a .996 $\overline{R}^2$, has a SEE of $22.37 billion. This implies that the equation is able to generate PCE82 projections for 1965 to 1986 that typically come within $22.37 billion of the PCE82 actual values. Using the same criterion, the latter model, with a .63 $\overline{R}^2$, has a smaller SEE of $19.49 billion. The first difference model, therefore, has a better record of accuracy.

A regression using the percent change (rather than the first difference) between PCE82 and DPI82 is also analyzed. Once again, the positive autocorrelation problem disappears. However, the fit is not as good as the equation with the first difference. That is, the R^2, the F-statistic, and the independent variable's t-statistic are all lower in the percent-change equation.

Before accepting the equation in Table 6-7, the tests for multicollinearity and stability need to be reviewed. Since the equation has only one independent variable, multicollinearity can be dismissed as a potential danger. In testing for stability, the latest (1986) observation for CHPCE82 and CHDPI82 is removed and the regression is rerun. The new specification does not deviate significantly from the origi-

---

[*] As noted in Chapter 5, the fitted values of the dependent variable (Y_{if}) are calculated by substituting the actual values of the independent variable (X_i), which in this case is real disposable income, into the regression equation. From here, the SEE can be calculated using the formula

$$\sqrt{\frac{\sum (Y_i - Y_{if})^2}{n - 2}}$$

where Y_i represents the actual values, Y_{if} the fitted values, and n the number of observations.

nal parameters presented in Table 6-7. Therefore, it appears that the data set contains a sufficient number of observations or degrees of freedom.

Other than a brief description in Chapter Five, little has been said concerning the constant or intercept term (a) in the regression equation. As previously defined, the constant represents the value of Y when the explanatory variable(s) equal zero. Its primary role is in helping to set the equation line so that the variances above the line offset those below (Figure 5-1 in Chapter Five).

Although many software programs provide a t-statistic for the constant term, most forecasters concern themselves only with the equation coefficients and do not examine the constant's significance. This does not imply, however, that the constant should be removed from the equation. While the constant term can be suppressed by running the equation through the origin, this action will adversely impact the regression. Leaving out the constant unfairly enhances the importance (t-statistic) of the independent variable's coefficients, making them look better than they should. Moreover, it can also distort the equation's specification. In conclusion, the constant term should neither be left out of the equation, nor should any implications be drawn from its value.

Summary

This chapter has applied the major validity tests to actual regressions in order to determine the appropriateness of the resulting equations. As we see, having a good historical fit (high $\overline{R}^2$ and F-statistic) is not sufficient in itself for accepting the model. The equation must also be free from collinearity among the independent variables, serial correlation between the error terms, and instability in its coefficients.

In our initial exercises, we have dealt with simple regressions. In the coming chapter we will examine multiple-regression model building. While it requires more in the way of resources and involvement, the tests and concepts discussed over the past two chapters are completely adaptable to this new environment.

7

Causal Model Building II

The objective of Causal Model Building I was to provide the reader with the fundamental concepts of constructing regression models. To facilitate that process, simple regressions were utilized as examples. With the basic elements in place, we can now examine more intricate model-building procedures. For this purpose, the exercises presented will encompass multiple regression, that is, having more than one explanatory variable.

This chapter has been divided into two sections. The first section (Exercises Three, Four and Five) deals with multiple-regression models based on annual data while the second (Exercises Six and Seven) examines equations developed from monthly and quarterly series.

Note that the numbering of the exercises continues sequentially from the previous chapter. In this way, each causal-modeling exercise in Chapters Six and Seven can be referred to easily.

Part One—Annual Models

Exercise Three

A forecasting analyst for a southern electric utility wants to develop a causal model for projecting electric sales to the company's commercial customers. The commercial sector primarily involves businesses in retail and wholesale trade, finance, insurance, real estate, and other service activities.

The analyst hypothesizes that commercial sales are likely to be impacted by the dynamics of the local economy. That is, the economic vitality and growth of a region directly influence both the number of commercial companies in the local area and their electrical consumption. The relative price of electricity, which is the ratio between electricity costs and other consumer items, is also expected to affect sales. Here an inverse relationship is anticipated since an increase in the relative price discourages electricity sales, while a decrease boosts consumption. Finally, weather conditions should also explain electricity sales since temperatures affect the amount of energy needed for cooling and heating.

The analyst has identified certain economic series which serve as surrogates for these explanatory factors. Commercial employment, personal income, population, and the number of residential customers are potential candidates for representing economic trends in the local community.

The relative price of electricity, also known as the real price, monitors the pace at which electricity costs change in contrast to other products that the commercial customer purchases. In this example, the Implicit Price Deflator for Business is used to represent the variety of products that the commercial firm can choose from. A good representative of weather is cooling- and heating-degree days, which are calculated by the National Oceanic and Atmospheric Administration (NOAA) for all regional areas.

In developing the data base, a modeler often has difficulty obtaining up-to-date regional income and employment information. This is particularly a problem for smaller regional units such as counties. One series which our analyst obtains on a current basis is the number of residential customers served by the utility. This number is very exact because the electric company counts each customer and does not have to derive the series from a sample. Therefore, residential customers appears to be appropriate for representing local business activity from the standpoint of timeliness and completeness.

Before it is accepted, however, the analyst must test the residential series to determine if it is statistically the most acceptable representative of the economy. This is accomplished by running three simple regressions with commercial energy sales as the dependent variable, and interchanging personal income, commercial employment, and residential customers as the explanatory variable. The results indicate that residential customers provides the best historical explanation (highest $\bar{R}^2$) or fit to commercial energy sales.

In fact, the regression relating movements in residential customers (RESCUS) and commercial electricity sales (COMENG) has an extremely high $\bar{R}^2$ of .996, denoting a close relationship between the two series. While an $\bar{R}^2$ of this magnitude is usually a source of suspicion, the plot of these series in Figure 7-1 provides an explanation. In this graph, the two data sets have moved together quite closely over the time period examined. The pertinent information from the commercial sales/residential customer regression is provided in Table 7-1.

Despite this close fit, the equation suffers from positive serial correlation as indicated by its low D-W value. As we are now aware, serial or autocorrelation reflects a pattern in the residual (error terms) which could represent explanatory variables that have not yet been identified. This problem should diminish with the addition of the price and weather variables to the equation.

Figure 7-1. Commercial Electricity Sales versus Residential Customers.

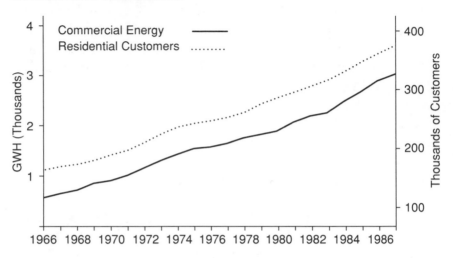

Source: Tampa Electric Company

Table 7-2 adds the relative-electricity-price (COMCTS) series to residential customers in explaining historical commercial energy sales. Although the explanatory power ($\bar{R}^2$) of the original equation is considerable, the new variable improves the fit from .9963 to .9969.

Table 7-1.   Regression Results: COMENG = f(RESCUS).

Sample:	1966–1987
Equation:	COMENG = $a + b_1 \times$ RESCUS
	COMENG = $-1370.7 + 12.9 \times$ RESCUS
	$(t = 74.9)$
$\bar{R}^2$:	.9963
F-statistic:	5608.17
D-W:	0.69
Number of Observations:	22
Degrees of Freedom:	20

Table 7-2. Regression Results: COMENG = f(RESCUS, COMCTS).

Sample: 1966–1987

Equation:
COMENG = $a + b_1 \times$ RESCUS $+ b_2 \times$ COMCTS
COMENG = $-1211.3 + 13.1 \times$ RESCUS
$$(t = 74.9)$$
$$+ \; -86.0 \times \text{COMCTS}$$
$$(t = -2.3)$$

$\bar{R}^2$:	.9969
F-statistic:	3397.68
D-W:	0.96

Correlation Matrix:

	COMENG	RESCUS	COMCTS
COMENG	1.00	0.998	0.42
RESCUS	0.998	1.000	0.44
COMCTS	0.42	0.44	1.00

Number of Observations:	22
Degrees of Freedom:	19

Looking at the *t*-ratios for the explanatory variables, the new specification shows them both to be significant. However, the *t*-value of the price variable is just above the acceptable limit at the 95% confidence level. The fact that the RESCUS *t*-ratio of 74.9 is well above the COMCTS value of -2.3 gives us more certainty that RESCUS is significant.

Also noteworthy is that the explanatory variables have the appropriate signs associated with their coefficients. Specifically, RESCUS is directly related to COMENG. This is reasonable since a rise in RESCUS implies the need for more commercial services which, in turn, should lead to additional firms and electricity sales. The negative sign on COMCTS is also consistent with economic theory since an increase in the relative price of electricity has the opposite effect on electrical consumption.

The addition of COMCTS to the regression also improves the D-W statistic from 0.69 to 0.96 because part of the error pattern in the original regression has been identified as belonging to the COMCTS variable. Finally, it is important in a multiple regression to examine the correlation matrix to determine if there is an unusually close relationship between the independent or explanatory variables. In this regression, the RESCUS and COMCTS variables are not closely correlated (r = .44).

The next step for the analyst is to include the weather series (TDD) as an explanatory variable along with RESCUS and COMCTS. TDD stands for total heating-and-cooling-degree days. Degree days are calculated as the absolute value of the difference between each day's average temperature and 65 degrees. When warmer summers and colder winters occur, the result is wider temperature variations, greater total degree days, and more heating and cooling. The relationship between TDD and COMENG, therefore, should be positive, as an increasing number of degree days produces a rise in electricity consumption. Table 7-3, which contains this new explanatory variable, indicates that TDD has the appropriate sign. In addition, the TDD variable is significant, albeit marginally, with a t-ratio of 2.2.

Once again, the addition of an independent variable improves the $\bar{R}^2$ value (.9969 to .9974), as well as the D-W statistic (0.96 to 1.25). Thus, it further explains a portion of the previous pattern in the residual or error term. Also important is that the new explanatory series does not correlate closely with any of the other independent variables.

Table 7-3. Regression Results: COMENG = f(RESCUS, COMCTS, TDD).

Sample: 1966–1987
Equation:

COMENG = $a + b_1 \times$ RESCUS + $b_2 \times$ COMCTS
$\qquad\qquad + b_3 \times$ TDD
COMENG = $-1560.4 + 13.0 \times$ RESCUS
$\qquad\qquad\qquad (t = 80.2)$
$\qquad\qquad + -83.7 \times$ COMCTS $+ 0.089 \times$ TDD
$\qquad\qquad\quad (t = -2.4) \qquad\qquad (t = 2.2)$

$\bar{R}^2$:   .9974
F-statistic: 2721.84
D-W: 1.25

Correlation Matrix:

	COMENG	RESCUS	COMCTS	TDD
COMENG	1.00	0.998	0.42	0.22
RESCUS	0.998	1.00	0.44	0.20
COMCTS	0.42	0.44	1.00	0.06
TDD	0.22	0.20	0.06	1.00

Number of
Observations: 22
Degreees of
Freedom: 19

From the example, we have observed that model building is a process of trial and error. It is always possible that a better specification can be developed by experimenting with various alternative structures. These additional regressions, however, should have theoretical merit.

On this note, our utility analyst seeks to further improve the model. In the original hypothesis, it was assumed that changes in economic activity (RESCUS) and price (COMCTS) immediately impacted commercial energy sales (COMENG). It is reasonable, however, to suppose that a time lag exists between movements in RESCUS and COMCTS and their impact on

COMENG. That is, a period of time could elapse before an increase in the demand for commercial services elicits a response from the business sector. Likewise, commercial businesses might not react to changing energy prices until the influence substantially alters expenses and profits.

With this rethinking of the hypothesis, further regressions are examined which use a time lag of one year for the RESCUS and COMCTS explanatory variables. This produces an improved equation in Table 7-4. The new specification retains the original independent variables of COMCTS and TDD, but

---

Table 7-4. Regression Results: COMENG $= f$(RESCUS(-1), COMCTS, TDD).

Sample: 1966–1987
Equation:

$$\text{COMENG} = a + b_1 \times \text{RESCUS}(-1) + b_2 \times \text{COMCTS} + b_3 \times \text{TDD}$$

$$\text{COMENG} = -1461.1 + 13.71 \times \text{RESCUS}(-1)$$
$$(t = 92.1)$$
$$-169.8 \times \text{COMCTS} + 0.103 \times \text{TDD}$$
$$(t = -5.6) \qquad (t = 2.9)$$

$\bar{R}^2$:	.9981
F-statistic:	3594.84
SEE:	37.01
D-W:	1.85

Correlation Matrix:

	COMENG	RESCUS(-1)	COMCTS	TDD
COMENG	1.00	0.997	0.42	0.22
RESCUS(-1)	0.997	1.000	0.47	0.19
COMCTS	0.42	0.47	1.00	0.06
TDD	0.22	0.19	0.06	1.00

Number of
  Observations: 22
Degrees of
  Freedom: 19

replaces RESCUS with a one-year lag for residential customers (RESCUS(-1)).

The new equation improves the historical fit ($\overline{R}^2$), as well as the significance of all of the explanatory variables. It also results in a jump in the D-W statistic from 1.25 to 1.85, with the latest value indicating no autocorrelation among the error terms.

A lagged independent variable, when theoretically appropriate, is also helpful in developing a projection. For example, a forecast for COMENG based on the equation in Table 7-4 requires future estimates for RESCUS(-1), COMCTS, and TDD. Supplying projections for the explanatory variables often necessitates considerable research. In the case of RESCUS(-1), however, last year's residential customer value can be utilized to develop this year's forecast because of the lag in the explanatory variable. Thus, estimates of only two (COMCTS and TDD) rather than three explanatory variables are needed for developing the one-year COMENG projection.

Summary

In this example, we have expanded our analysis to encompass the data-gathering process. While this topic will be examined in more detail in Chapter Nine, the reader can begin to appreciate its importance in model building.

From the exercise, we see that multiple regressions are more complex than simple regressions. Fortunately, the same general principles and tests apply to both types of equations. Given the numerous interrelationships in the real world, most causal modeling will involve equations with several explanatory variables.

It is important to note that the final structure represents only one of many possible specifications and routes that can be taken in arriving at a workable model. In fact, rather than building a multiple regression equation one variable at a time, many analysts use an approach called stepwise regression. In this procedure, all potential explanatory variables are evaluated as the program chooses the one most closely related to the dependent variable and adds those which improve the fit of the equation ($\overline{R}^2$).

A limitation of the stepwise approach is that the selected independent variables have not been tested for multicollinearity. Still, the procedure is useful for sorting through series where the forecaster has many possible explanatory variables.

Exercise Four

Although the issue of model stability has already been defined, consideration is paramount in this exercise. As previously stated, the integrity of the coefficient values is the key to regression analysis. When a model is unstable, the independent variable coefficients are prone to volatility. Such instability is almost always due to insufficient observations. However, there is no hard and fast rule for the number of observations necessary to develop a statistically-acceptable equation. Therefore, a decision on the appropriate size of the data set has to be determined subjectively. In Chapter Five, it was noted that the minimum acceptable degrees of freedom can vary between 15 and 30 depending on the forecaster. A relatively small number of degrees warrants extreme concern over the possibility of unstable coefficients. As the degrees of freedom rise, the analyst's concern will diminish. Still, it doesn't hurt to test all equations for this possible problem.

An analyst with the Bureau of Mines is interested in projecting U. S. phosphate-rock production. Phosphate, a key ingredient in agricultural fertilizers, is sold both domestically and internationally. The analyst hypothesizes that surrogates for domestic-phosphate demand could include real Gross National Product, as well as farm income and farm production measures. A popular proxy for foreign-market demand is the U. S. dollar's trade-weighted value. This is because a strengthening in the dollar versus international currencies increases the cost of U. S. phosphate overseas, reducing its foreign demand. On the other hand, a declining dollar reduces the price of U. S. phosphate products in world markets, making the products more attractive to foreign purchasers.

The regressing of various combinations from the above hypothesis results in the model specified in Table 7-5. In this equation, the dependent variable

---

Table 7-5. Regression Results: MINING = f(GNP72, DOLLAR).

Sample: 1967–1982

Equation:
MINING = $a + b_1 \times$ GNP72 + $b_2 \times$ DOLLAR
MINING = 31896 + 32.5 × GNP72 −287.1 × DOLLAR
                    ($t = 5.9$)   ($t = -2.4$)

$\bar{R}^2$:   .74
F-Statistic: 22.46
D-W: 1.09

Correlation Matrix:

	MINING	GNP72	DOLLAR
MINING	1.00	0.82	−0.43
GNP72	0.82	1.00	−0.15
DOLLAR	−0.43	−0.15	1.00

Number of
  Observations: 16
Degrees of
  Freedom: 13

(MINING) is shown to be closely related to historic movements in real Gross National Product (GNP72)[*] and the trade-weighted value of the dollar (DOLLAR).

Looking at the "goodness of fit" measures, we find that the equation has an $\bar{R}^2$ value of .74. This signifies that nearly three-fourths of the historical movement in MINING is accounted for by the equation. A check of the t-ratios indicates that both explanatory variables (GNP82 and DOLLAR) are significant at the 95% confidence level. In addition, the signs attached to the independent variables conform to expectations and economic theory. In the domestic market, the production of phosphate moves directly with the course of U. S. economic activity (GNP72). For the DOLLAR variable, the negative coefficient suggests an inverse relationship, with a declining dollar bolstering foreign phosphate sales and vice versa.

The analyst is particularly surprised that the GNP72 variable, which represents general economic activity, performed better than farm income and production in explaining phosphate-fertilizer output. This is because the farm economy's fortunes are closely tied to the national economy.

The F-statistic of 22.46 indicates that the equation is significant at the 95% confidence level in explaining the historical movements in the dependent variable. Since there is more than one independent variable, a check of the correlation matrix should be made to see if GNP72 and DOLLAR are multicollinear. The matrix shows no close correlation

---

[*]The GNP data is periodically rebenchmarked to a new year. This example involves national data that was based in 1972. During a 1985 data revision, a new base period of 1982 (see Exercise Two) was established.

between the explanatory variables. The D-W statistic is in the grey area where it's not possible to determine whether or not the residuals are autocorrelated. Within this area, the forecaster can decide whether to adjust the equation using the Cochrane-Orcutt procedure or to utilize the model in its present form.

Because of data limitations, the regression encompasses only 16 observations and 13 degrees of freedom. As previously noted, the probability of model instability increases as the number of observations declines. To test for stability, the most recent data point is removed and the regression is respecified. In this example, the 1982 observations for MINING, GNP72 and DOLLAR are dropped and the new equation is presented in Table 7-6.

A quick glance at the new specification indicates that the original model in Table 7-5 is unstable. Evidence is contained in the new parameter values, which have changed dramatically. Also critical is that the sign on the DOLLAR coefficient has gone from negative to positive.[*]

Adding more observations to the data base should solve this deficiency. In some cases, this can be done only by waiting for future observations. In other instances, the analyst is able to locate earlier data. A third solution is to change the regression from its annual form to a semiannual or quarterly format. This allows the equation to encompass more data points for the same time period. Models with other than annual data will be discussed in Exercises Six and Seven.

---

[*]Interestingly enough, the $\bar{R}^2$ and the F-statistic of the new equation have increased. This illustrates the need for the analyst to examine more than just the "goodness of fit" tests in developing an equation.

Table 7-6.   Regression Results: MINING = f(GNP72, DOLLAR).

Sample: 1967–1981
Equation:

MINING = $a + b_1 \times$ GNP72 $+ b_2 \times$ DOLLAR
MINING = $-27900 + 44.0 \times$ GNP72 $+ 144.5 \times$ DOLLAR
                       ($t = 10.2$)   ($t = 1.2$)

$\bar{R}^2$:   .90
F-Statistic: 64.27
D-W: 1.30
Number of
  Observations: 15
Degrees of
  Freedom: 12

Summary

The problem of multicollinearity was addressed in Exercise One, while serial correlation was presented in Exercises Two and Three. With this examination of the stability question, we have covered the three major non-"goodness of fit" considerations that are likely to be experienced in building a time-series regression.

Up to now, the exercises have exclusively dealt with time-series regressions in which the observations span a period of years. In the following example, a cross-sectional regression model will be constructed, relating data from one point in time. These two types of regression, time-series and cross-sectional, are developed in much the same way. Moreover, "goodness of fit," multicollinearity, and stability considerations are important to both in examining statistical integrity. Their primary difference, as we will see in this example, is in the testing of the residual or error term.

Exercise Five

The owner of a major-league baseball team is desperate to improve the financial situation of the organization, which has been unprofitable over the past few years. To achieve this objective, a consultant is hired to study the industry and uncover those factors that are significant to financial success. To quantify the impact of these major elements, the consultant decides to construct a regression model.

The owner and consultant both agree that the key to profitability is healthy ballpark attendance. Thus, the model structure targets this as the dependent variable. Next, it is hypothesized that the factors influencing attendance include (1) the ability of the team to win games; and (2) the population of the team's locality. The relationship between attendance and the number of victories is expected to be strongly positive, as they should rise and fall together. The same is expected of population, as a larger city's greater population base should draw more fans to the games.

With this framework, a cross-sectional regression is developed using the preliminary form of

$$\text{attendance} = f(\text{wins, population})$$

The model is based on 1987 data from the 26 major-league baseball teams.

Since the consultant expects the number of team victories (WIN) to have a major influence on attendance (ATTEND), this relationship is examined first. Interestingly, the results in Table 7-7 imply that WIN is not greatly explanatory in describing ATTEND. Instead, the R^2 of .26 indicates that only about 25% of the variation in team attendance is explained by the number of wins. Still, the 3.1 t-value for the independent variable WIN represents a significant relationship with ATTEND. In addition, the positive

---

Table 7-7. Regression Results: ATTEND = f(WIN).

Equation:	ATTEND = $a + b_1 \times$ WIN
	ATTEND = $-0.568 + 0.0317 \times$ WIN
	$(t = 3.1)$
$\overline{R}^2$:	.26
F-Statistic:	9.71
Number of	
Observations:	26
Degrees of	
Freedom:	24

---

sign on the WIN coefficient agrees with the hypothesized direct relationship between victories and attendance.

Since a cross-sectional regression examines observations from the same time period, serial correlation is not a concern. Therefore, testing for autocorrelation with the D-W statistic is not necessary in this analysis. Heteroskedasticity, or the nonconstant variance in the residuals, is, however, a potential danger and will be tested for after the preliminary specification of the equation is complete.

The addition of the population variable (POP) to the equation has a positive impact on the regression's "goodness of fit." POP represents the number of people in the metropolitan areas where each team is located. For those cities which have two teams—such as New York, Chicago, and Los Angeles—the area population has been divided by two.

In Table 7-8, the new equation with WIN and POP has increased the $\overline{R}^2$ to .41. Moreover, the POP variable's coefficient has the correctly-hypothesized sign, as well as a significant t-statistic. Finally, the F-statistic of 9.82 is above the 3.42 minimum-acceptable level for 23 degrees of freedom and two explanatory variables derived from Table 6-4.

Table 7-8.   Regression Results: ATTEND = f(WIN, POP).

Equation:
ATTEND $= a + b_1 \times$ WIN $+ b_2 \times$ POP
ATTEND $= -0.706 + 0.0280 \times$ WIN $+ 0.1185 \times$ POP
$\quad\quad\quad\quad\quad$ ($t = 3.1$) $\quad\quad\quad\quad\quad\quad$ ($t = 2.7$)

$\bar{R}^2$: $\quad\quad\quad\quad\quad$ .41
F-Statistic: $\quad\quad$ 9.82

Correlation Matrix:

	ATTEND	WIN	POP
ATTEND	1.00	0.54	0.49
WIN	0.54	1.00	0.15
POP	0.49	0.15	1.00

Number of
Observations: $\quad$ 26
Degrees of
Freedom: $\quad\quad$ 23

Because the equation has two independent variables, a test for multicollinearity is necessary. An examination of the correlation matrix indicates that there is no close relationship between WIN and POP.

Despite the improved statistics, the consultant feels that an important determinant is still missing from the equation. Certainly the past record of the teams should have a bearing on 1987 attendance. That is, teams that have performed well in recent years will likely have substantial fan support, even if the club has faltered in the latest season.

From this hypothesis, a new variable called CHAMP is introduced which measures the previous performance of the franchise. To understand this variable better, some background on the baseball championship process is necessary. The 26 baseball teams are broken into two leagues (National and American), each having two divisions (East and West). The individual teams play 162 games to determine the four division champions. The two champions from each league then take part in a playoff to determine that league's participant in the World Series. The new variable, CHAMP, represents the number of division championships each team has won over the past three years. This variable reflects the past success of the teams and should be directly related to ATTEND.

The addition of CHAMP in Table 7-9 has a favorable influence on the equation's statistical fit. The $\overline{R}^2$ indicates that 62% of the movement in attendance can now be accounted for by the equation. The F-statistic, which measures the significance of the equation, is well above the acceptable minimum. As we know, this implies that the independent vari-

---

Table 7-9. Regression Results: ATTEND = f(WIN, POP, CHAMP).

Equation:
$$ATTEND = a + b_1 \times WIN + b_2 \times POP + b_3 \times CHAMP$$
$$ATTEND = -0.614 + 0.0250 \times WIN + 0.1009 \times POP$$
$$(t = 3.4) \qquad\qquad (t = 2.9)$$
$$+ 0.4646 \times CHAMP$$
$$(t = 3.7)$$

$\overline{R}^2$:	.62
F-Statistic:	14.82
SEE:	0.36

Correlation Matrix:

	ATTEND	WIN	POP	CHAMP
ATTEND	1.00	0.54	0.49	0.57
WIN	0.54	1.00	0.15	0.13
POP	0.49	0.15	1.00	0.15
CHAMP	0.57	0.13	0.15	1.00

Number of Observations:	26
Degrees of Freedom:	22

ables, taken together, are more significant than zero in explaining the dependent variable.

Looking at the individual explanatory series (WIN,POP, and CHAMP), each is significant and also has the correct sign on its coefficient. Moreover, the correlation matrix indicates that there is no strong relationship between any of the independent variables.

At this point, the consultant believes that the equation has captured the dominant factors influencing ATTEND. However, testing for heteroskedasticity in a cross-sectional regression will help determine if an explanatory variable is missing. We've seen that heteroskedasticity occurs when the equation's residuals have a nonconstant variance; that is, the error term is increasing or decreasing over the range of observations. Existence of a rising or falling error pattern probably represents a series that has been omitted.

A common approach for identifying heteroskedasticity is the Park Test. Its objective is to correlate the log of the squared residuals (errors) against one or more of the equation's independent variables. In this example, the residuals represent the difference between each team's actual attendance and its attendance as estimated from the regression equation. Since the explanatory variable has a broad or nonconstant range over its data set, a strong relationship with the error term implies that the latter also fluctuates in a nonconstant manner.

As a first step, the Park Test requires calculating the residuals of the equation, which usually is done by the computer software package used to specify the equation. The residuals are then squared and the natural log of the series is computed.

This series, called ln RES in our example, is regressed against the log of the primary independent variable to determine how closely the series are correlated. In the model equation, the three explanatory variables are similar in significance (t-value). However, only in WIN and POP is there a substantial pattern of variation within the data set. Therefore, the consultant regresses ln RES individually against ln WIN and ln POP.

In the regression ln RES = f(ln WIN), the t-statistic for ln WIN is 0.70, well below the minimum significance level of 2.0. Since ln WIN is not closely related to ln RES, the residual does not display a nonconstant variance. That is, its variance is constant or homoskedastic. The t-value of ln POP (1.0) is only slightly higher in its regression against ln RES, thus bringing us to a similar conclusion. Heteroskedasticity, therefore, does not appear to be a problem in the equation, as there is no significant correlation between the residuals and the explanatory variables. From this, the consultant concludes that the major explanatory variables have been identified.

Having completed the model specification, the consultant proceeds with an analysis of the equation results. The obvious inference from the model is that a baseball franchise should have healthy attendance if it fields a strong team every year and is located in a large metropolitan area.

More specific information can be obtained from the equation coefficients, which quantify the impact of the explanatory variables (WIN, POP, and CHAMP) on attendance. Examining the individual coefficients, a team can expect to increase annual attendance by 250,000 if they win an additional ten games during the season. This impact is calculated by multiplying the coefficient assigned to WIN (.0250) by 10, which yields a .250 million (250,000) increase in ATTEND (Table 7-10). Using the same approach, attendance will rise by around 100,000 for every million addi-

Table 7-10. Impact of Explanatory Variables on Attendance.

Explanatory Variable	Coefficient		Change in Explanatory Variable		Impact on ATTEND (millions)
WIN	0.0250	×	10	=	.250
POP (millions)	0.1009	×	1	=	.101
CHAMP	0.4646	×	1	=	.465

tional people that reside in a metropolitan area. Most dramatic is the impact of a division championship, which is worth an extra 465,000 customers. This effect appears to be reasonable given the media attention and fan fervor related to winning a title.

While the coefficients play a valuable role in analyzing the influence of the explanatory variables, they should be used with caution. The forecaster must be careful that the independent variables are not extrapolated beyond the actual data. For example, the CHAMP data set ranges from 0 to 2. It is important that the analyst does not consider the effect of more than two championships in measuring the benefits to be gained from this variable.

The consultant has taken the analysis one step further in Table 7-11 by examining the relative situations of the individual franchises. This table contains the fitted equation values, as well as the actual observations for each of the 26 teams. Once again, the fitted values for each club are calculated by substituting their actual wins, population, and championships into the final regression equation. In addition, the residuals, or the difference between the actual and estimated values, have also been computed.

The equation, as we now know, represents the relative influence of the explanatory variables across all the teams. The consultant is interested in identifying those cities which differ considerably from this norm.

Table 7-11. Team Attendance Comparison.

Team	Actual	Fitted	Residual	Residual Plot — Under-achievers	Over-achievers
Cleveland	1.078	1.193	−0.115	I　*	I
Seattle	1.134	1.567	−0.433	*I	I
Pittsburgh	1.161	1.617	−0.456	*I	I
Chicago (A.L.)	1.208	1.723	−0.515	*　I	I
Atlanta	1.217	1.372	−0.155	I　*	I
San Diego	1.454	1.697	−0.243	I*	I
Oakland	1.679	1.702	−0.023	I　　*	I
Texas	1.763	1.633	0.130	I	*　I
Baltimore	1.836	1.292	0.544	I	I　*
Montreal	1.850	1.962	−0.112	I　*	I
Milwaukee	1.909	1.821	0.088	I	*　I
Houston	1.910	2.113	−0.203	I　*	I
San Francisco	1.917	1.927	−0.010	I　　*	I
Chicago (N.L.)	2.035	2.163	−0.128	I　*	I
Detroit	2.062	2.763	−0.701	*　I	I
Minnesota	2.082	1.742	0.340	I	*I
Philadelphia	2.100	1.970	0.130	I	*　I
Cincinnati	2.185	1.656	0.529	I	I　*
Boston	2.232	2.213	0.019	I	*　I
Kansas City	2.392	2.540	−0.148	I　*	I
New York (A.L.)	2.428	2.517	−0.089	I　*	I
California	2.696	2.380	0.316	I	*I
Toronto	2.778	2.592	0.186	I	*　I
Los Angeles	2.797	2.330	0.467	I	I　*
New York (N.L.)	3.034	3.057	−0.023	I　　*	I
St. Louis	3.072	2.466	0.606	I	I　*
				−.36　　　　0	.36

That is, those cities with the largest residual or error terms. A boundary of plus or minus one SEE is used in examining the residuals. From previous discussions, approximately 67% of the errors should fall inside this band, while 33% will be outside.

With this information, the consultant can note those teams whose actual attendance was considerably different from the model calculation during 1987. These are the teams with large residuals outside the error band. In the table, four cities (Baltimore, Cincinnati, Los Angeles, and St. Louis) attracted more fans than would be expected based on the equation and their specific wins, population, and championships. These clubs can be considered as overachievers in 1987 given the determinants of attendance and the conditions in their franchise. There are also four underachieving teams (Seattle, Pittsburgh, Chicago White Sox, and Detroit) who drew fewer fans than anticipated from the equation results.

Naturally, this represents only one year of analysis. It would be useful for the consultant to examine other years to see if certain teams are consistently outside the bandwidth. Still, these results provide important information about the factors that drive baseball franchises.

Summary

In Exercise Five, we explored the world of cross-sectional regression, including its similarities and differences with the time-series variety. The example also illustrated how an equation's coefficients can be interpreted and utilized for obtaining a deeper understanding of the subject. From this, the coefficients take on a new importance as does the need for examining the model results to ensure that they are reasonable.

Part Two—Monthly and Quarterly Models

From the causal-modeling concepts first described in Chapter Five, we have progressed through several real-life exercises, starting with a simple regression and progressing to equations with three explanatory variables. These examples have provided some common situations that forecasters face in model building.

All these examples, however, have dealt with annual data. The next section concludes our causal-modeling work by developing equations from quarterly and monthly observations. The good news is that the intra-year data base has the potential for considerably more observations that an annual series, resolving any degrees-of-freedom limitations. The bad news is that quarterly and monthly data require an additional consideration—the treatment of seasonal patterns.

In Exercises Six and Seven, we will build on our knowledge and examine more sophisticated equations involving seasonality, dummy variables and nonlinear relationships.

Exercise Six

Fairly Well-Built Homes is a large, residential development company with offices throughout the United States. It specializes in building both single and multi-family structures, including apartments and condominiums. Mr. Fairly, the owner, is concerned about the sensitivity of the housing industry to economic activity. He has asked his research department to develop a model which can be used for projecting national housing starts on a short-term basis. With this forecast, he hopes the company can better plan for future contingencies.

The analyst working on the project determines

Figure 7-2. United States Housing Starts.

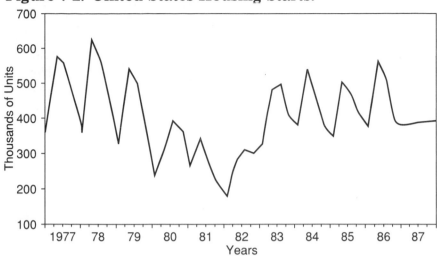

Source: Bureau of the Census, Department of Commerce.

that a quarterly model will provide Mr. Fairly with the timely forecast he is seeking. The first step is to plot the historical data for national housing starts. Figure 7-2, which graphs the data, suggests that the housing series is extremely volatile. Data that fluctuate dramatically are always more difficult to forecast. However, a certain portion of the movement appears to be related to seasonal patterns. The analyst makes a note of this and moves on to hypothesizing those variables likely to influence housing starts.

Demographics, income, price, and interest rates are known to be most important in explaining housing movements. In developing these concepts, the analyst attempts to locate data series that accurately portray these factors and for which outside forecasts are available.

Looking at demographics, the rate of change in the number of households should impact housing sales in a direct manner, with increased growth in new families resulting in the demand for additional units. It is difficult, however, to obtain household data on a quarterly basis. Our analyst, therefore, chooses the change in U. S. population (aged 16 and over) as a surrogate for households because (1) the population series is available on a more timely basis, (2) it covers the basic household group, and (3) a forecast of population can readily be obtained.

Family income is also an important consideration in purchasing a home. To capture this influence, the percent change in disposable-income per capita, adjusted for inflation, is utilized. As family real or inflation-adjusted income expands, its ability to meet the monthly payment on a home should also improve. Thus, a direct relationship between income growth and housing starts is hypothesized.

The price of a home relative to other products purchased by the consumer should also be an explanatory variable. In this instance, an increase in the relative price of housing should have a negative, or inverse, influence on residential construction. To represent this real-price variable, we can adjust the average cost of a new home by the Implicit Price Deflator for Gross National Product.

Finally, interest rates must be considered. Similar to the income and price components, the real or inflation-adjusted interest rate is determined to be the best expression of this factor. In addition, the impact of the real interest rate on housing starts is anticipated to be negative, as higher borrowing costs drive down housing sales. For this variable, the mortgage rate is deflated, again, by the Implicit Price Deflator.

At this point, there are four potential explanatory variables. Household additions (1) and real-income growth (2) are expected to have positive signs on their coefficients, representing a direct relationship with the dependent variable (housing starts). On the other hand, the real price of a home (3) and the real interest rate (4) are assumed to have negative coefficients, reflecting an inverse relationship with residential activity.

The analyst also has had numerous discussions with representatives in the company's satellite offices. They are concerned about the slowdown in housing activity since 1987, particularly in the multifamily sector. It appears that tax legislation passed in late 1986 may have discouraged investments in apartments and condominiums.

Although the analyst wants to test this factor in the model specification, there is no quantifiable measure for tax legislation. This obstacle, however, is removed by using a "dummy" variable to represent the new tax code. A dummy quantifies an explanatory factor that cannot otherwise be expressed numerically by assigning a value of either 1 or 0 to represent whether the condition being measured exists or does not exist. For the tax legislation, a value of 0 is assigned to those quarters prior to the new tax law (before 1987), while a 1 is assigned for those periods after the legislation was enacted. A negative sign is expected on the dummy variable, as the tax legislation (value = 1) should have a downward impact on housing activity.

This still leaves the consideration of the seasonal patterns identified in the housing-starts plot in Figure 7-2. There are two methods for treating seasonality in regression analysis. In the first approach, both the dependent and independent variables are seasonally adjusted using a classical decomposition method. An exception to this is the interest rate, which is not usually adjusted for seasonality. In addition, the tax dummy developed by the analyst does not have a seasonal pattern. Once all the other series have been seasonally adjusted, however, the data are ready to be regressed.

The second approach is to create dummy variables which represent the seasonal influences. In this procedure, the first-quarter seasonal dummy is assigned values of 1,0,0, and 0, for the four quarters of each year, with 1 reflecting the first period's seasonal influence. For the second quarter, the assigned dummy values are 0,1,0, and 0, while the third quarter pattern is 0,0,1, and 0. A fourth-quarter dummy is not needed since the three seasonal dummies, when regressed, reflect their relationship to the fourth-quarter pattern. If monthly data are being examined, eleven seasonal dummies are used.

In this second method, all the variables should remain unadjusted. Therefore, the seasonal dummies incorporate not only the seasonal influence of the dependent variable, but also the seasonality of the independent series in the regression.

There are pros and cons to these two approaches. Proponents of the first method (seasonally adjusting all series) note that the degrees of freedom in the equation are improved since there are three less independent variables (the seasonal dummies) to restrain the data. Those utilizing the second approach state that the classical decomposition method (seasonally adjusting data) is not always appropriate. They believe that certain series are extremely difficult, if not impossible, to adjust in this manner (see Chapter Three).

Our analyst is particularly sensitive to this latter argument as a result of past difficulties in adjusting multifamily housing starts. Therefore, seasonal dummies are employed in constructing the model. In addition, 44 observations covering 1977 to 1987 are included in the data base to ensure sufficient degrees of freedom, even with the dummy variables.

Most forecasters examine the total effect of the seasonal dummies on the model equation rather than the individual significance of each. With this objective, the impact of the three seasonal variables on the regression's F-statistic is measured instead of each dummy's t-value being studied.

We have packed a great deal of discussion into the past several pages, and can organize these thoughts by separating the equation-building process into two steps. In the first stage, housing starts are regressed against the five orginally-hypothesized explanatory variables of population growth, income growth, price, mortgage rates, and tax legislation. In the second stage, the dummy seasonal variables are added to the regression as explanatory variables to determine if there is significant improvement in the equation's "goodness of fit."

Table 7-12 contains the first regression where the dependent variable is housing starts (HOUSE), and the independent variables are (1) change in population (POP), (2) change in real disposable income per capita (INCOME), (3) real home price (PRICE), (4) real interest rate (INT), and (5) the tax legislation dummy (TAXES). From this table, the $\overline{R}^2$ indicates that 31% of the historical movement in housing starts has been accounted for by the equation. This rather lackluster fit is further verified in that only two of the five independent variables are significant at the 95% confidence level. Other evidence is found in a low F-statistic, although it exceeds the 95% standard.

Still, the optimistic analyst is heartened by the fact that all the independent variables' coefficients match their hypothesized signs. Also noteworthy is the correlation matrix, which indicates that there is no multicollinearity between any of the five independent variables.

Table 7-12. Regression Results: HOUSE = f(POP, INCOME, INT, PRICE, TAXES).

Sample: 1977–1987

Equation:
HOUSE = a + b_1 × POP + b_2 × INCOME + b_3 × INT
        + b_4 × PRICE + b_5 × TAXES
HOUSE = 1326.1 + 140.4 × POP + 14.1 × INCOME
                        (t = 1.2)   (t = 0.8)
              −23.9 × INT − 7.1 × PRICE − 125.2 × TAXES
              (t = −3.1)   (t = −1.7)   (t = −2.2)

$\bar{R}^2$:   .31
F-Statistic: 4.85
D-W: 1.87

Correlation Matrix:

	HOUSE	POP	INCOME	INT	PRICE	TAXES
HOUSE	1.00	0.12	0.35	−0.39	−0.42	−0.04
POP	0.12	1.00	0.03	0.29	−0.23	−0.17
INCOME	0.35	0.03	1.00	−0.32	−0.31	0.07
INT	−0.39	0.29	−0.32	1.00	0.18	−0.59
PRICE	−0.42	−0.23	−0.31	0.18	1.00	0.02
TAXES	−0.04	−0.17	0.07	−0.59	0.02	1.00

Number of
  Observations: 44
Degrees of
  Freedom: 38

At this point, the three seasonal dummy variables are added to the regression in order to measure their impact on the equation. Table 7-13, representing this new specification, indicates a substantial improvement in the statistical significance of the regression. First, the $\bar{R}^2$ has jumped to 74%. Moreover, the addition of the seasonal dummies has enhanced the significance (t-statistic) of the five original independent variables. Most importantly, the three seasonal dummies have lifted the F-statistic to 16.43 from the

---

Table 7-13.   Regression Results: HOUSE = *f*(POP, INCOME, INT, PRICE, TAXES, DUM1, DUM2, DUM3).

Sample: 1977–1987

Equation:

$$\text{HOUSE} = a + b_1 \times \text{POP} + b_2 \times \text{INCOME} + b_3 \times \text{INT} \\ + b_4 \times \text{PRICE} + b_5 \times \text{TAXES} + b_6 \times \text{DUM1} \\ + b_7 \times \text{DUM2} + b_8 \times \text{DUM3}$$

$$\text{HOUSE} = 1350.8 + 245.6 \times \text{POP} + 19.0 \times \text{TAXES} \\ (t = 3.4) \qquad\qquad (t = 1.8) \\ -24.0 \times \text{INT} - 8.3 \times \text{PRICE} - 118.1 \times \text{TAXES} \\ (t = -5.1) \quad (t = -3.2) \qquad (t = -3.3) \\ -62.7 \times \text{DUM1} + 112.2 \times \text{DUM2} + 77.0 \times \text{DUM3} \\ (t = -2.7) \qquad (t = 4.8) \qquad\quad (t = 3.3)$$

$\overline{R}^2$:   .74
F-Statistic: 16.43
D-W: 1.69

---

original 4.85. This dramatic increase in the equation's ability to explain the historic movements in housing starts validates the importance of quantifying the seasonal element.

The coefficients on the seasonals also conform to expectations. The first-quarter negative value implies that housing activity in this period is below that of the fourth quarter, while second- and third-period levels are above the final quarter. Our analyst, from discussions with company employees, confirms that this is exactly the pattern experienced due to the harsh weather in many parts of the country between December and March.

Although the correlation matrix is not included in Table 7-13, an examination has been carried out with no evidence of multicollinearity between any of the independent variables. A check of the D-W statistic shows that autocorrelation does not appear to be a

---

Table 7-14. Correlations.

HOUSE (t) versus:

INCOME (t)	0.35	INT (t)	−0.39	PRICE (t)	−0.42
INCOME ($t-1$)	0.31	INT ($t-1$)	−0.38	PRICE ($t-1$)	−0.52
INCOME ($t-2$)	0.28	INT ($t-2$)	−0.34	PRICE ($t-2$)	−0.60
INCOME ($t-3$)	0.27	INT ($t-3$)	−0.29	PRICE ($t-3$)	−0.59
INCOME ($t-4$)	0.22	INT ($t-4$)	−0.24	PRICE ($t-4$)	−0.54

---

problem. Finally, the large number of observations and degrees of freedom ensures that the regression equation is stable.

Before presenting the model to Mr. Fairly, the analyst tests one other hypothesis in which the independent variables of income, interest rates, and price can possibly influence housing starts with some type of time lag. That is, changes in these variables may build up over several periods before impacting housing activity.

The analyst, therefore, develops correlations between HOUSE and the lagged series of INCOME, INT, and PRICE. The correlation coefficients (r) provided in Table 7-14, show that the closest relationship between HOUSE and the individual variables of INCOME and INT are in the corresponding time frame (period t). On the other hand, the strongest relationship between HOUSE and PRICE is when the latter variable has a two-period lag.

From this analysis, the regression in Table 7-13 is rcrun with the PRICE variable lagged two periods. The inclusion of this lagged relationship (Table 7-15) increases the $\overline{R}^2$ to .80 and the F-statistic to 23.15. In addition, the income variable in the previous regression is significant only at the 90% confidence level. Now, due to the improved fit, all of the independent variables are significant at the 95% confidence standard. Finally, a careful check of all the coefficient signs indicates no major changes from the original regression. The explanatory variable correlations are also examined to make sure that the equation dynamics remain intact.

Summary

In this exercise we have seen that building a model with quarterly data requires substantially more effort than one using annual observations. There is an advantage to the quarterly approach, however, in that a more current time frame can be employed in generating the appropriate sample size. For example, a quarterly data base covering five years supplies the

---

Table 7-15. Regression Results: HOUSE $= f$(POP, INCOME, INT, PRICE(-2), TAXES, DUM1, DUM2, DUM3).

Sample: 1977–1987

Equation:
$$\text{HOUSE} = a + b_1 \times \text{POP} + b_2 \times \text{INCOME} + b_3 \times \text{INT}$$
$$+ b_4 \times \text{PRICE}(-2) + b_5 \times \text{TAXES} + b_6 \times \text{DUM1}$$
$$+ b_7 \times \text{DUM2} + b_8 \times \text{DUM3}$$

$$\text{HOUSE} = 1526.8 + 161.6 \times \text{POP} + 19.8 \times \text{INCOME}$$
$$(t = 2.4) \qquad (t = 2.2)$$
$$-22.3 \times \text{INT} - 9.7 \times \text{PRICE}(-2) - 114.6 \times \text{TAXES}$$
$$(t = -5.5) \qquad (t = -5.0) \qquad (t = -3.7)$$
$$-65.8 \times \text{DUM1} + 90.1 \times \text{DUM2} + 61.4 \times \text{DUM3}$$
$$(t = -3.3) \qquad (t = 4.3) \qquad (t = 3.1)$$

$\bar{R}^2$:	.80
F-Statistic:	23.15
D-W:	1.79
Number of Observations:	44
Degrees of Freedom:	35

---

same number of observations as 20 years of annual data, allowing the analyst to incorporate more recent trends in developing the relationships between the model variables.

A monthly model, which will be presented in the next example, further defines the differences between annual data and those of a shorter duration. Like the quarterly format, the seasonal pattern will need to be treated in a monthly series. Yet, only two or three years of monthly data are necessary to provide a sufficient number of observations.

Exercise Seven

An automotive analyst for a New York City investment firm is interested in projecting new car purchases. By understanding the major factors that influence sales, the analyst hopes to better monitor the industry's health, and anticipate related stock market movements. The analyst wants the ability to forecast short-term, as well as several years out. Therefore, a model based on monthly observations is determined to be the best approach.

An examination of data sources indicates that seasonally-adjusted new car sales are available from federal-government publications. The series includes sales of both domestic and import models in the United States. A plot of this information (Figure 7-3) reveals that the series continues to fluctuate considerably even after seasonal adjustment. However, there is a cyclical pattern that is likely related to national economic activity.

Having viewed the data graph, our analyst is ready to develop a list of economic series that can possibly explain movements in automobile sales. One obvious determining factor is real or inflation-adjusted disposable income. The relationship between sales and

Figure 7-3. United States Automobile Sales.

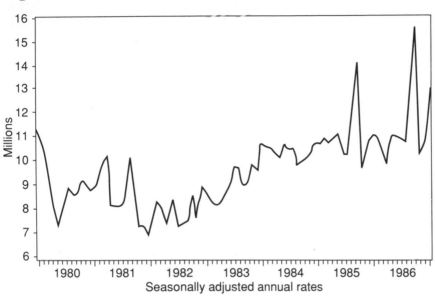

Seasonally adjusted annual rates

Source: Motor Vehicle Manufacturers Association; *Ward's Automotive Reports*;
Bureau of Economic Analysis, Department of Commerce.

income is expected to be positive (or direct), with the
two series moving together.

The cost of a new car relative to other items in
the household budget may also explain automobile
purchases. As noted earlier, this is called the real
price. The series is constructed by comparing the consumer price index for automobiles with the total index
of consumer goods and services (CPI-U). Auto purchases and price are expected to be inversely related,
as a decline in the relative price makes automobiles
more attractive to consumers. Naturally, the opposite
is true when car prices are rising faster than the "market basket" of goods represented by the CPI-U.

Since most new car purchases require a loan,
interest rates also should have an important influence
on the buying decision. As in Exercise Six, the real

or inflation-adjusted interest rate is examined. Like price, interest rates are expected to be inversely related to auto purchases as a higher rate increases the cost to the buyer. For the interest-rate variable, the analyst has adjusted the prime rate, which is tied to many consumer loans, by the CPI-U.

In summary, our analyst has identified three possible explanatory variables, including (1) real disposable income (INCOME), (2) the relative price of a new car (PRICE), and (3) the real interest rate (INT). Of these three, real disposable income is hypothesized to have a positive coefficient representing a direct relationship with automobile purchases (AUTO). Price and interest rates, on the other hand, should have negative signs on their coefficients, based on their inverse relationship with the dependent variable.

The analyst is also aware that these explanatory variables have the potential to impact automobile sales with some type of lag. As seen in our exercise with housing starts, the significance of a lagged relationship can be measured by examining the correlations between each of the three explanatory variables and sales.

In Table 7-16, PRICE has it strongest relationship to AUTO when it is lagged four or five months. INT, however, is most closely related to new-car sales in the same time frame (t). Finally, INCOME has a similar

Table 7-16. Correlations.

AUTO (t) versus:

INCOME (t)	0.76	PRICE (t)	−0.61	INT (t)	−0.10
INCOME $(t-1)$	0.76	PRICE $(t-1)$	−0.62	INT $(t-1)$	−0.10
INCOME $(t-2)$	0.75	PRICE $(t-2)$	−0.62	INT $(t-2)$	−0.07
INCOME $(t-3)$	0.75	PRICE $(t-3)$	−0.62	INT $(t-3)$	−0.06
INCOME $(t-4)$	0.76	PRICE $(t-4)$	−0.64	INT $(t-4)$	−0.07
INCOME $(t-5)$	0.75	PRICE $(t-5)$	−0.64	INT $(t-5)$	−0.06
INCOME $(t-6)$	0.73	PRICE $(t-6)$	−0.60	INT $(t-6)$	−0.03

Table 7-17. Regression Results: AUTO = f(INCOME, PRICE(-5), INT)

Sample: 1980–1986

Equation:
AUTO $= a + b_1 \times$ INCOME $+ b_2 \times$ PRICE(-5)
$\qquad + b_3 \times$ INT
AUTO $= 9.4 + 0.007 \times$ INCOME $- 14.9 \times$ PRICE(-5)
$\qquad\qquad\quad (t = 7.1) \qquad\qquad\quad (t = -2.1)$
$\qquad -.083 \times$ INT
$\qquad\quad (t = -1.9)$

$\bar{R}^2$:   .62
F-Statistic: 46.72
D-W: 1.38

Correlation Matrix:

	AUTO	INCOME	PRICE(-5)	INT
AUTO	1.00	0.76	-0.64	-0.10
INCOME	0.76	1.00	-0.63	0.11
PRICE(-5)	-0.64	-0.63	1.00	0.19
INT	-0.10	0.11	0.19	1.00

Number of
  *Observations:*84
Degrees of
  Freedom: 80

correlation to sales between t and $t-5$. From this, the analyst decides to use INCOME and INT in the present (t) time frame and to lag PRICE by $t-5$ in the model specification.

Table 7-17 contains the results of INCOME, PRICE(-5), and INT regressed against AUTO. It shows that 62% of the historical movement in automobile sales can be explained by the three explanatory variables. Moreover, the F-statistic value of 46.72 is comfortably above the minimum guideline, indicating that the equation is significant in replicating historical sales.

Looking at the t-statistics of the independent variables, we see INCOME and PRICE are significant at the 95% confidence level. Although INT's t-ratio of -1.9 is a little below the 95% standard, this variable is significant at the 90% limit. Also important is that the coefficient signs on each of the explanatory variables match their hypothesized relationship with sales.

The correlation matrix indicates that there is no strong relationship (multicollinearity) between any of the three explanatory variables. Finally, the seven years of monthly data provide 84 observations, which should satisfy any concerns about model instability.

The regression equation, however, is not without problems. Although the equation is significant in explaining historical auto sales, the analyst would like the $\overline{R}^2$ value to be higher. In addition, an examination of Table 6-5 in Chapter Six reveals that using a substantial number of observations has tightened the acceptable parameters for measuring autocorrelation. Given the 84 data points and three explanatory variables in this regression, any D-W value below 1.57 implies a serial-correlation problem. Since the D-W statistic of the regression is 1.38, it falls within the danger zone.

Both the fit of the equation and the D-W statistic might be improved by identifying additional explanatory variables for the model. Certainly, other economic criteria such as consumer liquidity and the cost of maintaining a car can be tested. Moreover, dummy variables representing events such as consumer rebate programs and industry work stoppages might strengthen the explanatory power of the equation, as well as reduce the nonrandom error.

An evaluation of additional variables does not provide any significant improvement to the equation. There is, however, another possible solution before using the Cochrane-Orcutt procedure to remove the

Figure 7-4. Linear and Nonlinear Functions.

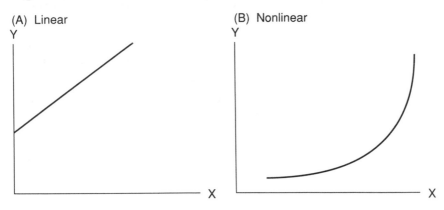

(A) Linear

(B) Nonlinear

autocorrelative pattern: to examine a nonlinear relationship between the variables in the equation.

Nonlinear Relationships

In the previous exercises, the model-development process emphasized linear relationships. This now-familiar form is illustrated in Figure 7-4(A), in which Y represents the dependent variable and X the independent variable. There are situations, however, where the relationship between the dependent and independent variables is nonlinear rather than linear. An example is presented in Figure 7-4(B).

In Chapter Five, we noted that regression analysis uses a linear equation to present the relationship between variables. Fortunately, many nonlinear relationships can also be accommodated in this format through transformation of the variables. The most common transformation utilizes natural logarithms of the series being examined. Where all the variables in the equation are converted to natural logs, the functional form is said to be log-linear. The forecaster, however, is not required to put every series in a logarithmic form. In those instances where some, but not all, of the variables are expressed in logarithmic terms, the form is considered to be partially or semi-logarithmic.

Where a logarithmic relationship is more appropriate than a linear format, the resulting regression provides a better fit to the historical data. This consideration brings us back to our equation in Table 7-17, which needs an improvement in its $\overline{R}^2$, as well as its D-W value. Having already explored the possibility of additional variables, our analyst now seeks to enhance the equation's fit by testing logarithmic relationships.

Income is usually one of the first variables to be examined in its logarithmic form. This is based on economic theory suggesting that as household income rises, proportionally less is consumed and more is saved. This hypothesis is best represented in a semi-logarithmic form where AUTO = f(ln INCOME).

The resulting equation in Table 7-18 substitutes ln INCOME for INCOME, but maintains the original

---

Table 7-18. Regression Results: AUTO = f(ln INCOME, PRICE(−5), INT)

Sample: 1980–1986

Equation:
AUTO = a + b_1 × ln INCOME + b_2 × PRICE(−5)
          + b_3 × INT
AUTO = −98.9 + 16.0 × ln INCOME − 15.1 × PRICE(−5)
                    (t = 7.3)   (t = −2.2)
          −.087 × INT
          (t = −2.0)

$\overline{R}^2$:   .63
F-Statistic: 47.60
D-W: 1.39
*Number of
  Observations:* 84
*Degrees of
  Freedom:*   80

(linear) PRICE(−5) and INT independent variables. This specification yields a minor improvement over the equation's linear form (Table 7-17), as all the major tests register small gains. A similar attempt to model the log of PRICE, however, does not enhance the equation's fit. Finally, INT cannot be tested in a logarithmic functional form because it has negative values in its data set (where the prime rate in certain months is below the inflation rate), and the log of a non-positive number cannot be calculated.

The examination of a semi-log equation for expressing the variable relationships is, therefore, of some help but has not resolved the D-W problem. In the next chapter we will introduce a simple procedure, similar to the Cochrane-Orcutt method, which adjusts for serial correlation and also ties the forecast line to the last actual data point.

Although our modeling exercise has been completed, let's discuss one final point concerning non-linear functions. In economic theory, the change in demand for a product that results from the change in another variable is referred to as elasticity. The two most common examples of elasticity measure price and income effects. In calculating price elasticity, the percent change in the quantity demanded is divided by the percent change in the price of that product. For example, if a 10% increase in the price of gasoline yields a 4% decrease in its demand, the price elasticity of this product is −0.4 (that is, −4% / +10%). In all but the most unusual cases, price elasticity has a negative sign.

Income elasticity is quite similar, as it represents the percent change in the demand for a product resulting from a percent change in income. The income elasticity for products such as jewelry, steaks, and automobiles should have a positive sign since income gains allow a higher standard of living. Black-and-white television demand, however, will likely have a negative income elasticity, as consumers will upgrade to a color set.

An important byproduct of a logarithmic transformation is that the coefficients assigned to the independent variables represent the elasticity between themselves and the dependent variable. The analyst, therefore, regresses ln INCOME, ln PRICE, and INT against ln AUTO to determine the price and income elasticity of automobile sales. The resulting equation of ln AUTO = -10.95 + 1.71 ln INCOME $- 1.19$ ln PRICE(-5) $- 0.010$ INT reveals an income elasticity of $+1.71$ and a price elasticity of -1.10. In both cases, the calculated values are considered to be substantial since they are greater than one.

Summary

During the past two chapters, many of the everyday challenges and obstacles in the causal-modeling process have been identified. At this time it might be useful to move from the detail of these exercises to a more sweeping philosophical discussion.

It should be clear at this point that causal model building, despite possessing a set of rules and procedures, allows the individual considerable innovation and freedom. The previous examples have presented only a few of many possible paths that can be pursued in constructing a regression. Moreover, some of the specific steps taken in these examples might not be popular with all forecasters.

One highly charged area of debate centers on the objectives of the model structure. Naturally there is the obvious goal of developing a structure which provides the most accurate forecast. More important is whether the modeler should be concerned with economic/business theory or the statistical results. Many forecasters feel that fine-tuning the model to improve its statistical fit is a superfluous step. They believe, rather, that the sole emphasis should be on developing an equation that adheres to economic theory.

Our examples have stressed both economic theory and statistical fit. You might remember that the sign on the explanatory variable's coefficient has to agree with economic theory. But we have also spent considerable time attempting to improve the statistical results.

Certainly the specific purpose of the model is an important factor in weighing these two considerations. Where a model is developed to support an academic pursuit, the theoretical aspects of the structure should dominate. However, statistical tests also become important when a company's forecast techniques are being scrutinized by an independent outside body.

Now that we have explored the mechanics and procedures for building a causal model, it might be useful to practice these new skills by reconstructing some of the regressions in the exercises. The following appendix contains the data used for generating the forecasting equations in the past two chapters.

As previously noted, developing a regression requires the use of a computer software package. For those who have not yet purchased a program, Chapter Nine will provide a brief explanation of the more popular packages as well as a simple walkthrough of one of these programs.

Appendix to Chapter Seven

The following tables contain all of the data series used in the seven exercises in Chapters Six and Seven. They are identified exactly as in the examples. For more detail as to what the individual series represent, refer back to the specific exercise.

Table 7A-1. Exercise One.

	MANEMP (thousands)	GNP82 (billions of 1982 Dollars)	POP (thousands)
1966	24.5	2208.3	456.121
1967	24.9	2271.4	462.591
1968	25.3	2365.6	473.342
1969	27.4	2423.3	486.084
1970	26.0	2416.2	490.265
1971	27.7	2484.8	509.427
1972	28.7	2608.5	529.300
1973	30.0	2744.1	578.200
1974	29.1	2729.3	595.300
1975	27.8	2695.0	604.300
1976	26.4	2826.7	602.400
1977	29.8	2958.6	605.600
1978	31.4	3115.2	616.600
1979	33.6	3192.4	630.800
1980	32.5	3187.1	646.960
1981	34.5	3248.8	661.243
1982	33.4	3166.0	677.733
1983	33.6	3279.1	693.152
1984	36.9	3501.4	721.990
1985	38.2	3607.4	748.974
1986	36.0	3713.3	775.269
1987	36.6	3816.9	801.392

Source: Department of Labor and Employment Security, State of Florida; Bureau of Economic Analysis, Department of Commerce; Bureau of Economic and Business Research, University of Florida.

Table 7A-2. Exercise Two.

	PCE82	DPI82	CHPCE	CHDPI
		(billions of 1982 Dollars)		
1965	1,236.4	1,365.7	NA	NA
1966	1,298.9	1,431.3	62.5	65.6
1967	1,337.7	1,493.2	38.8	61.9
1968	1,405.9	1,551.3	68.2	58.1
1969	1,456.7	1,599.8	50.8	48.5
1970	1,492.0	1,668.1	35.3	68.3
1971	1,538.8	1,728.4	46.8	60.3
1972	1,621.9	1,797.4	83.1	69.0
1973	1,689.6	1,916.3	67.7	118.9
1974	1,674.0	1896.6	−15.6	−19.7
1975	1,711.9	1,931.7	37.9	35.1
1976	1,803.9	2,001.0	92.0	69.3
1977	1,883.8	2,066.6	79.9	65.6
1978	1,961.0	2,167.4	77.2	100.8
1979	2,004.4	2,212.6	43.4	45.2
1980	2,000.4	2,214.3	−4.0	1.7
1981	2,024.2	2,248.6	23.8	34.3
1982	2,050.7	2,261.5	26.5	12.9
1983	2,146.0	2,331.9	95.3	70.4
1984	2,246.3	2,470.6	100.3	138.7
1985	2,324.5	2,528.0	78.2	57.4
1986	2,418.6	2,603.7	94.1	75.7

Source: Bureau of Economic Analysis, Department of Commerce.

Table 7A-3. Exercise Three.

	COMENG (GWH)	RESCUS (thousands)	COMCTS (1982$)	TDD (Degree Days)
1965	589	156.435	2.75	3,695
1966	655	161.193	2.58	3,956
1967	727	165.693	2.40	3,643
1968	826	170.839	2.14	4,017
1969	960	177.472	2.05	4,103
1970	1,041	186.153	1.94	4,156
1971	1,165	195.702	1.81	3,977
1972	1,335	207.213	1.98	3,946
1973	1,501	221.251	1.90	4,199
1974	1,640	233.356	2.09	3,926
1975	1,767	239.215	2.48	4,489
1976	1,804	243.548	2.66	3,756
1977	1,884	249.362	2.59	4,416
1978	2,010	258.971	2.62	4,382
1979	2,084	270.939	2.66	4,084
1980	2,165	283.448	2.77	4,118
1981	2,370	293.677	2.80	4,036
1982	2,456	303.073	2.69	3,982
1983	2,598	313.824	2.45	3,887
1984	2,848	328.441	2.45	3,935
1985	3,114	344.611	2.39	4,611
1986	3,317	358.687	2.41	4,162
1987	3,470	372.796	2.35	3,885

Sources: Tampa Electric Company; Bureau of Economic Analysis, Department of Commerce; National Oceanic and Atmospheric Administration.

Table 7A-4. Exercise Four.

	MINING (thousands of tons)	GNP72 (billions of 1972 Dollars)	DOLLARS (1975 = 100)
1967	36,071	1,011.4	112.9
1968	37,415	1,058.1	114.4
1969	34,217	1,087.6	114.5
1970	35,136	1,085.6	112.7
1971	35,270	1,122.4	109.7
1972	37,034	1,185.9	103.2
1973	38,218	1,254.3	98.1
1974	41,437	1,246.3	99.3
1975	44,276	1,231.6	100.0
1976	44,662	1,298.2	104.4
1977	47,256	1,369.7	108.0
1978	50,037	1,438.6	102.5
1979	51,611	1,479.4	101.4
1980	54,415	1,474.0	101.5
1981	53,624	1,502.6	111.0
1982	37,414	1,475.5	127.4

Sources: Bureau of the Mines, Department of the Interior; Bureau of Economic Analysis, Department of Commerce; Board of Governors of the Federal Reserve System; Bureau of Labor Statistics, Department of Labor.

Table 7A-5. Exercise Five.

Team	ATTEND (millions)	WIN	POP (millions)	CHAMP
Cleveland	1.078	61	2.8	0
Seattle	1.134	78	2.3	0
Pittsburgh	1.161	80	2.3	0
Chicago (A.L.)	1.208	77	4.1	0
Atlanta	1.217	69	2.6	0
San Diego	1.454	65	2.2	1
Oakland	1.679	81	2.9	0
Texas	1.763	75	3.7	0
Baltimore	1.836	67	2.3	0
Montreal	1.850	91	3.0	0
Milwaukee	1.909	91	1.6	0
Houston	1.910	76	3.6	1
San Francisco	1.917	90	2.9	0
Chicago (N.L.)	2.035	76	4.1	1
Detroit	2.062	98	4.6	1
Minnesota	2.082	85	2.3	0
Philadelphia	2.100	80	5.8	0
Cincinnati	2.185	84	1.7	0
Boston	2.232	78	4.1	1
Kansas City	2.392	83	1.5	2
New York (A.L.)	2.428	89	9.0	0
California	2.696	75	6.5	1
Toronto	2.778	96	3.4	1
Los Angeles	2.797	73	6.5	1
New York (N.L.)	3.034	92	9.0	1
St. Louis	3.072	95	2.4	1

Source: *The World Almanac and Book of Facts,* 1988 and 1989 eds.;
Bureau of the Census, Department of Commerce.

Table 7A-6. Exercise Six.

	HOUSE (thousands)	POP (millions)	INCOME (percent)	INT (percent)	PRICE (1982 = 100)	TAXES
1976.1	280.8	0.739	0.9898	14.51	85.58	0
1976.2	439.3	0.699	−0.2061	14.29	87.36	0
1976.3	434.3	0.753	0.2003	14.23	88.33	0
1976.4	382.9	0.695	0.1299	14.06	87.44	0
1977.1	367.4	0.689	−0.1820	13.72	88.87	0
1977.2	581.1	0.741	0.6425	13.39	90.28	0
1977.3	561.5	0.778	1.5923	13.32	90.55	0
1977.4	477.1	0.710	0.0801	13.18	93.61	0
1978.1	362.0	0.689	0.7778	13.16	92.99	0
1978.2	624.5	0.696	1.1199	13.10	95.53	0
1978.3	563.6	0.740	0.2731	13.26	97.67	0
1978.4	470.2	0.759	0.5336	13.32	98.25	0
1979.1	325.6	0.732	−0.0008	13.44	99.47	0
1979.2	541.9	0.691	−0.5564	13.50	102.44	0
1979.3	498.2	0.753	0.4848	13.78	102.27	0
1979.4	379.3	0.855	−0.0655	14.09	102.22	0
1980.1	238.1	0.707	0.8574	14.68	102.90	0
1980.2	304.3	0.654	−1.9882	15.51	103.43	0
1980.3	388.3	0.695	0.7486	14.29	103.35	0
1980.4	361.5	0.583	0.6710	14.57	101.91	0
1981.1	264.2	0.585	−0.1839	14.91	102.96	0
1981.2	338.7	0.558	−0.5059	15.42	103.66	0
1981.3	270.3	0.576	0.5350	15.90	103.06	0

1981.4	210.9	0.577	−1.0616	16.52	102.90	0
1982.1	176.7	0.507	−0.9118	15.63	101.12	0
1982.2	274.0	0.523	0.0363	15.80	101.51	0
1982.3	309.2	0.502	−0.0618	15.33	99.70	0
1982.4	302.3	0.524	0.5279	13.74	97.64	0
1983.1	325.4	0.459	0.1352	13.02	98.93	0
1983.2	485.7	0.452	1.0646	12.08	98.45	0
1983.3	496.5	0.492	0.8294	11.97	100.48	0
1983.4	404.8	0.501	1.9959	11.71	98.67	0
1984.1	377.8	0.729	1.8275	11.44	98.12	0
1984.2	539.5	0.446	0.1782	11.29	100.00	0
1984.3	460.5	0.470	0.7119	11.54	99.54	0
1984.4	378.2	0.537	0.3442	11.64	99.91	0
1985.1	346.4	0.390	0.1818	11.04	100.18	0
1985.2	509.9	0.424	2.0394	10.78	98.73	0
1985.3	470.7	0.467	−1.0184	10.08	98.75	0
1985.4	417.8	0.528	1.0606	9.80	98.58	0
1986.1	374.2	0.884	1.0923	9.47	98.67	0
1986.2	558.7	0.496	0.9062	8.98	101.06	0
1986.3	490.3	0.515	−0.6374	8.92	99.74	0
1986.4	384.9	0.519	0.3069	8.59	97.13	0
1987.1	380.7	0.646	0.6862	8.00	99.48	1
1987.2	384.7	0.526	−0.9910	7.98	99.83	1
1987.3	392.8	0.489	1.1033	7.96	100.42	1
1987.4	398.9	0.451	1.4788	7.78	97.98	1

Source: Bureau of the Census, Department of Commerce; Bureau of Economic Analysis, Department of Commerce; Federal Home Loan Bank Board.

203

Table 7A-7. Exercise Six.

	DUM1	DUM2	DUM3		DUM1	DUM2	DUM3
1976.1	1	0	0	1982.1	1	0	0
1976.2	0	1	0	1982.2	0	1	0
1976.3	0	0	1	1982.3	0	0	1
1976.4	0	0	0	1982.4	0	0	0
1977.1	1	0	0	1983.1	1	0	0
1977.2	0	1	0	1983.2	0	1	0
1977.3	0	0	1	1983.3	0	0	1
1977.4	0	0	0	1983.4	0	0	0
1978.1	1	0	0	1984.1	1	0	0
1978.2	0	1	0	1984.2	0	1	0
1978.3	0	0	1	1984.3	0	0	1
1978.4	0	0	0	1984.4	0	0	0
1979.1	1	0	0	1985.1	1	0	0
1979.2	0	1	0	1985.2	0	1	0
1979.3	0	0	1	1985.3	0	0	1
1979.4	0	0	0	1985.4	0	0	0
1980.1	1	0	0	1986.1	1	0	0
1980.2	0	1	0	1986.2	0	1	0
1980.3	0	0	1	1986.3	0	0	1
1980.4	0	0	0	1986.4	0	0	0
1981.1	1	0	0	1987.1	1	0	0
1981.2	0	1	0	1987.2	0	1	0
1981.3	0	0	1	1987.3	0	0	1
1981.4	0	0	0	1987.4	0	0	0

Table 7A-8.   Exercise Seven.

	AUTO (millions)*	INCOME (billions of 1982$)*	PRICE	INT (percent)
1980.01	11.3	2235.3	1.001	1.33
1980.02	10.5	2227.4	1.014	1.48
1980.03	9.5	2214.2	1.016	3.63
1980.04	8.1	2193.2	1.018	5.11
1980.05	7.3	2180.2	1.017	2.18
1980.06	8.0	2183.4	1.008	−1.68
1980.07	8.9	2205.4	1.013	−1.72
1980.08	8.6	2206.2	1.013	−1.68
1980.09	8.7	2209.9	1.012	−0.44
1980.10	9.1	2228.4	1.009	1.15
1980.11	8.9	2236.5	1.011	3.44
1980.12	8.8	2251.3	1.010	7.95
1981.01	9.1	2245.5	1.016	8.45
1981.02	10.0	2240.9	1.029	8.09
1981.03	10.2	2242.4	1.032	7.50
1981.04	8.1	2239.2	1.032	7.13
1981.05	8.1	2230.0	1.033	9.77
1981.06	8.1	2235.9	1.032	10.46
1981.07	8.2	2259.4	1.030	9.66
1981.08	10.1	2266.4	1.026	9.63
1981.09	8.8	2263.0	1.021	9.11
1981.10	7.3	2264.7	1.026	8.21
1981.11	7.3	2254.7	1.030	7.28
1981.12	7.1	2241.7	1.029	6.81
1982.01	7.7	2240.1	1.026	7.30
1982.02	8.3	2244.3	1.016	8.89
1982.03	7.9	2252.8	1.007	9.71
1982.04	7.4	2272.9	0.995	9.94
1982.05	8.4	2264.3	0.995	9.77
1982.06	7.3	2245.7	1.008	9.39
1982.07	7.4	2267.2	1.013	9.77
1982.08	7.6	2261.6	1.012	8.49
1982.09	8.5	2261.5	1.007	8.49
1982.10	7.7	2264.8	1.005	7.45
1982.11	9.0	2278.5	1.007	7.25
1982.12	8.6	2285.2	1.008	7.63
1983.01	8.3	2287.6	1.000	7.41
1983.02	8.2	2283.7	0.989	7.52

Table 7A-8.　(continued).

	AUTO (millions)*	INCOME (billions of 1982$)*	PRICE	INT (percent)
1983.03	8.3	2293.9	0.980	6.86
1983.04	8.7	2305.5	0.989	6.56
1983.05	9.0	2311.5	0.997	7.02
1983.06	9.8	2316.5	1.001	7.92
1983.07	9.7	2339.9	1.004	8.07
1983.08	9.0	2325.7	1.007	8.33
1983.09	9.0	2340.5	1.006	8.10
1983.10	9.9	2371.8	1.008	8.11
1983.11	9.6	2392.7	1.011	7.76
1983.12	10.6	2413.5	1.009	7.20
1984.10	10.2	2484.5	1.001	8.38
1984.11	10.3	2492.6	1.003	7.74
1984.12	10.7	2511.6	1.001	7.11
1985.01	10.7	2524.3	0.996	7.04
1985.02	10.9	2512.3	0.990	6.98
1985.03	10.8	2491.6	0.993	6.76
1985.04	11.0	2556.5	1.000	6.84
1985.05	11.1	2598.2	1.000	6.56
1985.06	10.3	2535.9	0.998	6.05
1985.07	10.3	2537.0	0.997	5.94
1985.08	12.6	2533.7	0.991	6.15
1985.09	14.1	2535.6	0.985	6.32
1985.10	9.7	2552.2	0.986	6.26
1985.11	10.2	2552.0	0.990	5.92
1985.12	11.0	2584.3	0.990	5.73
1986.01	11.1	2587.9	0.986	5.61
1986.02	10.7	2615.6	0.975	6.32
1986.03	9.9	2640.0	0.950	6.84
1986.04	11.0	2668.8	0.932	7.21
1986.05	11.1	2654.5	0.937	6.94
1986.06	10.9	2644.5	0.941	6.76
1986.07	10.8	2646.4	0.929	6.55
1986.08	12.5	2643.9	0.917	6.32
1986.09	15.6	2641.6	0.915	5.74
1986.10	10.3	2645.2	0.916	5.96
1986.11	10.6	2647.4	0.920	6.21
1986.12	13.0	2655.6	0.921	6.37

* Seasonally Adjusted Annually Rated.
Sources: Motor Vehicle Manufacturers Association; *Ward's Automotive Reports*; Bureau of Economic Analysis, Department of Commerce; Board of Governors of the Federal Reserve System; Bureau of Labor Statistics, Department of Labor.

8

Forecasting from an Equation and Econometrics

In Chapters Six and Seven, we discussed the main considerations in constructing a causal-forecasting model. Our exercises emphasized two of the three major steps of causal model building including hypothesis formulation, and testing of a regression's statistical properties.

We are now ready to focus on step three, which is to utilize our equations for forecasting. As in model building, developing a forecast from an equation involves a set of standard practices. This chapter discusses the path from equation to forecast in three parts. The first part explains how to evaluate the forecasting capabilities of the equation followed by the second part, specific steps for calculating a forecast from the equation. The third part examines the development of alternative scenarios.

The final topic of this chapter draws on our previous knowledge to explain the most sophisticated area of causal modeling: econometrics. In this presentation, we see how economic theory and regression analysis can be merged into an interdependent forecasting structure.

The Equation Model's Forecastability

The final equations in the examples from the past two chapters represent what the analysts believed were the best statistical expressions of the data. These "winning" equations, as we are now aware, provided the most theoretically- and statistically-complete explanation of the dependent variable.

By using these models for forecasting, the analysts are assuming that the equations will continue to excel in the future, which appears to be a reasonable supposition. Still, before forecasting with these equations, the analyst should examine them in order to gain some insight into their future performance.

Perhaps the simplest means of evaluating the model's forecasting ability is to examine the equation's accuracy in replicating the most recent values of the dependent variable (Y). In this approach, the analyst measures the proximity of the equation's estimate of Y to the actual Y values during the current period. [Once again, the Y estimate for any past time period is calculated by substituting the actual values of the independent variable(s) into the regression equation.] This approach is especially useful in choosing a winner when several equations have satisfied the major statistical tests.

A more rigorous test of the "forecastability" of an equation is to break the data set into two segments. If there are 40 data points, the first group might be given 35 observations and the second group five. A new regression is developed from the 35 data points, then the five explanatory series values from the second group are supplied to this new equation to calculate projections for the dependent variable Y. The accuracy of the model is measured by comparing these five forecasts for Y with the actual Y values from the second set.

The separation of the data into two groups allows the new equation to be independently developed from the observations it is being tested against. This process is as close to a real life forecasting situation as can be created.

The MANEMP (manufacturing employment) equation from Chapter Six provides an example of this concept. In this regression, there are 22 annual points covering the 1966–1987 period. These observations, however, represent a relatively small data set. Accordingly, the analyst needs to ensure that the first data group maintains a sufficient supply of points for the new equation to be statistically valid. This is accomplished by removing the 1987 observation and rerunning the regression, exactly as in the stability-testing process.

The resulting equation for the 1966–1986 time frame is MANEMP = 4.91 + 0.0088 × GNP82. By substituting the actual 1987 GNP82 value of \$3816.9 billion into the equation, a 1987-MANEMP projection of 38.5 thousand is calculated. This estimate compares favorably with the 36.6 thousand actual-employment level for 1987, providing the forecaster with some comfort as to the equation's near-term forecasting accuracy.

The forecaster can carry this testing even further by removing both the 1986 and 1987 observations, then projecting MANEMP for those years with the new equation. This process can be continued until the analyst becomes concerned about the stability of the new specification.

The Forecast Calculation

A major strength of regression analysis is the ease with which the equation can be solved to yield a result for the dependent or forecasted variable. For example, the parameters of the 1966-1987 equation in Exercise One are MANEMP = 5.84 + 0.0085 × GNP82. As we have observed, MANEMP is calculated for a given year by providing a value for GNP82. While a computer is capable of generating the calculations, an analyst can perform a "sanity check" by replicating the work on a calculator.

The primary purpose of any model equation, of course, is to produce a forecast. To this end, the forecaster needs projections for the explanatory or independent variables. Using the above equation, a forecast for MANEMP requires a future estimate for GNP82. From this, we begin to understand the importance of choosing explanatory variables for which projections are available.

A projection of 1988 MANEMP, therefore, requires a 1988 estimate for GNP82. Having previously planned for this contingency, the analyst has secured a projection from an economic bank letter that the agency receives regularly. Applying the GNP82 estimate to the equation, the analyst calculates a 1988 solution for MANEMP. The 1988 MANEMP results are contained in Table 8-1, along with those of the previous year.

Looking at the computation process, the GNP82 projection calls for a three-percent increase in 1988 to $3931.4 billion from the previous year's level of $3816.9 billion. Multiplying the 1988 GNP82 figure by its coefficient of 0.0085 and adding the constant of 5.84 yields a 1988 MANEMP value of 39.3 thousand. Any forecast of MANEMP, however, must be consistent with the previous year's actual value. In this instance the 1987 MANEMP observation serves as the

Table 8-1. MANEMP Equation Solution.

Year	Actual MANEMP (thousands)	Model MANEMP	GNP82 (billions of 1982 $)
1987	36.6	38.3	3816.9
1988	—	39.3	3931.4

jumping-off point from which the 1988 forecast is developed.

Unless an equation fits the historic data perfectly ($\overline{R}^2$ of 1.00), the model solution which corresponds to the last year of actual data is not likely to match the observation. In this example, plugging the actual 1987 GNP82 value into the equation yields a 1987 MANEMP solution of 38.3 thousand, which is above the actual 1987 MANEMP figure of 36.6 thousand. Of course, the solution could just as likely have been below the actual value.

Methods of Adjusting

There are several methods of tying the model solution to the last actual data point in deriving a forecast. The first method is called the Percent Change or Delta Approach. While it is the simplest technique we will be discussing, it is also the least rigorous from a statistical standpoint. In addition, it is only applicable for short-term forecasts.

In the Percent Change Method, the percent change projected by the model equation is applied to the last actual observation. Looking at our example, the percent change between the 1987 and the 1988 MANEMP model solutions is calculated. To do this, the 39.3 is compared to the 38.3 to yield an expected 1988 growth of 2.6% [((39.3 − 38.3)/38.3) ×100]. Next, the 1987 actual value of 36.6 is multiplied by the 2.6% growth rate (36.6 × 1.026) to yield a MANEMP forecast of 37.6. In this way, the growth implied by the model solution between 1987 and 1988 is applied to the 1987 actual value to provide a forecast which is linked to the historical MANEMP data series.

If this adjustment is not made, the 1988 model solution of 39.3 thousand represents an unreasonably strong 7.4% increase over the 1987 actual level. This is considerably higher than the 2.6% gain the model predicts.

The objective of any adjustment, therefore, is to move from the jumping-off point (last actual observation) to the forecast. A major limitation of the percent change adjustment method, however, is that we never return to the equation line. For example, applying the percent change in the model solution over a longer period (such as 1987 to 1997) to the actual 1987 value places the long-term forecast below the long-term model solution (Figure 8-1). In fact, it is the same percentage distance below the long-term solution line as the original 1987 variance. Naturally, if the 1987

Figure 8-1. The Percent Change Method's Dilemma.

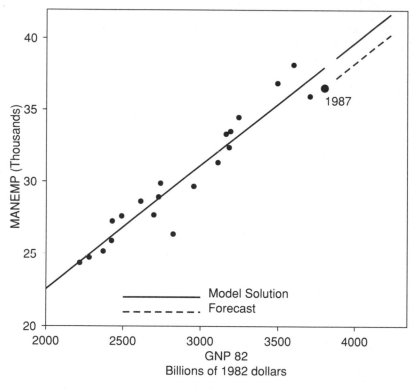

actual value is above the 1987 model solution, the percent change adjustment places the long-term forecast above the long-term model solution.

The second technique, known as the Addfactor Method, solves this long-run dilemma and provides for an orderly transition from the jumping-off point to the long-term model solution. It is appropriate both in the short term and the long term.

The Addfactor Method also corrects for any autocorrelation difficulties by adjusting the equation results by a factor called rho. Rho, you might remember from a previous discussion, measures the serial correlation in the error terms. The job of Cochrane-Orcutt and similar procedures is to calculate rho and reestimate the equation without this factor.

Remember also that the D-W statistic measures the pattern in the error. In fact, rho and the D-W value are related since they examine the same phenomenon. This bond is embodied in the formula rho = 1 − (D-W/2), which provides a simple procedure for approximating their relationship.

The Addfactor Method ties the model solution to the last data point and removes the autocorrelation influence of the last observed error. The process involves several simple steps which we will go through in detail.

The first step is to calculate the variance between the last actual data point and its corresponding model solution. In our example, the last actual MANEMP data point is 36.6 in 1987. Once again, the corresponding model solution for 1987 is 38.3 (Table 8-1). Subtracting the model solution from the actual value results in a variance of −1.7.

Next, the rho factor is estimated. Substituting the MANEMP equation's D-W statistic of 1.26 into the above formula yields a rho value of .37 [1 − (1.26/2)]. From here, the forecaster calculates the first future-year's model solution. This would be the 1988 model value of 39.3. This figure is adjusted by the 1987 actual versus model variance (−1.7) times rho (.37). This resulting value of −0.6 is added (hence the term addfactor) to the model solution of 39.3 to yield a 1988 MANEMP forecast of 38.7.

Let's look at a slow-motion replay of the MANEMP calculation to see the five easy pieces of the addfactor process.

Step 1. Measure the variance between the last actual data point (1987) and its corresponding model solution. From Table 8-1, the difference is 36.6 − 38.3 = −1.7.

Step 2. Compute the rho factor using the equation $\rho = 1 - (D\text{-}W/2)$. Inserting the equation's D-W statistic into the formula yields 1 − (1.26 / 2) or .37.

Step 3. Using the 1988 GNP82 estimate, solve the equation for MANEMP. The 1988 model solution is 39.3.

Step 4. Multiply the 1987 variance (−1.7) by the rho factor (.37) to produce an addfactor value of −0.6.

Step 5. Apply the addfactor value of −0.6 to the 1988 model solution of 39.3 which results in a 1988 MANEMP forecast of 38.7.

Before getting too comfortable, we should go on and calculate forecasts for future years in case management requires more than a one-year projection. While this involves further computations, the hardest work is behind us. For the 1989 MANEMP forecast, the model solution is adjusted by .37 (same rho factor as before) times the 1988 adjustment of −0.6.

Table 8-2. MANEMP Forecast Development with Addfactors.

	GNP82 Estimate (bill. of 1982 $)	MANEMP Model Solution (thousands)	Addfactor Calculation	MANEMP Forecast (thousands)
1988	3,931.4	39.3	$-1.7 \times .37 = -0.6$	38.7
1989	4,049.3	40.3	$-0.6 \times .37 = -0.2$	40.1
1990	4,170.8	41.3	$-0.2 \times .37 = -0.1$	41.2
1991	4,295.9	42.4	$-0.1 \times .37 = 0.0$	42.4

Therefore, the -0.2 addfactor value for 1989 is added to the model solution of 40.3 to arrive at a 1989 MANEMP forecast of 40.1 (Table 8-2).

For the example in Table 8-2, the addfactor adjustment process, which links the 1987 starting point to the forecast line, takes four years. The time frame for the adjustment, however, varies from equation to equation depending on the D-W value and the variance at the jumping-off point. This is highlighted further in our next section.

The addfactor process enables the forecaster to tie the model equation to the last actual data point. It does this by supplying a transition value (addfactor) for each year that is used for adjusting the model solution value. Figure 8-2 allows us to visualize the course of the addfactor adjustment in Table 8-2.

Now that we have the hang of it, let's work through one more example of the addfactor adjustment process. In this exercise, we'll generate a forecast using the multiple regression for COMENG (commercial electricity sales) developed in the previous chapter.

The parameters of the equation are COMENG = $-1461.1 + 13.71 [RESCUS(-1)] - 169.8 (COMCTS) + 0.103 (TDD)$. In solving for COMENG in 1988, the process is simplified because RESCUS is lagged.

Figure 8-2. Addfactor Adjustment from Table 8-2.

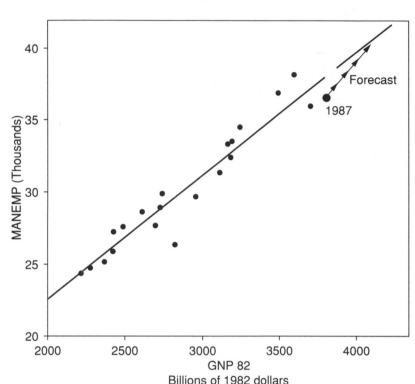

For this explanatory variable, the 1987 value is utilized in the equation. For COMCTS, however, a 1988 estimate is obtained from the company's Rate Department. Finally, weather cannot be projected a year in advance, or even a week, with any accuracy. Therefore, the analyst uses the average annual TDD for the period encompassed by the model equation (1966–1987). With the equation parameters and the future estimate of the explanatory variables, the analyst calculates a 1988 solution for COMENG. Using the same general approach, a COMENG solution is also developed for 1989. Both calculations are summarized in Table 8-3.

Table 8-3. COMENG Equation Solution.

	Actual COMENG (GWH)	Model COMENG (GWH)	RESCUS(−1) (Thousands)	COMCTS (1982 $)	TDD
1987	3,470	3,458	358.7	2.35	3,885
1988	—	3,679	372.8	2.30	4,076
1989	—	3,863	386.2	2.30	4,076

As in the MANEMP equation, the 1987 actual value for COMENG in Table 8-3 varies from the model solution obtained by inserting the explanatory variables into the equation. In the COMENG example, however, the actual data point of 3470 GWH is above the 3458 GWH model result. This differs from the MANEMP equation, where the 1987 actual fell below the solution.

In developing a COMENG forecast for 1988, the 1987 actual-versus-model variation of 12 is multiplied by the rho factor of .075 [1 − (1.85 / 2)] which yields an addfactor of 1. This addfactor is applied to the 1988 model solution of 3679 to arrive at a 1988 FORECAST of 3680 (Table 8-4).

For 1989, the addfactor calculation drops out, signifying that the transition from the 1987 starting point to the forecast line is complete. From 1989 onward, the model solution becomes the forecast.

Table 8-4. COMENG Forecast Development with Addfactors.

	COMENG Model Solution (GWH)	Addfactor Calculation	COMENG Forecast (GWH)
1988	3,679	12 × .075 = 1	3,680
1989	3,863	1 × .075 = 0	3,863

This example is quite different from the MAN-EMP equation. As previously noted, the 1987 COM-ENG starting point is above the model solution, while the MANEMP point is below. In addition, the COMENG transition period requires only two years, while the MANEMP equation has a four-year adjustment. There are two reasons for this longer time frame. First, the 1987 COMENG variance between actual and model, measured as a percent, is smaller (0.3%) than the 1987 MANEMP deviation (4.4%). More importantly, the COMENG equation's D-W value is closer to 2.0, requiring a smaller rho adjustment for serial correlation.

While we have presented two methods of adjustment, there are other addfactor approaches for making the transition between the last actual data point and the forecast line. One involves a constant increment, applied to all future model solution values, which is mathematically or subjectively determined. Since the adjustment represents a fixed value for all periods, it can be rolled into the constant (a) term of the model equation.

Alternative Forecasts

Now that we know how to produce a forecast from an equation, we can consider multiple projections. In many cases, a company will require alternative forecasts in addition to a base case or most-likely outcome. This provides a range of possible "what if" scenarios for exploring other strategies. The most common pattern is for the forecaster to generate a high and low projection representing a band around the base case.

There are two general approaches to supplying additional forecasts. The most popular is to develop alternative scenarios which examine several paths that might be taken by the model's explanatory variables. The analyst, in developing these future economic scenarios, needs to make sure that each case is reasonable and internally consistent. For example, a scenario that assumes more rapid inflation than the base case should also anticipate higher interest rates. This is where experience and an understanding of economics play an important role in the process.

The starting point for developing alternative economic scenarios is to review the assumptions utilized in the base-case projection. In the 1988/1989 COMENG forecast presented in Tables 8-3 and 8-4, the driving variables include RESCUS(-1), COMCTS, and TDD. A high scenario should anticipate more favorable economic circumstances than the base case. This usually takes the form of faster growth and milder inflation. Therefore, the anticipated RESCUS level in the high case is above that of the base case. In addition, the high case can reasonably assume a lower COMCTS level than the base scenario. Since weather is a noneconomic variable, it remains constant in both cases. The low scenario expects slower growth and higher prices than the base case. With these guidelines, the analyst has developed the economic projections contained in Table 8-5.

Examining the specific assumptions, the RESCUS values for 1988 are fixed at 372.8 for all scenarios since they represent a lagged actual value. For 1989, however, the RESCUS growth from the previous year is 3.6% in the base-case, with 4.1% and 3.1% projected

Table 8-5. Economic Scenario Assumptions.

	RESCUS(-1) (thousands)			COMCTS (1982 $)			TDD (Degree Days)		
	Low	Base	High	Low	Base	High	Low	Base	High
1988	372.8	372.8	372.8	2.35	2.30	2.25	4,076	4,076	4,076
1989	384.3	386.2	388.1	2.37	2.30	2.23	4,076	4,076	4,076

Table 8-6. COMENG Alternative Forecasts (GWH).

COMENG Model Solution			Add-	Forecast		
Low	Base	High	factors	Low	Base	High
1988 3,671	3,679	3,688	1	3,672	3,680	3,689
1989 3,825	3,863	3,901	0	3,825	3,863	3,901
Annual Percent Change						
1988				5.8%	6.1%	6.3%
1989				4.2%	5.0%	5.7%

for the high and low scenarios, respectively. For the COMCTS inputs, the low case expects a higher cost and the high case a lower cost than the base assumption in both 1988 and 1989.

The development of 1988/1989 high- and low-COMENG forecasts requires applying the new assumptions to the model equation. The computations are then adjusted by the same addfactors as the base-case projection. The resultant model solutions and forecasts for the various scenarios are in Table 8-6.

As expected from the forecast, the more favorable assumptions of the high scenario have yielded higher projected growth in 1988 and 1989 than under the base case. On the other hand, the lower growth scenario has led to the opposite relationship between the low and base cases.

The forecast band around the base-case projection is particularly narrow in 1988 as only 17 GWH separate the high and low cases. This is because COMCTS has been the only variable altered in creating the alternative scenarios. Although the TDD variable is held constant in developing the high and low bands, it might be useful to study the effects of warmer and cooler weather using past variations from the norm. This would widen the forecast range and provide a more complete examination of possible outcomes.

While the projections have been taken forward

two years, the analyst has the option to forecast over a longer period. We are chiefly interested, however, in the causal model's ability to quantify the impact of various scenarios. This is a valuable feature, not available in time-series approaches, that many analysts feel is worth the extra time and resources required for developing causal models.

Another technique for supplying bands or a range around the base case is through the standard error of the estimate (SEE). In Chapter Five, the SEE is described as measuring the difference between the regression equation's calculated Y values and the actual Y values. Stated more simply, the SEE is the past error or residual not explained by the equation.

We also showed in Exercise One (Chapter Six) how the SEE can be used to band the forecast. Because a normally-distributed data series has 95% of its values within two standard deviations of its mean, this concept can be tied to the SEE and the regression equation. Specifically, two SEEs on either side of the forecast line represent an approximate band in which the analyst can be 95% confident that the actual value will fall.

Let's create these bands using the COMENG equation. In the specification relating COMENG to RESCUS(-1), COMCTS, and TDD, the historic SEE is calculated to be 37 GWH. From Table 8-4, the base-case forecast developed from the COMENG equation line is 3,680 GWH in 1988 and 3,863 GWH in 1989. The application of plus and minus two SEE to these base forecasts results in a range from 3,606 to 3,754 in 1988, and 3,789 to 3,937 in 1989 (Table 8-7).

Table 8-7. COMENG Banded Forecast (GWH).

	Base Forecast	± Two SEE	Range
1988	3,680	± 74	3,606 to 3,754
1989	3,863	± 74	3,789 to 3,937

The range in Table 8-7 represents a fairly tight band around the base forecast because the COMENG equation fit is extremely good ($\overline{R}^2$ of .996), minimizing the SEE or typical error. As the explanatory power of an equation declines, the SEE increases and the 95% confidence band will widen (observations held constant).

This 95% confidence interval, or band, hinges on two important conditions. First, the band assumes that the future estimates for the explanatory variables are correct. Secondly, the relationship between COMENG and its explanatory variables, embodied in the equation parameters, is assumed to continue unchanged into the future. Both these assumptions are asking a lot of the forecast process. That is, the analyst should be considerably suprised (and pleased) if the actual 1988/1989 values for the independent variables exactly match their projections. In addition, some minor deviations in the future parameters can be expected as the relationships are dynamic and change through time.

Thus, the implications of the 95% confidence interval need to be tempered by the fact that this range is based on rather rigid assumptions. Still, the banding process provides management with useful insights on future possible outcomes which can guide them in their planning.

Econometrics

Beginning with Chapter Five's discussion on the basics of causal modeling, we have moved forward through simple regression to the more sophisticated process of multiple regression. Our final stop in causal modeling is econometrics, which represents a further enhancement to the multiple regression approach. Econometrics is commonly defined as a series of interrelated regression equations that are based on economic theory. It should be noted, however, that the term econometrics is sometimes applied to the total range of business regressions including single equations with one explanatory variable.

The advantage of econometrics over the simpler causal methods is that its structure is more reflective of the real world, in which economic phenomena are highly interdependent. A simplified three-equation econometric model will better help us appreciate this point.

1. $A = f(B,C)$
2. $B = f(A,D)$
3. $C = f(D,F)$

In the first equation, the dependent variable A is a function of independent variables B and C. In equations two and three, B and C are dependent variables whose values are derived within the model. Thus, the solutions from equations two and three become inputs to the first equation. This format, in which independent variables from one equation are determined in another part of the model, is a unique feature of econometrics.

To get this model started, variables D and F are brought in from outside the structure. Inputs which are provided in this manner are called *exogenous* variables, while those variables which are solved for inside the structure (A, B, and C) are defined as *endogenous* variables. From this, we see clearly the difference between a regression model and an econometric model. In a regression structure, all the independent or explanatory series are exogenous, supplied from outside sources. In an econometric construct, certain of the independent variables are endogenous as they are solved in one equation and carried forward to other equations.

Another feature of an econometric model is that it can allow for *cross dependencies*, or the mutual dependence of two series. The above model illustrates this concept: B has an impact on A in the first equation, but A also helps to determine B in equation two.

A real life example of cross dependency is the relationship between the money supply and economic activity. Macroeconomic theory proposes that movements in the money supply influence economic activity. It also suggests that economic activity has a reciprocal effect on the stock of money. Following the mechanisms set forth by Neo-Keynesian theory, an increase in the money supply lowers interest rates. This, in turn, stimulates business investment and consumer purchases, bolstering aggregate demand and income. Finally, the higher level of business transactions resulting from expanded activity leads to a greater demand for money.

Calculating the values for mutually-dependent variables A and B in the above model involves solving equations one and two simultaneously. Specifically, it requires finding a value for A and B which satisfies both equations.

A structure which contains the dual causality of simultaneous equations is often considered to provide a more realistic replication of market dynamics. With this advantage, however, comes a greater degree of difficulty in generating these equations. The ordinary least-squares approach is not appropriate for developing the variable coefficients in a set of simultaneous equations because it produces biased results. Instead, a process called "two stage least squares" is required to calculate the equation parameters. In this procedure, the A variable is reestimated as a first step. These new A values are then substituted into equation two and used in the specification of that function.

The detail involved in specifying simultaneous equations requires a level of mathematical understanding beyond the scope of this primer. Moreover, an econometric model encompassing real-world relationships can be constructed without using simultaneous equations. Let's examine a nonsimultaneous econometric structure that was developed using ordinary least squares and the concepts that we have discussed over the past four chapters.

A Regional Economic Structure. The Tampa Electric Regional Economic-Demographic Model (TEREM) is an econometric structure which circumvents the issue of simultaneity, but maintains the pertinent economic interrelationships. Tampa Electric Company, an electric utility in Florida, does a great deal of long-term planning. As part of this process, the company has built TEREM to forecast population, employment, housing, and income. These economic projections are then placed into an electricity consumption model to generate forecasts for electric energy sales and peak demand on the system. The latter projection provides the basis for planning future electricity-generating facilities.

TEREM, an annual model, is comprised of 17 equations housed within four major sectors (Figure 8-3). The structure is a combination of two concepts—a cohort survival algorithm* and an econometric framework. Our purpose in the following discussion is briefly to present TEREM's dynamics and provide an overview of how an econometric model operates.

---

* A cohort survival algorithm takes an initial population and ages it forward to include the addition of births and the removal of deaths. For future years, these adjustments are made by using fertility and death rate projections.

Figure 8-3. Tampa Electric Economic/Demographic Model.

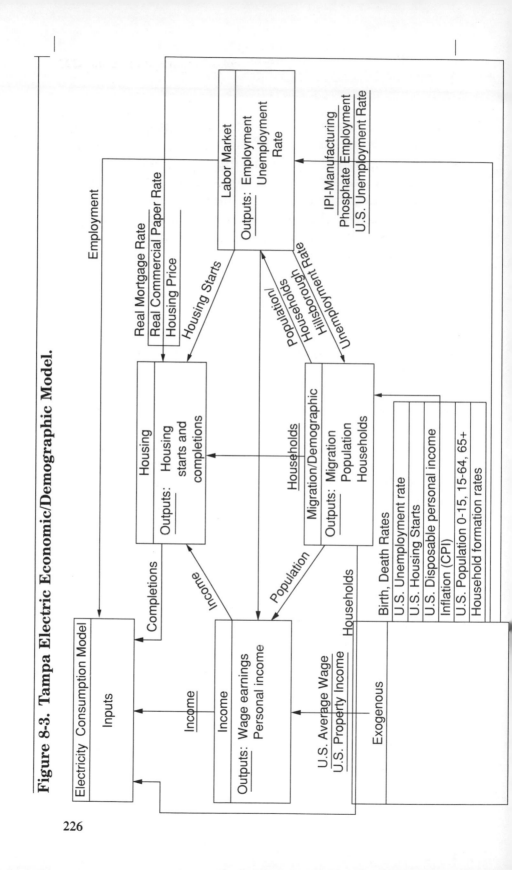

Migration/Demographic Sector. The Migration/ Demographic sector, the nucleus of TEREM, provides a forecast of population and households. This section contains regression equations for projecting population inflows (migration) into the utility's area using economic criteria as the explanatory variables. To accomplish this, it forecasts migration for three age groups including children (0–14), work-age population (15–64), and retirees (65+).

Looking at the work-age (15–64) equation, it has been determined that migration can be explained by (1) the relative strength of the local economy as reflected in the ratio of the local unemployment rate to the national unemployment rate; (2) the health of the national economy as represented by real disposable personal income; and (3) the strength of the housing market, which is measured through national housing starts. Retiree (65+) migration, likewise, is determined by economic considerations. Somewhat differently, 0–14 age-group migration is related to the flow of work-age population into the area.

Using these three regressions, we can examine the steps taken to arrive at a population/household forecast.

1. The starting point of the model is to calculate the work-age migration equation for the coming year. This requires supplying inputs for the exogenous variables of national housing starts, real disposable personal income and national unemployment.

2. The work-age migration solution then becomes an endogenous variable and is used for calculating the children's migration equation.

3. Retiree migration is computed and aggregated with the other two age groups to obtain total migration.

4. These migration results are then adjusted for expected births and deaths to yield the projected change in local population.

5. This projected change is added to the previous year's population level to arrive at forecasted population for the coming year.

6. Finally, household-formation rates are applied to the population forecast to yield a household, or residential customer projection.

Housing Sector. From here, TEREM moves to the Housing sector which contains equations for projecting single-family, multifamily, and mobile-home additions. All three regressions use a similar framework where housing starts are explained by new households and the real interest rate. For solving these equations, the household input is provided by the model's Migration/Demographic section. The real interest rate, however, is an exogenous variable which is brought into the model.

Labor Sector. From Housing, the model shifts to the Labor sector. The purpose of this component is to forecast employment as well as the unemployment rate for the local economy. This is accomplished through four manufacturing employment equations, commercial/government employment equations, and an unemployment rate equation.

The manufacturing regressions relate local manufacturing employment to the level of national economic activity. This, of course, requires an outside projection for the national economic variable. One industry group, however, also supplies products to the local construction sector. In this equation, local housing starts is an explanatory variable and is provided by the Housing section.

The commercial and government employment equations are driven by local population and household trends. The projections for these variables are supplied by the Migration/Demographic sector.

The Labor group's final equation calculates the local unemployment rate, which is explained by (1) Tampa employment trends, (2) the national unemployment rate, and (3) the prior period's jobless rate. The employment-trend variable is supplied internally by combining the solutions from the previous employment equations. In addition, the past jobless rate for the local area is also obtained from within the model. A projection of the national unemployment rate, however, is provided from an outside source.

You might remember from our discussion of the Migration/Demographic section that the local unemployment rate is an important explanatory variable in forecasting work-age migration. Therefore, once it is computed in the Labor section, the unemployment rate becomes an input in calculating migration for the coming period.

Income Sector. The final sector takes the employment solutions generated in the Labor sector and merges them with an average-wage equation to generate a projection for employment earnings. This, in turn, becomes the major explanatory variable in the model's final equation, which forecasts local personal income.

Having completed our walk-through of TEREM, it is important to note that an issue often debated in econometric circles is the size of the model. While there is no specific rule as to the optimal number of equations that a structure should have, some guidance can be gained through understanding the primary objective of a model.

There are generally two types of econometric structures—those developed for policy analysis and those utilized for forecasting. In policy analysis, the model's primary focus is to examine the economic impact of various courses of action. These types of models are usually found at the state- and Federal-government level, and examine tax and monetary considerations. Models geared for this type of analysis tend to be large since all significant effects need to be encompassed.

Forecasting structures are usually smaller than policy models since they do not require the same level of detail. This is because accuracy is the key objective in forecasting, and more detail does not necessarily provide greater accuracy. Therefore, most forecasters follow the maxim that their models should be as simple as possible—but not too simple.

Perhaps the greatest advantage of an econometric model is its ability to pull together all the important economic factors into a cohesive, interrelated structure. If the equations have correctly been specified using appropriate economic theorems, the resulting group of equations provides the forecaster with consistent, reasonable projections. In our example, the population, employment, housing, and income forecasts developed within the structure should relate to each other in a realistic and consistent manner.

Still, the forecaster needs to be on guard in gathering outside projections for running the model. If numerous sources of outside information are used, the analyst must make sure that these inputs are in accord with one another. For example, an inflation forecast from one source might conflict with an interest-rate projection from another source. To ensure that there are no inconsistencies among the exogenous inputs, the forecaster must attempt to get as many outside assumptions as possible from one source.

Summary

This chapter marks the completion of our work on causal modeling. Having covered the major points in this primer, the reader might want to examine other books on this subject. One of the more popular texts is *Econometric Models and Economic Forecasts*, by R.S. Pindyck and D.L. Rubinfeld. Other excellent publications on regression analysis and econometrics are contained in the consolidated references at the end of Chapter Eleven.

At this point in the text, the reader has been exposed to the major elements of quantitative forecasting including the most widely-used time series and regression approaches. From here, Chapter Nine will examine tracking of the forecast, the data-collection effort and the role of computers in forecasting.

9

Tracking the Forecast/Locating Data and Using Computers

In the first eight chapters, we have focused on mastering the elements of quantitative model building. During this period, we have become familiar with the mathematical procedures for developing time-series and causal models. Having completed this task, Chapter Nine attempts to tie up some loose ends by discussing (1) the tracking of the forecast, (2) locating data, and (3) using computers.

These three elements are necessary ingredients in forecasting. In building quantitative structures, data quality is an important component for ensuring a sound model. In addition, the tremendous technological advances in computers have simplified all aspects of forecasting. Finally, it is important to remember that the forecasting process is dynamic. Tracking devices indicate whether adjustments in the projected trend and/or revisions to the model structure need to be made.

Tracking the Forecast

We have thus far described a process that involves establishing a methodology, examining the model results, and releasing the forecast for implementation into the company's planning function. Many are under the misconception that the forecast process ends at this point; that is, that the forecast group lies dormant until the next planning cycle. This is not the case because the function involves much more than developing a model and issuing a projection. Once the forecast is released, the next step is to establish a procedure which closely monitors and measures its performance.

This process, called tracking the forecast, provides an early-warning system as to possible problems with the projection. In addition, the analyst uses the results of this device to determine whether a forecast revision is needed. By quickly uncovering and correcting any divergencies in the forecast, the company can take the appropriate course of action. This, of course, plays a key role in the economic survival of the firm (and the forecaster).

The Method

The objective of this chapter is to present a simple system for monitoring the forecast. The most common tracking methods measure forecast accuracy. The reasoning is that any substantial deviation between the forecast and the actual trends will be reflected in a growing forecast error. Should the error become significant, the forecaster will want to revise the projection.

There are four steps to developing a simple monitoring device.

Step One: The first step involves the establishment of a procedure for comparing the forecast for a given week/month/quarter with the actual values for the same period. This process calculates the level difference, as well as the percent variance between each individual forecast point and its corresponding observation.

Table 9-1, which examines the performance of the Acme Steel Company's 1985 sales tonnage projection,

Table 9-1. Acme Steel Company Sales for 1985 (Thousands of Short Tons).

Month	Monthly (1) Actual	(2) Forecast	Variance (3) Level	(4) Percent	Cumulative (5) Actual	(6) Forecast	Variance (7) Level	(8) Percent
Jan.	77.8	86.4	−8.6	−10.0%	77.8	86.4	−8.6	−10.0%
Feb.	74.7	82.9	−8.2	−9.9	152.5	169.3	−16.8	−9.9
Mar.	75.8	84.5	−8.7	−10.3	228.3	253.8	−25.5	−10.0

presents this comparison. In this table, columns 1 and 2 contain the actual data points and their corresponding forecasts, while columns 3 and 4 provide a forecast comparison.

In column 3, the forecast error is calculated as the difference between the actual and projected. Looking at the first observation, the January forecast of 86.4 thousand tons is subtracted from the January actual of 77.8 thousand tons to yield a −8.6 variance. In column 4, this variance is displayed as a percent by dividing the −8.6 error in column 3 by the forecast (86.4), and then multiplying by 100.

The variance calculations in columns 3 and 4 are similar to those discussed in Chapter One.* In Table 9-1, however, the signs on the accuracy measures have been maintained. This provides the analyst with a clear signal should the forecast be consistently above (−) or below (+) the actual pattern.

Interpretation of the forecast variance in columns 3 and 4 is straightforward. If the actual and forecasted trend patterns move closely together over time, the table will reveal small positive and negative deviations which represent the random element (I) in the actual data. Should the table indicate large errors which are consistently above or below the forecast, this reflects an actual trend that is diverging from the projected trend.

Step Two. Having established a mechanism for analyzing the forecast error for each point, the next step

---

*In column 4, the percent forecast variance is calculated using the formula [(actual − forecast) / forecast] × 100. This deviates slightly from the example in Chapter One which uses the format [(actual − forecast) / actual] × 100. Either of these two forms is appropriate as long as the forecaster applies one method consistently throughout the data set being examined.

is to examine the projection on a cumulative basis. This is the purpose of columns 5 through 8. In columns 5 and 6, the cumulative year-to-date total of the actual and forecast values are calculated. For March, the cumulative year-to-date figures include the aggregated values from January through March. Columns 7 and 8 measure the variance of these cumulative values using the same approach as the calculations in columns 3 and 4.

Step Three. Step three establishes a ceiling, or limit, on the allowable size of the cumulative forecast error. When this guideline is exceeded, it provides a signal that a forecast revision is necessay. In many companies, the average historical forecast error is utilized as the ceiling. Also needed is a minimum time period before the error guideline is invoked. This allows any random forecast variations to work themselves out.

Using the example in Table 9-1, the average annual forecast error for Acme product sales over the past five years has been 4%. Therefore, the variance guideline, or ceiling, is set at this level. In addition, the forecast group has determined that a minimum period of three months is necessary to see if an error pattern is developing.

By March, there is an obvious pattern in the data. In each month, actual sales have been well below forecast. By the end of March, the cumulative forecast error is 10%. Since this is two and one half times the size of the acceptable ceiling, the company decides to revise their projection to incorporate the most recent data trends.

Step Four. The final step involves revising the forecast. If the method used for projecting sales is a time-series application, the model is respecified using the latest data. From our examples in Chapters Two and Three, this is done by adding the recent observations to the data base and choosing the alpha or time period that provides the smallest historic error.

Should the forecast model be a causal approach, however, a more intricate analysis is required. First, the basis for the forecast error is considered. Either the 10% variance is due to incorrect projections of the equation's explanatory variables (input error), an incorrectly-specified model (model error), or some combination of the two.

A variance resulting from input error is the easiest situation to remedy. To determine if this is the source of the problem, the actual values of the explanatory variables for January through March are put into the model equation. Should the new sales calculations from the equation closely match the actual January–March values (col. 1), then the past forecast error has been due to faulty inputs. A revised sales forecast for April to December is developed by supplying the model with updated estimates of the explanatory variables.

Model error due to an inadequate equation specification involves considerably more time and resources to resolve. It is almost always the result of changing forces in an industry. In fact, the United States economy can be characterized as a dynamically shifting structure. Thus, the forecaster can expect that the factors driving a company's sales will be altered over time, requiring model adjustments. Because of this fact of life, most forecasters periodically review the explanatory variables in their equations.

Let's examine a situation where model error exists. As background, we need to review the development of Acme's original forecasting equation. The company uses a multiple regression approach with three explanatory variables for projecting company product sales (SALES). The first variable is the Industrial Production Index (IPI), representing national economic activity. The relationship between IPI and SALES is expected to be positive. The second independent variable is local nonresidential construction adjusted for inflation (NONRES82). Since the company's steel products are used in the construction of office buildings, the coefficient assigned to NONRES82 is also expected to be positive. The final explanatory variable is the real price of steel (PRICE). This, of course, should have an inverse, or negative, relationship with SALES.

The model, therefore, has the form SALES = f (IPI, NONRES82, PRICE). The regression equation resulting from this hypothesis is determined to be statistically significant according to the tests presented in Chapter Five. In addition, it does a solid job of projecting Acme's sales between 1980 and 1984.

In Table 9-1, however, we have noticed a substantial forecast error for the first three months of 1985. As part of step four, the forecast group takes the actual January–March values for IPI, NONRES82 and PRICE and places them into the equation. The recalculation of SALES for the January–March period, based on the new inputs, continues to be significantly above the reported sales figures for that period. Therefore, it is determined that the 1985 variance is due to model error rather than input error.

This requires that the forecast group return to the drawing board and respecify the model. Our previous comparison of actual sales and the SALES equation indicates that the model is overforecasting because Acme sales have been noticeably weak since the end of 1984. A thorough review of company records reveals that a growing portion of new construction is substituting steel imports for Acme products. It is the group's contention that the U.S. dollar's strength versus other currencies during this period is the reason behind this trend. That is, the rising value of the dollar has made foreign imports cheaper in the United States, thus giving them a competitive edge over Acme.

It appears that a trade or exchange-rate variable should be added to Acme's forecast model. After some deliberation, the forecast group decides to use a dummy variable to represent the dollar's exchange rate. A zero is assigned to those periods when the dollar has been relatively weak, while a 1 is assigned to the most recent time frame when the dollar has strengthened. A negative sign is expected on the trade variable coefficient as a stronger dollar reduces Acme sales and vice versa.

The inclusion of this new series leads to a new equation where SALES = f(IPI, NONRES82, PRICE, TRADE DUMMY). The resulting regression proves to be statistically sound. Even more important, the introduction of the trade dummy brings the model results in line with actual product sales for the first three months of 1985. From here, the latest forecasts for the independent variables are input into the equation and a new SALES projection is calculated.

In summary, tracking the forecast allows for the quick identification of any significant deviation between the actual and expected trends. The discovery of a substantial forecast error, of course, necessitates a revision. In certain cases, this revision involves a simple adjustment, while in other cases it can require a complete overhaul of the model. In the latter case, the forecaster must revisit the total modeling process and reexamine the underlying factors that impact the company.

The Use of Judgment in the Forecast Process

In past discussions, we have emphasized the mechanical procedures that underlie the quantitative forecasting techniques, and rightfully so, since they are the foundation of these methods. At this time, however, we need to discuss another important element of the quantitative forecast process—the use of judgment.

Chapter Ten will present in some detail the methods where judgment and intuition play a primary role. These, of course, have previously been identified as the qualitative approaches. Right now, our comments will be confined to the integration of judgmental actions into the mathematical methods.

Judgment is related to experience, and is ingrained in all the steps of the forecast process. For example, judgment provides the basis for developing the list of hypothesized variables to be tested in arriving at an equation. Judgment is also necessary in determining the data series to represent these variables. For instance, there are a number of inflation measures that can be used in adjusting a series. The forecaster decides which one is most appropriate.

Despite the seeming rigidity of statistical tests, judgment also plays a role in model specification. We have seen that the gray area of the D-W statistic is subject to different interpretations by forecasters. The same can be said about the tests that measure significance. Some modelers require an independent variable's t-statistic to be significant within 95% confidence before it is accepted in the equation. On the other hand, certain forecasters include all variables that have appropriate coefficient signs in their model, no matter how low their individual t-statistics.

Judgment can also enter into the type of modeling structure employed. Whether a time-series or causal-model approach is instituted sometimes depends on a forecaster's intuition. In certain cases, individuals might choose one method over another simply because they perceive that management views it favorably.

At the other end of the process, judgment is often utilized for adjusting the model's output. To most forecasters, the solutions from a mathematical structure represent a general guideline rather than a sacred truth. They feel that the path outlined by the model can be judgmentally altered within a reasonable boundary to allow for the individual's own expectations.

There are times when judgment is used for determining if a forecast revision is necessary. In the Acme sales example, the three-month error of 10% is well above the 4% tolerance band, making the decision to revise the forecast simple. But what if the variance is 4.5% rather than 10%? With the variance so close to the allowable limit, the forecaster might not feel justified in changing the projection.

Because forecasting is an art as well as a science, there is substantial room for these judgmental considerations. Certainly, the basic elements of forecasting should not be ignored or overridden. Still, certain aspects that appear to be rigid, like the t-ratio and D-W rules of thumb, have more flexibility than at first glance.

As the individual obtains forecasting experience, judgmental expertise also grows. Therefore, the beginner might feel more comfortable by closely following the general principles and procedures during the first forecasting expeditions. As time goes by, however, the forecaster will be able to incorporate the element of judgment into the process. A good understanding of the basic processes plus good judgmental skills should always lead to reasonable and accurate projections.

Data

In our model-building exercises, little has been said about the data being analyzed. However, data collection is a significant part of the forecast process. In fact, understanding the strengths and weaknesses of the data is as important as understanding the forecasting methods. The objective of this section is to present the special considerations in gathering data for the forecast process. Specifically, we will be discussing 1) the forecast's influence on data gathering, 2) the primary elements of data integrity, and 3) where to locate data.

The Forecast's Impact on Data

The company's forecasting objectives have a major impact on the characteristics of the collected data. Perhaps the main consideration is the forecast-time horizon, or the length of the projection. Should the company be interested in developing a long-term forecast, the model utilized will likely be based on quarterly or annual data. If the corporation is primarily focusing on the short-term, its model structure and data requirements will focus on weekly or monthly information. Therefore, the time frame of the data is related to the forecast-time horizon.

The level of detail in the data gathering process is also affected by the forecast goals. If the forecaster is charged with examining the company's overall financial outlook, the emphasis will be on the firm's total products and revenues. In this regard, aggregate rather than specific product data is required in the modeling process. Should sales or production forecasts of individual product lines be the objective, then more detailed information and models are needed.

The department in which the forecaster is located also has a major influence on the model and its data requirements. In the corporate planning section, the focus is usually on longer-term projections involving a total company perspective. A forecaster in the production department, however, is often involved in making weekly projections for individual products.

The variable used to measure the company's business activity also influences data needs. Most firms are interested in projecting their volume of sales. This can be represented by the number of automobiles, tons of steel, or kilowatt hours sold by the firm, depending on its specific industry.

In some instances, however, data is only available in dollar amounts. It is important to remember that through time, movements in dollar-denominated data contain both volume and inflation trends. Said differently, a change in a series' dollar value includes a change in volume or activity, as well as a change in price.

To isolate the volume trends, the price or inflation effect is removed from the data. The example below separates U.S. retail sales (in dollars) into its volume and price components. The first step in this process is to find a suitable price series with which to measure inflation. In this example, the Consumer Price Index (CPI-U) is utilized since it measures price movements in retail goods and services. Other popular inflation series include the Producer Price Index (PPI) and the Implicit Price Deflator (IPD) from the Gross National Product accounts.

Once an appropriate series has been identified, the price values for a given time period are matched with the corresponding values of the dollar denominated data. In Table 9-2, U.S. retail sales for 1987 and 1988 are aligned with their respective CPI-U values. Mechanically, the CPI-U value for each year is divided

Table 9-2. Deflating U.S. Retail Sales.

Year	Retail Sales (Bill. of Dollars)	Percent Change	CPI-U (1982–84 = 1.00)	Percent Change	Retail Sales (Bill. of 1982–1984$)	Percent Change
1988	1,612.4	6.7%	1.183	4.1%	1,363.0	2.5%
1987	1,510.6	—	1.136	—	1,329.8	—

Source: Bureau of the Census, Department of Commerce; Bureau of Labor Statistics, Department of Labor.

into the retail-sales figure to remove inflation. For 1988, this calculation is $1,612.4 divided by 1.183 which yields $1,363.0.

In the example, retail sales increased 6.7% from 1987 to 1988. To calculate this percent, we apply the previously introduced formula [($1,612.4 − $1,510.6) / $1,510.6] × 100. Over the same period, inflation was 4.1% utilizing the same procedure. Finally, the volume change, or the increase in economic activity, was 2.5%. This volume growth is often called the "real" increase and is presented in a form called constant dollars. That is, inflation has been removed or held constant. In this instance, the period of constancy is 1982 to 1984 since this is the base year for the CPI-U. From this, the $1,363.0 level represents the cost of 1988 sales ($1,612.4) if they had been purchased in 1982 to 1984.

Data Integrity

It is imperative that the forecaster be familiar with the quality of the data being utilized. Within this area, the three major considerations are accuracy, consistency and availability.

Accuracy of a data set can be evaluated by examining the methodology used for gathering the information. Data is derived either from a sample or the total population. The method chosen tells the forecaster a great deal about the data's accuracy. Data developed from a sample use only a portion of the total universe being measured. If the sample is generated using a statistically appropriate technique, the characteristics of the data sample should closely reflect that universe.

The size of the sample also has an important bearing on its reliability. For example, a monthly household survey of approximately 60,000 is used to estimate the nation's unemployment rate. While this sample provides reliable estimates for the total United States, accuracy declines when the results are disaggregated to the state level because a greater percent of the total universe must be sampled in smaller areas to maintain the same accuracy as the national estimate.

Survey results for the states, therefore, contain a much wider band of possible error than the national figure. In certain cases, state unemployment rates can vary as much as 1% from month to month before it is considered to be anything more than sampling error. Because of these relatively wide variations, state unemployment rates should be used with care. Specifically, state and national movements cannot be interpreted in the same manner.

By understanding how data is developed, the analyst has a better handle on the capabilities of the model derived from this information. In this regard, most government data is generated from samples. Moreover, the reporting agency provides the user with the important facts as to the survey's size and statistical significance.

Population or census data involve the counting of each element in the universe being measured. Every ten years a national census is taken in which economic and demographic information is generated. In addition, company records are usually of the census variety since all production, sales, and expenses are monitored. All things being equal, data developed from a population is preferred to that from a sample.

Consistency in a series is another important quality consideration. In certain instances, a series might add a new category. Where it does, the past data need to be adjusted for this new definition, or the new data adjusted to the old definition. The government usually makes the necessary adjustments to put a series on a consistent basis where the definition has changed.

Within a company, however, this is not always the case. Care should be taken to make sure the series has been developed through time using consistent measuring criteria.

The final concern is the availability of the data. Often a series is found which measures an important variable in the forecast process. It might not, however, be available on an ongoing basis. If the data is from the Government's census, it surely will not be available every year. In fact, it might not even be collected during the next census. This possibility should be taken into consideration since it will be necessary to update the model.

Trends in Data Quality

Much has been written about the recent deterioration in the quality of government data. At the federal, state and local levels, the budget pressures of the 1980s have resulted in the elimination of certain data collection efforts, as well as the downsizing of various surveys.

A good portion of these cutbacks have occurred at the Department of Labor, which generates employment and price measures. Several industry-wage surveys, for example, have been phased out over the past decade. Even more significant has been the loss of geographical coverage in the CPI-U due to a reduction in the number of cities sampled. This has limited price monitoring activities, which is particuarly disturbing since CPI-U movements are tied to federal government programs,[*] income tax brackets, and labor contracts.

The budget crunch has also delayed needed improvements in aging data-gathering procedures.

---

[*] Some of these programs include Social Security, Civil Service retirees and survivors, veterans benefits plus many social services such as food stamps and school lunches.

Efforts to include services in the PPI have been put off due to money considerations. This is also the case in the proposed reweighting of certain series to reflect the declining role of manufacturing.

Other data inaccuracies result from methodological shortcomings rather than sampling problems. Foreign-trade figures, for instance, have been found to overstate the United States trade deficit. These difficulties have been traced to a systematic under-counting of American exports as well as the inclusion of insurance and freight costs in imports but not exports. Because the trade numbers affect investor expectations, this distortion can have a dramatic impact on stock and bond markets.

Despite these limitations, the United States government produces the most timely, extensive, and accurate data of any country in the world. Users, however, should be familiar with the strengths and weaknesses of the series they are employing in their forecast models.

Data Sources

There are three major sources of data, including (1) the government (federal, state, local), (2) industry trade associations, and (3) company records. As previously noted, the United States government produces a wide range of statistics on a regular basis. The bulk of national economic series are generated by four agencies including the Bureau of Labor Statistics, Bureau of the Census, Bureau of Economic Analysis, and the Federal Reserve Board.

Trade associations are another important source of data. They provide detailed information on industry-specific series and supply information not otherwise available through government sources.

Company records, of course, are also of critical importance. From these files come sales, revenue, product price and other important series necessary for developing a company-specific model.

While the individual can often locate the specific company and industry information needed, government-generated data is more difficult to find. There are, however, five publications that contain a considerable amount of the pertinent economic data necessary for the model-development process. These include

1. Statistical Abstract of the United States. This is an annual publication produced by the Bureau of the Census, Department of Commerce. The abstract contains most of the major U.S. economic/demographic information in one central location. Its primary feature, however, is its ability to identify data sources. The researcher need only look in the back index to locate the tables related to the subject of interest. While these tables might not have all the information required, they provide the source of the information so that additional data can be obtained. Also important, the past data for many of the series contained in the abstract are found in *Historical Statistics of the United States: Colonial Times to 1970, Part I and Part II.*

2. Survey of Current Business. This document, also known as the SCB, is published on a monthly basis by the Bureau of Economic Analysis, Department of Commerce. It provides many national economic series in the "blue page" section of its publication. However, it is more well known for containing the National Income and Product Accounts, which include the quarterly Gross National Product data. The SCB also publishes state and local income numbers, as well as capital expenditure information. The historical data for the series presented in the SCB are contained in *Business Statistics: 1986.*

3. *Monthly Labor Review*. As the title implies, this is a monthly document published by the Bureau of Labor Statistics (BLS), U.S. Department of Labor. Since the Labor Department is responsible for generating the CPI-U, the PPI and all employment data series, this information is reported in this document. The *Handbook of Labor Statistics*, produced by the BLS on an annual basis, provides the historical data for many of the series in the *Monthly Labor Review*.

4. *Federal Reserve Bulletin*. This is a monthly publication released by the Board of Governors of the Federal Reserve. It provides all major monetary data, including the monetary aggregates (money supply) and interest rates. The Bulletin also publishes the Industrial Production Index and capacity utilization, which are computed by the Federal Reserve Board.

5. *Economic Report of the President*. This report is released every January by the President's Council of Economic Advisors. While the bulk of this report discusses recent developments in the national economy, an excellent statistical section provides historical data for the major economic series.

All of these publications can be found in the library, usually in the business section. While we have mentioned them here as excellent sources of information for providing the raw material needed in model building, they also contain useful economic articles.

There are also reference publications that attempt to compile and organize the various informational sources. Two of these are *Economic Sourcebook of Government Statistics* by Hoel, Clarkson and Miller, and *Business Information Sources* by Lorna Daniells. Although they use different formats, these books share a similar objective, which is to provide a centralized roster of the major economic series and their sources. Another reference resource is provided by Oryx Press of Phoenix, Arizona in a series of reference guides for locating information in the areas of federal data bases, stocks and bonds, and money, banking and finance.

The above publications represent only a small portion of the data resources available. Some other prominent sources of information, including several that contain projections, are listed below. Taken together, these publications provide a good starting point for gathering the information needed in model development.

- *Employment and Earnings* is a monthly publication produced by the Bureau of Labor Statistics which provides employment and wage detail by industry and geographic area. Historical data for these series are found in *Employment and Earnings, States and Areas.*

- *Employment Projections for 1995: Data and Methods* (Bulletin 2253) is a report from the Bureau of Labor Statistics which contains a forecast of employment by industry.

- *Projections of the Population of States, by Age, Sex, and Race: 1988 to 2010* (Series P-25, No. 1017) is published by the Bureau of Census and provides detailed population forecasts.

- *Labor Force Statistics Derived from the Current Population Survey, 1948–87* provides important employment data including breakdowns by age, sex, and race.

- *CPI Detailed Report* and *Producer Price Indexes* are published monthly by the Bureau of Labor Statistics and contain tables of all the series in their respective indices.

- *The National Income and Product Accounts of the United States, 1929–1982* is produced by the Bureau of Economic Analysis of the Department of Commerce. It contains further historic detail on the national income and product accounts in addition to that supplied in *Business Statistics*.
- *Annual Energy Outlook* is a publication of the Energy Information Administration, U.S. Department of Energy. This report provides an analysis of the major energy issues, and includes numerous tables and projections.
- *U.S. Industrial Outlook* is produced annually by the International Trade Administration of the Department of Commerce. This report contains an analysis of specific industries, including future expectations of activity.
- *1985 OBERS BEA Regional Projections* provides population, employment, and income forecasts for metropolitan areas as well as states. This publication can be obtained from the Regional group of the Bureau of Economic Analysis, Department of Commerce.
- Federal Reserve Bank Publications—The Federal Reserve system is comprised of twelve member banks located in Atlanta, Boston, Chicago, Cleveland, Dallas, Kansas City, Minneapolis, New York, Philadelphia, Richmond, San Francisco, and St. Louis. Each bank publishes data and reports on monetary and macroeconomic topics that are available to the public.

Computers

The advent of microcomputers has brought forecasting out of the shadows and onto the desktop. In the 1960s and 1970s, any type of rigorous forecasting technique required the use of large mainframe computers and considerable programming skills. Today, however, individuals can generate their own forecasts with a microcomputer and a software package. This new accessability to the tools has inspired a surge of interest in forecasting.

As always, there are various considerations in choosing the appropriate software package. One of the primary concerns is to be aware of the forecasting techniques provided in the program. Some packages are strong on time-series methods but do not sufficiently address regressions and econometrics. Other packages are directed toward causal modeling with little attention to time-series applications. There are numerous packages, of course, that fall within these two extremes.

It is also important that the program contain the necessary tests for examining statistical significance. Some software packages, for example, have the ability to generate an ordinary least-squares equation. However, they may provide only the $\overline{R}^2$ value while leaving out the other major measures. If any of the tests discussed in Chapter Five are omitted, it is impossible to fully determine an equation's statistical integrity.

Find out also if the software is compatible with your computer system. The more sophisticated forecasting packages often require considerable memory and a coprocessing chip to speed the calculative function. The make of the computer is another critical issue. Most programs are produced for IBM-PC models and compatible machines. For other types, like Apple, the user should check to see if the software is available.

Cost, of course, cannot be ignored. The price of a forecasting program can vary from as low as $50 to over $1000, with most falling in the $200 to $800 range. Just like other products, the adage "you get what you pay for" applies to software packages. The final decision as to how much to spend depends on the importance of the forecast and the individual's resources.

Over the past several years, numerous packages have been developed which provide the forecaster with the ability to construct a model, manage the data files, and perform the calculations. Several of the more popular programs are briefly discussed below. The intent of this section is not to cover this subject in great detail, but to get individuals started in locating the package that best suits their needs.

Also keep in mind that the forecasting software industry is highly competitive. Thus, the package descriptions provided below can become obsolete very quickly. To solve this dilemma, company telephone numbers have been included so that individuals can obtain the most recent program literature.

Forecast Master

Forecast Master is one of the most complete forecasting packages on the market. It has the capability to develop time-series models as well as causal techniques. Moreover, it possesses a wide range of applications from the simple to the sophisticated within these categories. Under time-series methods, the program allows for simple- and higher-order exponential smoothing, seasonal adjustment, Winter's model, and linear/curvilinear trend fitting, as well as the more advanced Box-Jenkins, state space, and vector autoregression procedures. In the causal school, single/multiple regression and econometric techniques are all available. Also important is that the major statistical tests are included in *Forecast Master's* output.

Because of its sophistication, considerable work is necessary to become familiar with the numerous features of the program. It is available for IBM® PC™, PC/XT™, PC/AT™, PS/2™ and compatible machines, and requires 512K of memory as well as a 8087 coprocessor chip. Its cost is $795. For further information, contact Scientific Systems, Inc., 54 Cambridge Park Drive, Cambridge, MA, 02140 (617-661-6364).

MicroTSP™

MicroTSP™ has been around for most of the 1980s and has a good track record of performance. Its primary emphasis is on causal modeling since it contains all the tools and tests necessary for single/multiple regression and econometric modeling. However, it also has time-series capabilities including exponential smoothing, seasonal adjustment and Box-Jenkins. It is extremely user friendly, and the forecaster can become familiar with its capabilities rather quickly.

The program requires 512K of memory and is available on IBM® PC™, PC/XT™, PC/AT™, PS/2™ and compatible machines. It can optionally be used with a math coprocessor. The cost is $595. Further information can be obtained by writing Quantitative Micro Software, 4521 Campus Drive, Suite 336, Irvine, CA, 92715 (714-856-3368).

ESP®

ESP®, a pseudonym for Econometric Software Package, has been adapted to the PC from the mainframe. This is an extremely comprehensive causal modeling structure, covering the most sophisticated regression and econometric procedures. In addition, it provides on-line help to the user. The program is limited, however, to simple exponential smoothing and Box-Jenkins models in the time-series area. *ESP*® requires 320K of memory and is available on IBM® PC™, PC/AT™, PS/2™ and compatible computers. The cost of the program is $795 and there is an advanced version which sells for $1295. Further information can be obtained by writing or calling Mikros, Inc., 76 Bedford Street, Suite 33, Lexington, MA, 02173 (617-861-8852).

RATS

RATS, like *MicroTSP*™, is one of the pioneers of microcomputer forecasting software. It is almost exclusively an econometrics package, offering all the necessary elements for causal modeling. Its time-series application is limited to the sophisticated time-series methods of Box-Jenkins and vector autoregression. *RATS* is available on both IBM microcomputers (and compatibles) and Macintosh (Apple) machines. Its cost is $300 and it requires 348K of memory. Further information can be obtained by writing or calling VAR Econometrics, P.O. Box 1818, Evanston, IL, 60204-1818 (312-864-8772).

PROBE-PC™

PROBE-PC™ is another forecasting program that was originally developed for a mainframe computer. It provides both time-series and causal applications, including seasonal adjustment, exponential smoothing, Winter's equations, plus regression and econometric techniques. Similar to *ESP*®, *PROBE-PC*™ provides on-line help. At $1600, it is one of the more expensive packages. Further detail can be obtained by writing or calling Concurrent Technologies, 26 Broadway, Suite 1264, New York, NY, 10004 (800-345-3895) or (212-248-7233).

Listed below are other software packages available to the forecaster. Once again, the methods and tests contained in the programs should be investigated before a purchase is made.

1,2,3 Forecast	1,2,3 Forecast, P.O. Box 12582, Salem, OR, 97309 (503-585-8314).
Wisard Forecaster	Wisard Software Company, P.O. Box 19730, Green Bay, WI, 54307 (414-436-2341).
SPSS-X Trends™	SPSS Inc., 444 N. Michigan Avenue, Chicago, IL, 60611 (312-329-3330).
Futurecast™	Futurion Associates, Inc. 4067 Greensburg Pike, Pittsburgh, PA, 15221 (412-271-2127).
SmartForecasts II	Smart Software, 392 Concord Avenue, Belmont, MA, 02178 (617-489-2743).
Predict	Unison Technology, 410 Rouser Road, Bldg. One, Coraopolis, PA, 15108 (412-773-3428).

Using a Software Package

The first excursion into computer forecasting requires overcoming the psychological barrier presented by a new piece of machinery as well as the operational obstacles presented by the software program. In order to meet the challenge, let's walk through an example of running a regression on the microcomputer.

All the causal-modeling examples previously presented have been generated using the *MicroTSP*™ software. While there are other packages that do as good a job, the user friendliness of TSP fits in well with our purpose of providing a simple example. In the following exercise, we will cover the program commands for setting up the data files and specifying the regression equation.

Exercise

1. Starting with a dual-drive microcomputer, the user inserts the DOS system disk in the A (left side) drive and boots up the machine. From here, the DOS disk

is removed and the *MicroTSP*™ disk is inserted in its place (drive A). The program is initiated by typing in the letters TSP and pressing the enter key.

Summary of Steps

Type in TSP   Press enter key

2. An inventory, or menu, of all the important command keys appears at the bottom of the screen. Each has a key number preceding it. Pressing the CREATE, or F2 key on the left hand side of the keyboard elicits a prompt which queries the user as to the type of data to be used: (U) Undated, (A) Annual, (Q) Quarterly, or (M) Monthly. Since an annual regression model is being constructed, we type in A and hit the enter key.

Summary of Steps

Press F2 (CREATE FUNCTION)
Prompt will appear: (U) Undated
                                   (A) Annual
                                   (Q) Quarterly
                                   (M) Monthly
Type in A   Press enter key

3. The program prompts the user for the time frame of the regressions. The period that the equation is to cover is 1965 to 1988. Thus, the user types in 1965 next to the first prompt of STARTING DATE?, and 1988 for the second prompt of ENDING DATE?

Summary of Steps

Prompt will appear: Starting Date?
Type in 1965   Press enter key
Prompt will appear: Ending Date?
Type in 1988   Press enter key

4. The forecaster is ready to input the data series. In this regression, the two series being examined are real personal consumption expenditures and real disposable personal income.[*] First, the user hits the F1 (KEYS) button to provide a new menu with different functions. After pressing the F7, or DATA function, key, the program asks the individual to identify the file name of the data. Since the consumption series is to be created first, the series name of PCE82 is typed in and the enter key is pressed. With the supplied series name, the program provides the 1965 identifier for the first year of the time frame. The user types in the PCE82 value (1236.4) for that year and presses the enter key. This results in a prompt for the next year (1966), to which the user responds by typing in that year's PCE82 value (1298.9). After the last observation (1988) is inserted, the user simply types in END and the file is complete.

Summary of Steps

Press F1 (KEYS FUNCTION)
Press F7 (DATA FUNCTION)

Prompt will appear:	Name of Series?
Type in PCE82	Press enter key
Prompt will appear:	1965
Type in 1236.4	Press enter key
Prompt will appear:	1966
Type in 1298.9	Press enter key

Continue this process until the 1988 value has been typed in. Then type END and press enter key.

5. The same process is employed for creating the DPI82 file representing real disposable personal income. Now the forecaster is ready to generate a

---

[*]You might remember that these are the data series from Exercise Two in Chapter Six.

regression equation in which real personal consumption expenditures (PCE82) = f [real disposable personal income (DPI82)]. To begin the process, the user types in LS, which stands for least squares. The program returns with the prompt DEPENDENT VARIABLE? By typing in PCE82 and pressing the enter key, the program prompt comes back with INDEPENDENT VARIABLES? Here, the user types in C for the constant or y intercept followed by the explantory variable DPI82.

Summary of Steps

Type in LS	Press enter key
Prompt will appear:	Dependent Variable?
Type in PCE82	Press enter key
Prompt will appear:	Independent Variable List?
Type in c DPI82	Press enter key

6. Within seconds, the regression is calculated and flashed on the screen. The regression results include the equation coefficients, $\overline{R}^2$, standard error of the estimate, t-ratios, F-statistic, D-W statistic and other important tests. If the forecaster likes the equation results, the process is complete.

This introduction has covered only a few of the various features of the TSP software. For example, the forecaster is also able to alter the regression's time frame, add new series and lag the independent or explanatory variables. From this brief discussion, however, you can see the simplicity that computers have brought to forecasting.

10

Qualitative Methods

At this point, we have reached another milestone in our forecasting discussion. That is, time to reassess the "big picture." The focus of the first nine chapters has been on the quantitative methods of forecasting. These approaches are most likely to be found in a formalized forecasting process. Moreover, considerable research has taken place in this area, resulting in a well-defined body of procedures and techniques.

The second major category of forecasting encompasses the qualitative methods. Although not as developed as the mathematical approaches, they are also quite popular. As previously noted, there are two main groups under the qualitative banner: technological and judgmental. These groups, like the two quantitative divisions, are distinct from each other, as they serve specific purposes. In the following chapter we will examine the most widely-used approaches within these areas.

Quantitative versus Qualitative

Before embarking on a description of the qualitative methods, it is important to touch on the primary differences between the qualitative and quantitative schools. First, the qualitative methods usually do not utilize historical data. In addition, when data are included in the process, they are not rigorously examined and analyzed. By contrast, in quantitative methods, data serve as the basis for developing a projection.

What the qualitative school uses as its raw material is expert judgment. That is, intuition rather than data is the primary source from which the forecasting process unfolds. Since expert judgment serves as the foundation, the qualitative approaches do not utilize mathematical formulas. On the other hand, the quantitative methods rely exclusively on statistical and mathematical expressions in their procedures.

Technological Methods

The technological approaches are geared to projecting new technology and product applications. Of the two qualitative groups, they are the most removed from the quantitative techniques.

A closer look at the technological methods reveals that past data are never used as they are neither available nor relevant. That is, each new technology or product is so unique that empirical evidence from similar applications is largely ignored. Therefore, the judgment of the forecaster is the primary factor in developing a projection.

Because the forecaster's expertise is the key, technological methods do not follow a standardized set of procedures as do the mathematically-oriented quantitative approaches. And with their reliance on subjectivity, the technological techniques usually produce a range of possibilities rather than a single point forecast. In fact, the forecast might not be quantified at all. This, of course, makes it quite difficult later on to examine forecast accuracy.

The technological approaches are primarily utilized for long-term forecasts. In addition, they are not appropriate for developing highly-detailed projections. Thus, an hourly production forecast of a specific item would not be generated using a technological method.

Growth Curves

The growth curve is one of the most commonly utilized technological methods. You might remember from the time-series discussion of Chapter Four that a forecast was developed by fitting a curve to historical data. Technological growth curves have a similar objective of employing a curve to represent a future pattern. The significant difference, however, is that historical data are either not available or not relevant in the technological approach. Instead, expert judgment provides the foundation for determining the shape and type of curve.

One of the more widely used growth curve approaches is the S curve, which begins with a slow ascent, followed by a sharp acceleration, and then a leveling-off or plateau (Figure 10-1). Its popularity stems from its applicability to many technical and business situations. That is, the S-curve form is characteristic of many technological and market phenomena.

Figure 10-1. Example of an S Curve.

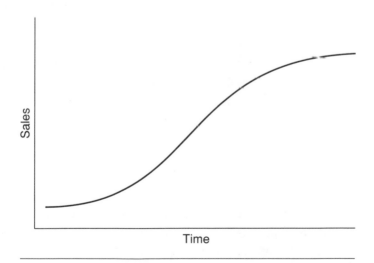

The sale of videocassette recorders provides an example of this form. In the early 1980s, purchases were modest as the product had to be introduced to the potential market. The completion of this education process and a technology-driven price decline, however, led to a dramatic acceleration in recorder sales during the mid-1980s. In recent years, this momentum has subsided as the rising portion of households that own a recorder has reduced the potential market. At some future point, sales will likely level off as additional purchases will be primarily for replacement or to new households.

This pattern, of course, relates to industries as well as specific products. For example, the data processing industry realized substantial growth between 1980 and 1985, but has recently advanced at a more moderate pace. The steel, auto, and electric-utility industries also have had similar experiences. The path of the S curve followed by a product/company/industry as it moves from infancy to maturity is often referred to in microeconomics as the life cycle.

What causes this type of pattern? In technology, the restraining factors leading to the curve's plateau are often natural or scientific limits. This can be exemplified in the maximum speed of an object or the maximum efficiency of light which cannot be surpassed. Said differently, these are physical boundaries related to the scientific makeup of the world.

In the business environment, the upper limits are usually the result of market saturation and the production function. We have touched on the first consideration, where product sales decelerate as the item moves toward full market penetration. This is a view from the demand side. The production function, however, can impact a product's receptivity from the supply or cost side. In the short run, an increasing labor input with a fixed capital stock eventually has an adverse impact on productivity. In microeconomics this is known as the point of diminishing marginal returns. Over the long run, the exhausting of economies of scale produces the same effect. The result, in both cases, is that declining production efficiencies cause spiralling costs. This leads to higher product prices and a reduction in product popularity.

In summary, S curves are popular because many technological and business phenomena fit its form. In the technological field, scientific limits are the vehicle behind the flattening of the curve. For business applications, market penetration plus the short- and long-term production functions are major factors behind the S-curve shape.

The implementation of a growth curve to project a new technology or product requires some critical decisions by the forecaster. The first is the projected shape of the curve, or in other words, whether the proposed form is to be exponential, S shaped or some other variety. The choice has a significant influence on the projected course of the item. If the form is determined to be exponential, the path is expected to be consistently rising at a constant percent rate. An S curve shape, as we know, proposes something quite different as it anticipates an eventual flattening in the long run. These divergent courses can have dramatically different implications as to the expected success or failure of the product (Figure 10-2).

Another important consideration is the present location of the technology or product on the curve. Even if the shape is correctly anticipated, the forecaster should know the present location of the item on the curve. An incorrect starting point can have an adverse impact on the planning process that evolves from the forecast.

Thus, growth curves, like all forecasting techniques, have the elements of uncertainty and risk. In

Figure 10-2. Comparison of Exponential and S Curves.

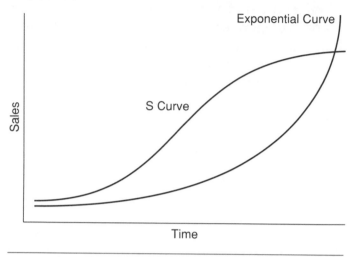

the considerations of shape and location, the forecaster's expert judgment is the primary determinant.

The Delphi Method

Another widely acknowledged technological method is the Delphi method. Developed at the Rand Corporation in the 1950s, this method arrives at a projection through independently surveying a group of experts. A panel serves as the medium for assessing the experts with a coordinator pulling the whole effort together. In fact, the coordinator plays a crucial role in this approach as the primary objective in gathering the information is to keep the individual respondents isolated.

The first step in implementing this method is to choose a panel of experts and to select the coordinator. As in all technological methods, the participants' expert judgment provides the vehicle for developing the forecast. Therefore, the experience and expertise of the panel members are a significant consideration in their selection.

Once the panel is identified, the individual members are independently queried about the forecast subject. This independent examination is to prevent the panelists from influencing each other's responses, thereby minimizing social or peer pressure.

The initial observations of the respondents are sent back to the coordinator who compiles the results. At this point, there is likely to be some divergence among the individual panelist's opinions. To reduce this range, the coordinator provides each panelist with the consensus view. Those panelists that deviate significantly from the consensus are asked to support their position.

This reevaluation step introduces a measure of peer pressure to the process. However, this approach allows those individuals that differ from the group, but do not feel strongly about their position, to modify their views. Moreover, it provides a forum for those members that hold strong beliefs about their position to enumerate the reasons.

Once the panelists have reexamined their original positions, the coordinator compiles the results. Most likely, the original bands have been tightened. If the coordinator want to further narrow the bands, this step is repeated. If the coordinator is satisfied with the results, the forecast process is finished.

It is important to note that unanimity among the panelists is not necessary. Indeed, a range of opinions is to be expected as a single answer is not the objective.

In summary, the two technological methods presented above are considerably different than the quantitative approaches discussed over the first nine chapters of the text. Yet, there are some common elements.

The growth curves described in the technological section have similar shapes and objectives as those developed in the quantitative discussion. Moreover, experience and judgment is a necessary element under either approach.

Judgmental Methods

The second category of qualitative methods is the judgmental variety, which are generally more simplistic and less expensive than the technological methods. While the simplicity of the judgmental methods enhances their popularity, it also results in biases that can often impact the credibility of the forecast. These limitations will be discussed later on in the chapter. For now, four of the most popular judgmental approaches will be presented.

Jury of Executive Opinion

Known for its simplicity, the jury of executive opinion arrives at a projection through a group session or meeting. During the meeting, a consensus forecast is hammered out as the participants present their positions and then move toward some common ground.

An enhancement to this process is to gather experts from various areas of the company, including sales, production, finance, and personnel. This approach provides the group with a broader based level of expertise, thus improving the forecast process. Moreover, the acceptability of the projection should be an easier task since the major company departments have participated in its development.

Another approach is to supply the individual group members with background information prior to the meeting. This historical data on sales and other important series provides the members with a perspective from which to generate a projection. However, the data do not have to be analyzed in any statistically rigorous fashion, as in a quantitative approach. Instead, the information serves as a foundation for group members to formulate their expectations as to future trends.

Still another variation is for the group leader to request written projections from the individual members. From them, the leader develops a forecast by combining the individual estimates. While this sounds similar to the Delphi approach, the leader is not required to isolate the members from peer pressure or to weigh their inputs equally. In fact, the group leader is given considerable latitude, such as allowing his or her own projection the most weight.

The advantage of the jury of executive opinion is in the relative ease and quickness with which the method can be implemented. Moreover, it does not require elaborate statistical analysis. When executives from various disciplines are brought together, it provides a forum for specialized viewpoints and also emphasizes teamwork.

However, this technique has considerable limitations. First, the accuracy of this approach is almost always inferior to the more rigorous quantitative methods. In addition, executives are usually more knowledgable on general subjects and less able to provide forecast detail. Finally, the resulting projection can be influenced by the most powerful member of the group, usually the leader. This can negate the advantage of specialized viewpoints and lead to damaging forecast biases.

Sales Force Estimation

The sales force estimation method develops a projection by soliciting the viewpoints of sales personnel. The most popular format is to have each salesperson project their volume of activity for the coming year. These forecasts are then aggregated to generate company sales estimates.

Similar to the jury of executive opinion, there are variations to this general theme which improve the process. One alternative is to have sales managers in the different districts check the individual projections for reasonability. Taking this one step further, the managers can independently develop a projection for their area which is then compared to the aggregated estimates of the salespeople in their group. Finally, the company might ask their distributors to provide sales projections as a complement to the individual estimates. The objective of these enhancements is to provide a check on the individual sales forecasts. As previously noted, any check or balance in the forecast process helps to assure it credibility.

One advantage of using sales force estimates is that their closeness to the market allows for more detailed projections. That is, forecasts can be provided by product line, geographic area and individual customer. In addition, their proximity to the market place allows sales members to identify emerging trends more quickly than company executives. This factor is felt to give sales force projections superiority over those of the executive jury.

The disadvantages of this methodology, similar to the jury approach, are centered on the biases of the individual participants. Sales people may be either optimistic or pessimistic by nature, which impacts their forecasts. Also important is that political considerations could taint their projections. For example, many companies have quotas or minimums for their sales force members. If the individual forecasts also serve as quotas, low projections might result. In this situation, circumstances other than the actual market dynamics would be determining the forecast.

Expectations Survey

Both the jury of executive opinion and sales force estimates rely on the expert knowledge of individuals close to the market. In the case of the sales force approach, the individual's proximity to the market place is considered to be an advantage over the jury method since changing market patterns are more quickly identified.

The expectations survey, also called the anticipatory survey, goes one step farther than these two methods in getting close to the market place by sampling the purchasers of the product, whose behavior and preferences shape future market trends. Moreover, the expectations survey utilizes quantitative procedures in the sampling process, which can greatly reduce biases. Of course, while methodological biases have been minimized, there are still individual biases to deal with.

Expectations surveys are utilized at the national level for predicting short-term economic movements. The two most frequently monitored groups are consumers and businesses. Since consumer and business spending represents approximately 65% and 10% of the Gross National Product, respectively, an understanding of their purchasing plans provides a useful barometer of future business activity.

In the consumer sector, the most widely-noted surveys are published by the University of Michigan and the Conference Board. These surveys originally assessed consumer opinions every six months. The increased economic uncertainty of the 1970s and '80s, however, has resulted in the surveys being generated on a monthly basis.

Both these surveys measure the consumer's impressions on the health of the economy, as well as their future purchasing intentions. Naturally these two topics are closely linked. Should consumers feel pessimistic about the economy due to expectations of rising unemployment and inflation, their initial reaction is to reduce purchases of cars, homes, and appliances, commonly referred to as "big ticket" items. Therefore, questions concerning consumers' economic outlook and their spending intentions provide reinforcing evidence as to their future plans.

Examples of business investment surveys include a quarterly report by the Commerce Department and a biannual report by McGraw-Hill. In these surveys, individual companies within major industry groups are queried on their spending plans for plant and equipment over the next year. Evidence indicates that these surveys are usually more accurate than those in the consumer area. The reason is that business spending plans are developed well before the actual transaction takes place through an intricate evaluation and budgeting process. Once this process is completed and the plan approved, it is usually carried forth. Consumers, on the other hand, make their purchases more spontaneously, and their spending plans for the next six months, therefore, are more apt to be revised due to unforeseen circumstances.

Expectations surveys are not just limited to examining the national economy. Many companies use this approach to gather information concerning their customers' purchasing plans. This can take the form of a survey sample carried out by telephone, mail, or personal contact. In other instances, companies survey all of their customers if this is a reasonably small group. Electric utilities with several large customers are an example of this latter approach.

Expectations surveys are vulnerable to the same biases that hamper the other judgmental techniques. Companies that assess the future plans of their major purchasers have found them, on occasion, to be overly optimistic during an economic expansion and overly pessimistic during a period of business stagnation. Thus, despite rigorous methods of surveying, strong biases are ingrained in the process.

Judgmental Probability

Judgmental probability, also known as subjective probability, takes a very different approach to forecasting than the other qualitative methods. In this technique, all major outcomes are identified and assigned probabilities based on judgment and experience. By specifically examining the various possible outcomes, this method specifically addresses the problem of uncertainty in forecasting.

It is useful to note that there are two types of probability. The first category is defined as objective, or historical, as it encompasses probabilities which represent events that can be replicated. The simplest example is the coin toss. For this event, there are two possible outcomes since the coin will land either heads or tails. In addition, probabilities are assigned to each outcome by recreating the event. From numerous simulated coin tosses, the forecaster will find that the individual probabilities for the two possible outcomes are 50 percent.

In the second category, called subjective or judgmental probability, the event being projected cannot be replicated. In this situation, probabilities for the various outcomes are developed judgmentally using an individual's expertise. This subjective determination of the probabilities is the reason this method is under the qualitative school.

While the judgmental probability approach has numerous variations, one popular method uses three basic steps to generate a forecast.

Step 1. First, the analyst needs to identify the variable to be projected and the time frame of the forecast. At this point, an examination of the subject is necessary to catalog the possible paths or outcomes.

Step 2. From here, probabilities are judgmentally assigned to each outcome using the simple rules: (1) all the individual probabilities must sum to 100% (or 1); (2) no individual probability can be less than 0 or greater than 100% (or 1).

Step 3. The final step entails the multiplication of each outcome by its assigned probability. Summing these products for all outcomes yields the expected value or forecast. The expected value, therefore, is the weighted average of all outcomes and represents the most likely value given all possible outcomes and probabilities.

Exercise

Let's go through an example to see how the simple steps and rules described above are used to develop a forecast. Regal Bank is a large institution in New York City that is attempting to project a short-term interest rate (three-month Treasury bills) for the coming month. The purpose of the forecast is to determine an investment portfolio plan for the bank's assets. Should the bank anticipate an increase in rates, they will shift funds out of bonds and into cash. If they expect an interest rate decline, they will move in the opposite direction.

The Investment Committee, comprised of Ms. Eng, Mr. McAuley, and Ms. Kibbe, are charged with developing the forecast and investment plan. They use the judgmental probability approach for producing the interest rate projection. In their approach, a form containing the latest three-month Treasury bill rate and possible future outcomes for the coming month is circulated at the committee's monthly meeting.

The three members fill out their forms by assigning probabilities to the various outcomes. They adhere to the simple rules stated above, making sure that their total probabilities equal 100%, with no individual probability greater than 100%, or less than 0%. Their aggregated forms are provided in Table 10-1.

The accumulated results show that each of the committee members has assigned a high probability to interest rates rising over the coming month. Of the three, Ms. Eng appears to be the most bearish as to the future course of the Treasury-bill rate.

At this point, the individual member projections are consolidated into an average probability for each of the five outcomes. Since Ms. Kibbe is the group leader, she might give greater weight to her forecasts. Moreover, she might want Ms. Eng to explain why her forecast is more pessimistic than the other members. However, we assume for ease of calculation that each member's response is left in its original form and is equally weighted. The calculation of the probabilities, therefore, is a straightforward procedure in which the

---

Table 10-1. Treasury-bill Forecast for One Month.

Present Rate: 8%

| | \multicolumn{6}{c}{Probabilities} | | | | | |
	7.0%	7.5%	8.0%	8.5%	9.0%	Total
Ms. Kibbe	0	.10	.40	.40	.10	1.00
Mr. McAuley	0	.05	.35	.30	.30	1.00
Ms. Eng	0	.00	.30	.50	.20	1.00
Average	0	.05	.35	.40	.20	1.00

three observations under each of the outcomes from 7% to 9% is averaged.

From these averages, the expected or most likely value can be computed. This involves multiplying the individual outcomes by their average probabilities from Table 10-1 and summing the resulting products. In this example, the expected value is 8.38%, which represents the three-month Treasury-bill forecast for the coming month (Table 10-2).

While the expected value represents the group's point forecast, the distribution, or range, of the individual outcomes is also significant. From this forecast, the committee projects a 75% probability that rates will be in the 8.0% to 8.5% range over the next month. In addition, they feel 95% certain that the Treasury-bill rate will be either at the present level, or higher one month down the road.

Table 10-3 contains probabilities from a similar group in another bank (we will call them group B). Although group B probabilities differ from those of the Regal Bank Investment Committee, they have the same expected value. This group, however, believes that there is only an 85% probability that rates will stay level or rise. Therefore, there is less certainty in group B that rates will be the same level or higher one month from now, since their range of probabilities is spread out more over the various outcomes.

Table 10-2. Expected Value Calculation.

Outcome	$\times$	Probability	$=$	Product	
7.0%		0.00		0.00	
7.5%		0.05		0.38	
8.0%		0.35		2.80	
8.5%		0.40		3.40	
9.0%		0.20		1.80	
		1.00		8.38%	Expected Value

Table 10-3. Forecast Range Differentials.

Outcome	Probabilities	
	Regal Bank Committee	Group B
7.0%	0.00	0.05
7.5%	0.05	0.10
8.0%	0.35	0.25
8.5%	0.40	0.25
9.0%	0.20	0.35
Expected Value	8.38%	8.38%

Of course, the group B leader can apply peer pressure in an attempt to narrow the band by requiring those members at either end of this range to review their positions. The important point from this comparison, however, is that the analyst examine not only the expected value, but also the distribution of the projected outcomes.

Judgmental Biases and Limitations

No discussion of judgmental techniques is complete without a brief overview of the biases that can impact this methodology. In fact, the greatest source of inaccuracy within judgmental methods results from individual and group biases. In the quantitative school, the proper application of mathematical procedures minimizes these limitations. However, biases are inherent in the methodological framework of the judgmental processes, and this influences the resulting projections.

The two major categories of bias are individual and group. The primary source of individual bias is the limited ability of the human mind to process data objectively. Unlike a mathematical formula, an individual cannot treat each observation fairly. An example of this limitation is an analyst who remembers only data that supports his or her position.

Other factors can bias a forecast in addition to the inability to recollect past observations. A forecaster may judgmentally arrive at a projection which tells the company's executives what they want to hear. This "good news" bias is a common problem, and results from the individual's reluctance to be the messenger of unpleasant information.

The physical and/or mental condition of the forecaster might also affect a judgmental projection. A well-traveled hypothesis about the auto industry is that you should never purchase an automobile assembled on a Monday or a Friday. The basis for this belief is that workers are "recovering" from the weekend on Monday and getting ready for the weekend on Friday. This same parallel can be drawn about any endeavor, including forecasting. Certainly, a forecast might be more pessimistic than otherwise if the individual responsible for developing it is not feeling well.

Group biases are usually the result of the membership's desire to maintain harmony and cohesiveness. One potential product of the desire for harmony is the discouragement of viewpoints which differ from the consensus. Alternative opinions provide a necessary balance to an analysis and often raise warning signals concerning the group's present course. By suppressing these points, a valuable part of the forecast development process is eliminated.

Also noteworthy is that the leader or individual with the strongest opinion tends to prevail in a group setting. This poses the danger that more relevant ideas might not be considered due to the pressure for a unanimous decision.

It has also been found that groups lean toward riskier decisions than individuals because the members of the group feel insulated by a sense of shared responsibility. That is, should their forecast prove incorrect, the group is at fault rather than any of the individual members.

While individual and group biases will always be a part of the judgmental process, steps can be taken to minimize their effect. To guard against individual bias, the forecaster should solicit opinions from other qualified individuals on those considerations that serve as the foundation for the projection.

For minimizing group bias, it is imperative to foster an environment which allows for the free and unrestrained exchange of ideas. To achieve this objective, the group leader can play an important role by remaining neutral during the discussion and allowing the members to express their own opinions. In addition, the leader can actively solicit the pros and cons of an issue by specifically assigning these tasks to individual members.

The group should also invite guests into the meeting to provide other viewpoints. Finally, a periodic reexamination of the situation provides a forum for the development of further ideas and the discussion of any final doubts that the membership might have.

Summary

In this chapter we have discussed six methods of qualitative forecasting. Further information on these and other qualitative procedures can be found in *Sales Forecasting* by D. Hurwood, E. Grossman and E. Bailey, *Forecasting Methods for Management* by S. Makridakis and S.C. Wheelwright, and *Forecasting in Business and Economics* by C.W.J. Granger.

With the completion of this topic, we have finished our discussion on the major quantitative and qualitative forecasting techniques. During the course of this text, we have presented fifteen different methods for

Table 10-4. Forecasting Methods.

Quantitative	Qualitative
Time Series	*Technological*
1. Smoothing	1. Growth Curves
2. Seasonality	2. Delphi Method
3. Smoothing plus Seasonality	
4. Box-Jenkins	
5. Time Trends	
6. Indicators	
Causal	*Judgmental*
1. Simple Regression	1. Jury of Executive Opinion
2. Multiple Regression	2. Sales Force Estimation
3. Econometrics	3. Expectations Survey
	4. Judgmental Probability

developing a projection. As review, Table 10-4 contains an inventory of the techniques studied—similar to Figure 1-1 in the first chapter.

11

Choosing a Forecast Method/Presenting the Forecast

"Being a forecaster is always having to say you're sorry."

—Anonymous

In the past ten chapters, we have introduced a wide variety of forecasting methods to the reader. The next step is to determine when these methods should be applied. Over time, experience will help the forecaster decide on the appropriate method to use in a given situation. For a beginner, however, this brief discussion should help with the first few forays into forecasting.

Various factors are taken into account in choosing the right forecast technique for the occasion.* The most frequently considered criteria include (1) the forecast time frame, (2) the prevailing data patterns, (3) the strengths and weaknesses of the methods, (4) cost, and (5) accuracy. As part of our discussion, we will see that certain of these factors are intertwined. In addition, the forecaster may not consider all of these elements in the decision-making process. Finally, the order of importance for these criteria varies from forecaster to forecaster, although

---

* This presentation is based on a discussion in S. C. Wheelwright and S. Makridkis, *Forecasting Methods for Management*, 3rd Ed.

cost and accuracy usually are the most popular considerations.

Time Frame

The time horizon encompasses both the length of the forecast and the lead time necessary for its development. Usually the two are interrelated. For example, a company produces a twenty-year sales projection and updates it once or twice each year. In this situation, the forecast group is charged with providing a long-term projection and is given ample time for its development. However, when a weekly forecast is required, there is little available time for preparation since, by definition, the projection must be regenerated 52 times a year. Consequently, the longer-term projections tend to employ the more developed (and time-consuming) methods, while the shorter time frames use simpler techniques.

Forecasters usually distinguish between the three time horizons of short-, medium-, and long-term. Different industries, of course, have different perceptions as to the length of time covered by these categories. In the fashion industry, the long-term is thought to be one or two years, since styles change quickly. For electric utilities, where considerable lead time is necessary for planning power plants, the long-term is 20 to 30 years. Despite these varying viewpoints, the period covered by the forecast goes a long way in determining the method to be used.

The short-term can encompass a period of six months or less. At the one end of the spectrum are projections of extremely short duration—that is, weekly, daily and hourly. For this group, forecast updates are required on a frequent basis. In addition, the only data usually available within this time frame is the series being projected. Therefore, the forecaster is constrained by both time and data limitations.

These circumstances warrant a simple, formalized procedure that can be quickly implemented. Time-series methods are useful in this situation, since they are the easiest of the quantitative methods to develop, and require data for only the forecasted series. Of these, exponential smoothing is advantageous because of its minimal data requirements and its ability to allow more weight to the latest observation, and some weight to all data points. However, the jury of executive opinion and judgmental probability are also compatible with this time frame.

As the short-term forecast horizon lengthens, cyclical and seasonal factors become more significant. Still, time-series smoothing approaches continue to be appropriate. The Seasmooth method of double exponential smoothing with seasonal adjustment is particularly useful in this time frame.

Causal models, however, are also suitable at this point since most economic data are available on a monthly or quarterly basis. Still, a forecast horizon of one month might predispose the analyst toward the time-series approaches since frequent updates are involved.

The second category, the medium-term, covers the period from six months to five years. In this time horizon, the forecast is usually integrated into the company's planning process, requiring that projections be tied to future economic considerations. Therefore, a causal approach relating company activity to economic variables is the most popular method.

While the medium-term allows for the more sophisticated causal techniques, there is still room for time-series approaches. Many companies utilize a causal model as their lead forecasting tool, but also develop a simple time-series method to provide a check and balance to the process. In addition, leading indicators are useful during this time span where the business cycle is being projected.

Finally, any of the four judgmental approaches discussed also can be employed in the medium-term. Their lack of sophistication and statistical rigor, however, can limit their applicability. Moreover, their accuracy suffers dramatically as the forecast horizon lengthens.

The long-term generally applies to projections of five years or more. In the long-term, the trend is the dominant pattern, and forecast uncertainty is a significant consideration. Moreover, projections of this duration are often integrated into the corporate planning process since the forecast provides the foundation for determining the company's future strategy. This responsibility requires sophisticated forecasting procedures capable of incorporating new technologies and developments.

Certainly the technological methods are appropriate for this time period. Their ability to project the impact of future innovations and products is consistent with the primary considerations of this time frame. Causal models, however, are also appropriate for developing long-term projections. It is not unusual to see both these approaches implemented, with the causal model identifying the basic relationships, and the technological method examining potential future changes in these relationships.

Patterns in the Data

In Chapter Two, we discussed the various patterns that can be contained in a series, including (1) cyclical, (2) trend, (3) seasonal, and (4) irregular. The primary objective of the quantitative methods, you might remember, is to remove the irregular, or random, component from the data. Moreover, it has been noted that the plotting of a series provides important clues as to the patterns inherent in the data.

Trends measure the increasing, decreasing, or horizontal pattern in a series over time. Should a series have a horizontal pattern, a simple time-series approach provides the best technique for forecasting. The method used can be a naive approach or a first-order smoothing procedure such as simple moving average or single exponential smoothing.

Where a trend has an upward or downward tilt, causal methods, as well as time series trend lines, have been identified as proper forecasting tools. In addition, technological techniques such as growth curves are useful for projecting the trend pattern.

The above techniques are particularly appropriate where a trend is being measured over at least one business cycle. Forecasting, however, does not always follow precise definitions. Some analysts use the word *trend* to characterize the developments in a series during the past several months. Under this definition, the double exponential smoothing method is a solid approach for following short-term trends.

The cyclical pattern involves the upward and downward movements around the long-term growth trend. As previously discussed, the business cycle is the most difficult pattern to anticipate because there is no regularity to its duration or impact. A good example of its inability to repeat itself at constant intervals is the recent history of the national economy. During the last cycle, the recession, or downward phase, ran for eight months (November 1979 to July 1980), while the recovery, or upward portion lasted one year (July 1980 to July 1981). In total, the business cycle encompassed 20 months. This varied considerably from its predecessor, which covered a period of 72 months and experienced a deeper downturn as well as a steeper expansion.

As noted in Chapter Four, the mystery surrounding the business cycle makes it a popular topic for media discussion. The most frequently used tool for projecting swings in the national economy is the Index of Leading Economic Indicators. However, the expectations survey is also appropriate for forecasting business turning points. In addition, decomposition analysis using the X-11 version of Census II has the ability to identify cyclical patterns through a calculation called months of cyclical dominance.

Recurring movements within the year signify that the data have a seasonal element. In this situation, a classical decomposition method, such as the simple procedure outlined in Chapter Three, or a more sophisticated treatment like the X-11 program, can be used to remove the seasonality.

Although classical decomposition of the data is the usual approach for determining seasonality, one of our regression exercises adjusted for seasonality by modeling it as a dummy variable. In that example, the quarterly seasonal influences were treated as explanatory variables in the equation. It is important to reiterate that all series of weekly, monthly, and quarterly duration need to be seasonally adjusted, regardless of which method the analyst favors.

Strengths and Weaknesses of Methods

Another way to get the most out of a technique is to understand its strengths and weaknesses. Two common choices facing the forecaster when identifying the appropriate method are whether to use a time-series or causal technique, or a quantitative or judgmental technique.

Looking first at the time-series/causal comparison, the time-series approaches are almost always easier to develop and implement, requiring less expenditure of time and money.

The simplicity of these approaches, however, also serves as a limiting factor. We have already noted that time-series techniques determine only the underlying pattern of the data being projected. These methods do not have the ability to identify the elements driving the forecast. This can become crucial when the forecast is presented to senior management. In this forum, a company vice president might want an explanation of the economic variables influencing the course of sales, and might even request a quantification of a major factor such as price on the sales of a product. A time-series approach is not equipped to provide these answers. However, a causal model can enumerate the effects of the major explanatory variables on the forecasted series.

Another shortcoming of a time-series approach is that it supplies only a single projection. A causal method, on the other hand, can be used to develop alternative outcomes by substituting various assumptions for the explanatory variables into the model equation.

Causal models, of course, have their own distinct limitations. Because they are more sophisticated, considerable resources and expense are required in their development. In addition, future values for the explanatory variables are a necessary part of the forecast process, imposing an additional cost on the user.

The choice between quantitative and judgmental methods revolves around the forecaster's concern for statistical rigor. Certainly, a quantitatively derived projection is easier to defend than a judgmental forecast, since the statistical procedures are designed to minimize forecast biases. Consequently, companies whose forecasts are frequently examined by a third party usually choose a quantitative procedure for generating their projections.

Cost

Although cost is the fourth item of discussion, many firms consider this to be the primary consideration in determining the appropriate forecast method. This is certainly understandable given the competitive nature of the business world, and the need to maintain close control over expenditures.

Forecasting expenses can be broken into the standard divisions of fixed and variable costs. The first category represents developmental outlays such as gathering data, constructing the model, and implementing a procedure for continuing the process. The second group encompasses operational expenses related to storing, maintaining, and running the program.

The costs related to the various forecast methods differ considerably within these two categories. For example, the majority of expenses related to the qualitative approaches (technological and judgmental) are developmental. Causal methods can also require substantial developmental expenses, while time-series approaches are the least expensive to design and implement.

Causal models also have higher operation costs than time-series methods because of their more intricate nature. At the other extreme, qualitative operational expenses are negligible since their costs, as already noted, are incurred in the developmental stage.

Storage and operation costs have diminished greatly in recent years with the proliferation of microcomputers. In fact, the expanding capabilities of these smaller machines have caused a shift away from the more expensive mainframe computers.

The dramatic reduction in computer operating expenses has lowered the cost of quantitative methods relative to qualitative techniques. This has heightened interest in the quantitative approaches, especially the less intricate varieties of time-series and regression methods.

Despite this trend, causal methods are still generally more expensive than judgmental methods. However, the technological procedures are usually the most expensive, while time series are the least expensive because of their more simplified nature.

Accuracy

Accuracy and cost are closely linked because they are often considered simultaneously in choosing a method. Certainly, greater sophistication in the forecast process entails a greater expense to the company. In addition, a more developed procedure in many cases (although not all) enhances accuracy. Therefore, it is generally assumed that greater expense, in many cases, yields more developed methods and an increased potential for accuracy.

This, then, is the tradeoff that firms must grapple with when considering cost and accuracy. For certain companies, the penalty resulting from a less accurate forecast might be minimal. This is usually the case for certain nonperishable items, where extra inventories due to a faulty forecast does not impose a great hardship on the firm.

For other companies, the penalty for inaccurate forecasts can be considerable. In the electric utility industry, forecasts are used to plan power plant additions. If a utility has either a surplus or a deficit in its future generation, the result can be financially stressful. Where there is excess capacity, the public utility commission might not allow the firm to include the new plant in its rate base. If more generation is needed, the cost of purchasing from another company can be prohibitive.

These examples lead to a better understanding of why certain industries use sophisticated and expensive forecasting procedures, while others employ simpler, less expensive tools. Similar to most aspects of business, the benefits of forecast accuracy are weighed against the cost of the methods in determining the appropriate course of action.

Consensus Forecasting

Forecasting, like any other activity, has techniques and procedures that go in and out of fashion. In the 1960s, large econometric models which projected national economic activity were extremely popular. However, the volatility of the economy in the post-1973 time frame reduced the accuracy, as well as the popularity, of these models. In fact, many companies who built these structures have since abandoned them or greatly reduced their size.

The latest industry trend is the move toward consensus forecasting. A consensus forecast is developed by averaging projections from numerous sources. The philosophy behind this approach is that the individual forecaster's performance tends to be erratic from one year to the next. In addition, there is a high probability that the group or consensus projection will have a better record than the individual over a given period of time.

There have been numerous studies which support the belief that the group is more accurate than the individual. Victor Zarnowitz has published several articles on this topic. In addition, Peter Bernstein and Theodore Silber have found that consensus projections of national economic series are extremely accurate.*

Most forecasters agree that their performance is prone to sizable fluctuations on a year-to-year basis. The lack of assurance that last year's sterling performance will be repeated on a steady basis is one of the fundamental facts of forecast life. Indeed, the awareness that any particular projection can bomb makes the individual extremely humble during times of success.

One of the first publications to produce consensus forecasts was the *Blue Chip Economic Indicators*, which developed a group projection of economic activity and inflation based on experts from all over the country. At this time, more than 50 individual projections are used to arrive at their consensus estimate. They have also expanded their service to projecting interest rates.

Other sources of national consensus projections have also appeared in recent years. *The Wall Street Journal* develops a group forecast by polling prominent national economists on a timely basis. The *National Association of Business Economists* (NABE), whose membership encompasses most professional forecasters, provides a consensus projection three times a year.

The consensus rage has also spread to international projections and exchange rate forecasts. But

---

* Zarnowitz's studies include "The Accuracy of Individual and Group Forecasts from Business Outlook Surveys," *NBER Working Paper 1053,* December 1982, as well as one he did with Geoffrey Moore entitled "Forecasting Recessions under the Gramm-Rudman-Hollings Law," *NBER,* November 1986. Bernstein and Silber's article is "Are Economic Forecasters Worth Listening To?," *Harvard Business Review,* Sep.–Oct. 1984.

the acid test for consensus projections will be their accuracy in calling the next business cycle downturn. During the 1982 recession, the *Blue Chip* consensus projected continued economic growth (see Table 1-3 in Chapter One). A repeat of that occurrence could dampen the popularity of this approach.

Pulling the Forecast Process Together

This text has attempted to provide the reader with the major elements of the forecast process. We first focused on the mechanical procedures involved in moving from model development to the actual forecast. From that point, we examined when to use a particular method.

With the fundamentals of forecasting firmly in place, a general review of some important considerations is in order. The points we will be discussing in the following pages have been touched on throughout the book, but an organized presentation will be useful.

First, the forecaster should always strive for a fair and unbiased projection. Quantitative techniques are usually more compatible with this objective. However, judgmental methods can also achieve this goal through a concerted effort to minimize the biases inherent in their methodology.

Many forecasters attempt to contain both bias and error by using more than one technique. This multiple method approach is valuable because it provides an important check and balance to the process. The way that many companies employ this philosophy is to generate a forecast with their primary model and then compare these results with the outputs from a second, more simplistic method. In this way, any unreasonable projections from the first approach can be identified and adjusted.

A second major consideration is the need for the economic assumptions driving the forecast model to be continually monitored for consistency. As previously noted, consistency implies that the estimates of the various inputs are in sync. For example, expectations of a decline in economic activity is not consistent with a forecast for rising employment. In certain cases, a company might subscribe to a national forecasting service such as Data Resources Incorporated (DRI) or Wharton Econometrics to provide these inputs. Since these firms have large econometric models, the resulting economic forecasts are related. Other companies, however, develop their own econometric structure (like TEREM) to ensure consistent economic assumptions.

Finally, it is important to remember that the judgmental adjusting of a model's outputs is an acceptable practice. In some cases, this involves the simple smoothing of the model's projections. In other cases, the forecaster might fine tune the major assumptions. Also, the forecast can be adjusted for special events which are expected, but cannot in any way be processed into the model structure.

As stated previously, experience and judgment go hand in hand. During your initial forecasting efforts, it is usually good policy to stick closely with the results from the model. Later on, however, the forecaster can exercise judgment where it is deemed appropriate.

Presenting the Forecast

A forecast is like any other product in that it must be "sold" to its potential customer which, in most cases, will be upper management. The key to marketing, of course, is to have a good product. In forecasting, that generally means a reasonable projection, as well as a good track record.

In presenting the forecast, it is important to

emphasize the checks for reasonability and consistency that are part of the process. One of the most common is to review the recent record of accuracy. This should include a comparison of the latest forecast variance with the historic average. Where the recent error exceeds the average, it is useful to explain the factors behind this variance. If the major economic assumptions (input error) are the cause, explain the adjustments that have been implemented. Should the error be the result of changes in the industry's structure (model error), discuss the new variables that are now being considered in the forecast. By having command of the situation, you will make management more confident about the projection.

It is also imperative that management be informed of the major economic assumptions that underlie the forecast. This usually involves a discussion of the general economy's expected course during the next several years. The presentation should always seek to highlight the consistency and reasonableness of these assumptions.

The primary focus of the forecast presentation is, of course, on the company's sales projection. In discussing the outlook, link it with recent historic trends to provide a basis for management to view the forecast's reasonability. Graphs usually serve this purpose better than tables. However, some tables are necessary to provide management with the exact level and percent change that is expected.

During the presentation, the element of forecast uncertainty needs to be noted. This can be integrated into the process by using the words "expect" or "should," rather than "will," when discussing the future. While forecasters want to instill confidence in their projections, they should emphasize that some error is to be expected.

Finally, the forecaster should refrain from using any technical terms. For instance, references to $\overline{R}^2$, t-ratios and D-W tests must be avoided at all costs. Instead, statements concerning methodological points should be couched in layman's terms. This has the effect of bringing management and the forecast closer together. Forecasting is a simple process: its description should be also.

You now have the basic tools to develop, implement, and present your own projections. In forecasting, like any other discipline, hard work overcomes all obstacles. Since you have shown the perseverance to finish this book, you obviously are not afraid of hard work. In closing, we wish you great success in your forecasting career and hope that all your F-statistics are significant at the 95% confidence level.

References

Armstrong, J. Scott. 1978. *Long Range Forecasting, from Crystal Ball to Computer*. New York: John Wiley and Sons.

Granger, C.W.J. 1980. *Forecasting in Business and Economics*. New York: Academic Press.

Gujarati, D. 1978. *Basic Econometrics*. New York: McGraw-Hill.

Hanke, J.E., and A.G. Reitsch. 1989. *Business Forecasting*. 3rd ed. Boston: Allyn and Bacon.

Hoff, J.C. 1983. *A Practical Guide to Box-Jenkins Forecasting*. Belmont, Ca.: Lifetime Learning Publications.

Hurwood, D.L., E.S. Grossman, and E. L. Bailey. 1984. *Sales Forecasting*. New York: Conference Board.

Intriligator, M.D. 1978. *Econometric Models, Techniques, and Applications*. Englewood Cliffs, N.J.: Prentice-Hall.

Maddala, G.S. 1977. *Econometrics*. New York: McGraw-Hill.

Makridakis, S., and S.C. Wheelwright. 1989. *Forecasting Methods for Management.* 5th ed. New York: John Wiley and Sons.

Makridakis, S., S.C. Wheelwright, and V.E. McGee. 1983. *Forecasting: Methods and Applications.* 2nd ed. New York: John Wiley and Sons.

McAuley, J.J. 1986. *Economic Forecasting for Business: Concepts and Applications.* Englewood Cliffs, N.J.: Prentice-Hall.

Pankratz, A. 1983. *Forecasting with Univariate Box-Jenkins Models—Concepts and Cases.* New York: John Wiley and Sons.

Pindyck, R.S., and D.L. Rubinfeld. 1981. *Econometric Models and Economic Forecasts.* 2nd ed. New York: McGraw-Hill.

Studenmund, A.H., and H.J. Cassidy. 1987. *Using Econometrics.* Boston: Little, Brown and Company.

Glossary of Forecasting Terms

Autocorrelation Coefficient measures the relationship between any two series derived from the same data set. The coefficient will range from -1 (representing a strong inverse relationship) to $+1$ (which implies a strong direct relationship). Autocorrelations are used in developing a Box-Jenkins model.

Box-Jenkins Method one of the most sophisticated time-series techniques. This approach involves the identification of a model structure that is autoregressive (AR), moving average (MA), or autoregressive moving average (ARMA).

Causal Methods one of the two subcategories of the quantitative forecasting group. It develops a projection based on the mathematical relationship between the series being examined and those variables which influence or explain that series.

Coefficient of Correlation measures the relationship between any two series. It ranges from -1 (representing a strong inverse relationship) to $+1$ (which implies a strong direct relationship). The coefficient of correlation (r) is similar to the autocorrelation coefficient, except that it measures two independent series rather than series derived from the same data set.

Consensus Forecasting develops a projection by averaging forecasts from numerous sources. This has become a popular approach for generating national economic projections. For example, the *Blue Chip Economic Indicators* produces future estimates of U.S. economic activity, inflation, and interest rates by averaging forecasts from experts all over the country.

Cross-sectional Regression a type of regression that develops its equation from data representing one point in time.

Cyclical Pattern one of the four basic patterns that can be found in a data series. It represents the up and down movement in business activity around the long-term trend. The cycle is the most difficult pattern to identify and project.

Delphi Method a technological forecasting method that arrives at a projection by independently surveying a group of experts. An outside individual collects and coordinates the responses to prevent the experts from influencing each other.

Differencing used to create a new stationary series from two other series. Differencing is used in constructing Box-Jenkins models.

Econometrics a series of interrelated regression equations based on economic theory.

Endogenous Variables variables in an econometric model whose values are determined within the structure.

Expectations Survey a judgmental forecasting method which directly surveys the customers or individuals that impact product sales.

Exogenous Variables variables in an econometric model whose values are supplied from outside the structure.

Exponential Smoothing a time-series technique which uses a weighting factor (alpha) to develop a forecast. Exponential smoothing is considered to be superior to the moving average method because it assigns greater weight to the most recent observation, gives some influence to all data points, requires minimal data, and has more flexibility. Exponential techniques include first-order (single exponential smoothing), as well as higher-order (double and triple exponential smoothing) varieties.

***F*-Statistic** measures the significance, or fit, of a regression equation. In its simplest form, the F-statistic examines the equation's explained variance as a ratio of its unexplained variance. A common rule of thumb is that an F-statistic above 5 indicates that the regression equation is more significant than zero and can be utilized for forecasting.

Growth Curves a technological forecasting method which uses a judgmentally derived curve to represent a future pattern. The most popular of these is the S curve which begins with a slow ascent, is followed by a sharp acceleration, and then levels off.

Heteroskedasticity a condition in which the error term of the regression increases or decreases over the data set. Heteroskedasticity is similar to serial correlation in that the nonconstant pattern in the residuals can represent an explanatory variable that has been omitted from the equation.

Indicators a time-series forecasting method that attempts to identify short-term cyclical turning points. The best known example is the Index of Leading Economic Indicators, which anticipates movements in the national economy.

Irregular Pattern one of the four basic patterns in a data series. It represents unexplained variations in the data that result from collection errors or unexpected circumstances, such as strikes or wars.

Judgmental Methods one of the two subcategories of the qualitative forecasting group. These methods use subjectivity to arrive at a forecast.

Judgmental Probability a judgmental forecasting approach in which all major outcomes are identified and assigned probabilities in developing a projection.

Jury of Executive Opinion a judgmental forecasting method which develops a projection through a group session or meeting.

Mean Absolute Deviation (MAD) measures forecast accuracy by averaging the absolute values of the errors.

Mean Absolute Percentage Error (MAPE) measures the average absolute error as a percentage. This allows for the comparison of forecast variances among different series.

Mean Squared Error (MSE) measures forecast accuracy by taking an average of the squared errors. By squaring the variations, this approach penalizes large errors more than small errors.

Moving Average a smoothing technique which averages a given number of observations to develop a forecast. Moving average techniques can be first-order (simple moving average) or higher-order (double moving average).

Multicollinearity a condition where two or more independent variables in a regression equation are closely correlated. When multicollinearity occurs, the coefficients assigned to the independent variables are often misspecified. A common rule of thumb is that multicollinearity can be a potential problem when the coefficient of correlation (r) between any two independent variables is greater than .7.

Ordinary Least Squares a procedure for determining the parameters of a regression equation. Its specific objective is to develop an equation which minimizes the squared difference between the actual data and the corresponding points on the equation line.

Qualitative one of the two major forecasting groups. This approach utilizes expert judgment rather than mathematical procedures.

Quantitative one of the two major schools of forecasting. This group relies on statistical or mathematical methods.

R^2 also known as the coefficient of determination, it represents the percentage of the past movement in the dependent (forecasted) variable that has been accounted for by the independent (explanatory) variable(s) in the regression equation. The R^2 has a range between 0 and 1, with the equation having greater explanatory power as the value rises.

Regression Analysis the principal vehicle for developing a causal forecasting method. It provides a mathematical expression of the relationship between the series being projected and the series thought to impact it. The product of regression analysis is the regression equation, which has the linear form $Y = a + b_1X_1 + \cdots + b_nX_n$ where Y is the dependent variable to be projected, and X represents the independent (explanatory) variable(s) influencing Y. A simple regression has one explanatory variable, while a multiple regression has more than one explanatory variable.

Regression Coefficient the b value assigned to the independent (explanatory) variable(s) in a regression equation. It represents the change in the dependent, or forecasted, variable (Y) that results from a one-unit change in the independent variable (X).

Sales Force Estimation a judgmental forecasting method which develops a projection by aggregating the expectations of sales personnel.

Seasonal Adjustment removing the seasonal pattern from a data series. Once the data have been seasonally adjusted or deseasonalized, the forecaster can apply time-series techniques to eliminate the irregular pattern and identify the underlying trend.

Seasonal Pattern one of the four basic patterns that can be found in a data series. It represents movements in a series during a particular time of year (week, month, or quarter) that recur year after year due to climate/weather, social customs/holidays, and business policies.

Serial Correlation also known as autocorrelation, it is a condition where the regression's error terms are related over time; that is, where there is a pattern in the error. Serial correlation can indicate that another explanatory variable is needed in the regression equation. The common rule of thumb is that a Durbin-Watson statistic between 1.5 and 2.5 implies that we can be reasonably sure serial correlation is not a problem.

Smoothing Methods simple time-series forecasting approaches which average the data in some fashion to remove random variations and identify the underlying trend pattern. Exponential smoothing and moving averages are the most common smoothing methods.

Stability the utilization of sufficient data points so that the regression equation's parameters accurately estimate the actual relationship between the variables being examined.

Standard Deviation used to measure the variation of the individual elements in a series from the central value, or mean, of the series.

Standard Error of the Estimate represents the historical forecast error of the regression equation. It also can be employed to create a band, or range, around the equation model forecast.

***t*-Ratio** measures the significance of each independent (explanatory) variable in a regression by determining whether the regression coefficient is more significant than zero. A common rule of thumb is that the *t*-ratio for an independent variable should have an absolute value greater than 2 to be significant.

Technological Methods one of the two subcategories of the qualitative forecasting group. It uses a subjective approach to project new technologies and product applications.

Time-Series Regression a type of regression which develops the equation from data over a certain time frame.

Time-Series Methods one of the two subcategories of the quantitative forecasting group. It develops projections by examining the patterns in the data series.

Time Trend   a time-series method that fits a trend line to a data set. The line, which best reflects the shape of the series, can either be linear or curvilinear.

Trend Pattern   one of the four basic patterns that can be found in a data series. This represents the increasing, decreasing, or horizontal course of a data series over a period of time.

Index

A

Acceleration indicator structure, 97

Accuracy:
  average error, 6–7
  degrees of, 10–12
  as factor in choosing forecast method, 291–292
  mean absolute deviation (MAD), 7–8
  mean absolute percentage error (MAPE), 9, 302
  mean squared error (MSE), 8–9
  standard deviation, 9–10

Adaptive forecasting, 94

Addfactors, 143, 213–218, 220

Adjusted R^2, 118, 130, 136, 147, 149, 150

Annual Energy Outlook, 253

Annual models, multiple regression using, 153–175

Anticipatory survey, 273

Autocorrelation, 89, 91, 92, 93, 115, 124, 126, 137–143, 147, 149, 213

Autocorrelation coefficient, 89, 299

Autoregressive (AR) model, Box-Jenkins method, 89, 92, 93

Autoregressive moving average (ARMA) model, Box-Jenkins method, 90, 92, 93

Average error, 6–7

B

Blue Chip Economic Indicators, 293, 294, 299

Box-Jenkins method, 299
  identifying the model, 90–93
  special characteristics of, 87–90
  specifying and checking the model, 93

Bureau of the Census, 249, 250, 252

Bureau of Economic Analysis, 249, 250, 253

Bureau of Labor Statistics, 249, 251, 252

Business cycle, 95–96, 287–288

Business Information Sources, 251

Business Statistics: 1986, 150, 253

C

Causal methods, 3–4, 109, 285, 286, 287, 288, 299
  comparison between time-series methods and, 289
  costs related to, 290
  econometrics, 222–231
  measuring model equation significance, 114–128
  multiple regression, 111, 153–194

About the Author

Thomas Moore is Manager of Economic Planning and Forecasting at Tampa Electric Company and also teaches graduate courses in economics at the University of Tampa. He received an M.B.A. from Rutgers University and an M.A. in economics from Lehigh University. Prior to his position in the utility industry, the author worked in the Economic Research Department of Chemical Bank. He presently serves on the Governor's Council of Economic Advisors for the State of Florida. In addition, Mr. Moore has written various articles on forecasting and economics.